No Grid Survival Projects Bible

The Definitive Step-by-Step DIY Guide to Self-Sufficiency & Protecting Your Family from Any Crisis. Proven Strategies for Complete Resource and Security Independence

By

Morgan Ridgeway

Table of Contents

Disclaimer & Legal Notice

This document is provided solely for educational and entertainment purposes. While efforts have been made to ensure the information is accurate, up-to-date, reliable, and complete, no guarantees or warranties are made. The content should not be interpreted as legal, financial, medical, or any other type of professional advice. It is strongly recommended that readers consult a qualified professional before attempting to implement any ideas or techniques mentioned in this document.

By using this document, you agree that the author is not liable for any direct, indirect, incidental, or consequential damages resulting from the use or misuse of the information provided. This includes, but is not limited to, any losses due to errors, omissions, or inaccuracies.

Copyright © 2024

Getting Started

Thank you for choosing the No Grid Survival Projects Bible. We're excited to have you on board, and I want you to know that this book was crafted with care, dedication, and a true passion for helping individuals like you achieve complete self-sufficiency.

Living off the grid is about creating a balanced, interconnected system that supports both you and the environment. The No Grid Survival Projects Bible is your comprehensive guide, divided into 30 books, each focusing on a core aspect of self-reliant living. Together, these books provide a clear, step-by-step approach to gaining the essential knowledge and skills needed to establish, maintain, and flourish in an off-grid home.

Our goal was straightforward: to produce a guide that's both exhaustive and practical. Every piece of advice is grounded in real-world experience. What you'll learn here is designed to be actionable and effective, not just theory. This is a complete blueprint to help you embrace an independent, sustainable off-grid lifestyle.

Each book in this Bible builds toward a larger vision of complete self-reliance. Follow the sequence, and you'll develop the practical skills needed to address everything from selecting the ideal location, setting up renewable energy systems, and growing your own food, to creating a long-term plan that integrates all these elements and more.

Before you dive in, here what you can do:

1) Share how excited you are to start this adventure, we'd love to hear from you! Here's how to share:

    a) Create a short video of yourself with the book

    b) Snap a few pictures and share your thoughts

    c) Write a few sentences about what you're looking forward to

Scan the QR code below to share your thoughts! Your feedback helps others find the right tools for their off-grid lifestyle.

2) Go to the section "Unlock Your Exclusive Bonus Content" to access your additional resources.

Now, let's get started—there's a lot to cover, and you're in great hands!

1. Choosing the Right Off-Grid Location

Introduction to Location Planning

When it comes to transitioning to off-grid living, the most important decision you'll make early on is choosing the right location. Your land will be the foundation for every other aspect of your off-grid life, and finding the perfect spot will shape your experience for years to come. This decision is not just about where you'll build your home, but how the natural features of your environment will support your self-sufficient lifestyle.

You need to carefully evaluate key factors like access to resources, the quality of the land, the local climate, and proximity to essential amenities. By taking the time to fully understand what each location offers, you'll set yourself up for long-term success in your off-grid journey.

Access to Resources

One of the most critical elements in selecting your land is resource availability. Your off-grid success depends heavily on the land's ability to provide essentials like water, sunlight, and wood. A reliable water source is non-negotiable—whether it's a nearby stream, a natural well, or a rainfall collection system you plan to set up. Abundant sunlight is essential for solar power, and nearby trees can provide wood for building and fuel.

Expert Tip: Always visit the land during different seasons to see how resources like water and sunlight change throughout the year. A water source in the dry season might look different in the wet season, and sunlight patterns will affect your solar energy production.

Land Quality and Terrain Considerations

The quality of the land itself is just as important. Flat, fertile land is ideal for growing food and creating gardens that can sustain you year-round. You'll want to avoid rocky or heavily wooded areas unless you plan to clear significant space for your garden or home. Elevated land offers protection from potential flooding, which is especially critical if you live in a region prone to heavy rains or seasonal flooding.

Consider how easy it will be to develop the land. Are there natural obstacles like steep slopes or large rocks? Will you need to bring in equipment to level the ground or make it suitable for farming?

Expert Tip: If you're planning on growing your own food, test the soil quality before purchasing the land. Fertile soil is essential for a thriving garden. Avoid land that has poor drainage or is overly sandy unless you're prepared to invest time and resources into improving it.

Climate Considerations

Adapting your off-grid systems to your local climate is essential. Cold climates require efficient heating systems and insulation to keep you warm, while hot climates demand excellent ventilation and reliable water storage to keep you cool and hydrated. Consider how much effort and cost it will take to adapt the land to your climate needs.

Expert Tip: Think about seasonal temperature changes, storm risks, and how much precipitation the area receives. If you're in an area that gets a lot of snow or rain, make sure your water collection systems are designed to handle it, and plan for insulation that can withstand temperature extremes.

Evaluating the Land

Once you've outlined your priorities, it's time to carefully evaluate the land you're considering. This is where your preparation and attention to detail come into play.

How to Check if Land is Fertile

Before investing in land for off-grid living, it's essential to determine whether the soil is fertile enough to sustain your gardening and farming needs. Fertile land is the backbone of food production, ensuring that you can grow crops year-round without exhausting resources. Here are simple, practical ways to check soil fertility, including temperature, chemical, and empirical tests.

1. Soil Temperature Check

Soil temperature plays a significant role in plant growth. Ideal temperatures vary based on the crops you plan to grow, but a range of 55°F to 75°F is generally suitable for most plants.

Step-by-step guide:

- Use a soil thermometer. Insert it about 2–4 inches deep into the soil.
- Take readings in the morning and late afternoon to understand daily temperature fluctuations.
- Keep a record of the temperatures over a week to ensure they stay within an optimal range for your intended crops.

Expert Tip: Soil warms up slower than air, so early spring temperatures might not be ideal for immediate planting. Knowing this will help you plan better planting schedules.

2. Chemical Soil Test

A chemical soil test will give you detailed insight into the nutrient content and pH levels of your soil. Most plants thrive in slightly acidic to neutral soil, with a pH of 6.0–7.0.

Step-by-step guide:

- Purchase a DIY soil test kit from a garden store or send a sample to a local agricultural extension office.
- Take multiple samples from different areas of your land to ensure accuracy.
- Follow the instructions on the kit to test for essential nutrients like nitrogen (N), phosphorus (P), and potassium (K), which are vital for plant growth.
- Test the soil's pH using the same kit. If the pH is too high (alkaline) or too low (acidic), you can adjust it by adding lime or sulfur.

Expert Tip: If the soil is nutrient-deficient, consider adding compost, organic matter, or fertilizers to enrich it.

3. Empirical Tests

You can assess the soil quality by observing natural indicators and performing hands-on tests. These methods require no special equipment but give you valuable insights into the soil's structure and fertility.

Step-by-step guide:

- **Visual Check**: Look for signs of healthy plant growth and biodiversity. If the land is covered in green, thriving plants, it's a good indicator that the soil is fertile. Avoid areas where plants are sparse or weak.

- **Texture Test**: Take a handful of soil and squeeze it. If it forms a loose ball but crumbles easily, it has good structure. If it's too sandy (crumbles immediately) or too clay-like (forms a hard lump), you might need to amend the soil.
- **Water Absorption Test**: Dig a small hole (about 12 inches deep) and fill it with water. If the water drains within 30 minutes to 1 hour, the soil has good drainage. Poor drainage can lead to waterlogged soil, which harms plant roots.
- **Earthworm Count**: Dig a hole about 1 foot deep and sift through the soil for earthworms. A healthy soil should have at least five earthworms per square foot. Earthworms are a sign of rich, organic soil with good nutrient cycling.

Expert Tip: Soil that holds moisture without becoming waterlogged and is home to beneficial organisms like earthworms is a strong indicator of fertility.

4. Long-Term Observations

Spend time on the land during different seasons to see how the soil reacts to weather changes. Note how well the soil retains moisture after rain and how plants grow naturally in the area. Observing the soil over time provides deeper insights into its suitability for long-term agricultural use.

By performing these simple checks—soil temperature, chemical tests, and empirical observations—you'll gain a clear understanding of the land's fertility. This knowledge will help you make informed decisions about your off-grid food production and ensure your garden thrives. Remember, soil is a living ecosystem, and with the right care and attention, you can improve and maintain its fertility for years to come.

Key Resources and Terrain Considerations

Water: A key factor is having reliable access to a steady, clean water supply. Whether through a natural source, a drilled well, or rainwater harvesting, water access should be your top priority.

Sunlight: If you plan to rely on solar power, look for land with unobstructed access to sunlight for the majority of the day. Avoid areas where trees or mountains might block sunlight, especially during the winter months when sunlight is limited.

Wood: Access to a natural wood supply can be a huge benefit for building, heating, and cooking. Consider whether the land has a sustainable supply of wood that won't require you to travel far for fuel.

Flat Land for Food Production: Flat, fertile land is ideal for growing crops. It simplifies irrigation, and makes planting and harvesting easier. This will save you significant effort in the long term, as it allows for efficient farming and better use of natural water flows.

Elevated Land for Flood Protection: If you live in an area prone to heavy rainfall or flooding, elevated land can provide natural protection. You don't want your home or garden to be in a low-lying area that could flood during a storm.

Expert Tip: The natural features of the land should align with your off-grid goals. Look for land that has a balance of flat, arable land for gardening and elevated spots for building, as well as natural barriers like trees or hills that can shield you from wind or other elements.

Selecting the right location for your off-grid home is the most crucial step in ensuring your success. Take the time to evaluate all aspects of the land—its resources, climate adaptability, and terrain features—before making a final decision. The choices you make now will shape your future, so be thorough, patient, and meticulous in your planning.

Balancing Accessibility and Isolation

When choosing the location for your off-grid life, it's crucial to strike the right balance between isolation and accessibility. Many off-grid enthusiasts seek solitude and independence, but being too isolated can introduce challenges, especially when it comes to accessing services and resources.

Proximity to Services

Evaluate how far you want to be from essential services like hospitals, grocery stores, and community resources. While living closer to civilization may seem counter to the off-grid ethos, it can offer crucial support in times of need. Being near medical services or stores can be vital, especially in emergencies or if your self-sufficiency systems experience a breakdown.

On the other hand, living closer to services often comes with less privacy, more regulations, and increased human interaction. Deciding how much of this trade-off you are willing to make is key to determining your perfect location.

Isolation Factors

If privacy and solitude are what you're after, then choosing a more remote location might be appealing. However, the further you are from services, the more self-reliant you need to be. Regular trips for supplies or medical assistance could become challenging, especially in extreme weather or if you're relying on limited transportation options. It's equally important to make sure that your location is accessible year-round, as roads in remote areas can be prone to flooding or snow blockage.

Expert Tip: Finding the balance between isolation and access to services is key. While solitude offers independence, it's important to be realistic about the challenges of being too far from critical resources. Plan for potential emergencies and consider how easily you can reach help when needed.

Evaluating the Legal Landscape and Local Regulations

Before purchasing land and committing to off-grid living, it's vital to know the legal restrictions and local regulations in the area you're considering. Many areas have laws that impact everything from building codes to water rights, and failure to comply with these regulations could cause significant headaches later on.

Zoning Laws

Zoning laws dictate how land can be used and developed. In some areas, off-grid living is encouraged and supported, while in others, there are restrictions on water collection, composting toilets, and renewable energy systems. Research local zoning regulations to ensure that living off-grid and employing sustainable practices like solar panels, rainwater harvesting, or waste composting is permitted. Some municipalities may limit the extent to which you can modify your property or impose restrictions on alternative energy use.

Building Codes

Building codes vary greatly depending on your location. Some rural areas have very few restrictions, while others may require that you adhere to strict regulations regarding building design, structure stability, and safety standards. For example, certain structures like yurts or tiny homes might need special permits, and homes with alternative energy sources may need to meet specific guidelines. Ensure that any home you build complies with these codes, as failure to do so could lead to fines, forced modifications, or even demolition of non-compliant structures.

Water Rights and Land Use

Water is one of the most important resources for off-grid living. However, in some areas, access to water is regulated by law. Whether you plan to drill a well, collect rainwater, or tap into natural springs, it's essential to know your legal rights regarding water use. Some areas may have restrictions that limit how much water you can collect or use, especially in times of drought or if you're living near sensitive environmental areas. Make sure to understand these rules before committing to a piece of land.

Expert Tip: Consulting with a local lawyer or authorities is crucial before purchasing any land. They can help you navigate the legal landscape, ensuring that you adhere to local regulations to prevent any expensive legal complications later on. Having the right knowledge and legal groundwork in place will save you from unnecessary complications and allow you to fully enjoy the off-grid lifestyle.

Evaluating the Advantages and Disadvantages of Off-Grid Living

Deciding to live off-grid is a major commitment. It comes with incredible rewards, but also significant challenges. It's important to evaluate both the pros and cons to understand if this lifestyle aligns with your personal goals and capacity for self-reliance.

Advantages

- **Self-Sufficiency:**
  Living off-grid gives you control over your own resources—food, water, energy. You become less dependent on external systems, which creates a profound sense of freedom and independence. This level of autonomy can be empowering, as you are directly responsible for meeting your own needs.
- **Long-Term Savings:**

While the initial setup for an off-grid home may require an initial investment, but the long-term savings can be substantial. Once you have established renewable energy sources and sustainable food production, ongoing costs are minimal. You are no longer paying utility bills or relying on supermarkets for basic sustenance.

- **Sustainability:**
  Living off-grid offers the opportunity to significantly minimize your environmental footprint. By harnessing renewable energy sources like solar or wind, managing waste independently, and growing your own food, you can establish a sustainable lifestyle that benefits both you and the planet. It's an ideal option for those dedicated to lowering their carbon emissions and living in harmony with nature.

Disadvantages

- **Maintenance:**
  Being self-sufficient means that you are responsible for maintaining every aspect of your home and systems. From solar panels to water storage, all the systems need regular care and attention. If something breaks, you'll need to fix it yourself or find an expert, which can be both expensive and time-consuming, especially in remote locations.
- **Isolation:**
  One of the most common challenges of off-grid living is the sense of isolation. While seclusion can be peaceful and liberating, it also means that you're further from essential services like healthcare or stores. In an emergency, help might take longer to arrive, and simple tasks like getting supplies can become more complex.
- **Initial Investment:**

The initial expenses for establishing an off-grid lifestyle can be quite high. Solar panels, water systems, home construction, and land acquisition all require significant financial investment. For some, this can be a barrier to getting started. However, it's important to remember that after the initial setup, ongoing costs are minimal.

Expert Tip: Carefully consider these factors before making the leap to off-grid living. You'll need resilience, flexibility, and a commitment to long-term planning to make it work. It's a lifestyle that demands constant learning, problem-solving, and adaptability.

Addressing Challenges Related to Climate, Geography, and Self-Sufficiency

Your land's climate, geography, and ability to support self-sufficient systems are key to your success in off-grid living. These factors will shape your entire lifestyle, from the resources you can tap into to the challenges you'll face daily.

Climate

Living off-grid in extreme climates requires thoughtful planning.

- **Cold Climates:** In colder regions, you'll need to prioritize insulation, efficient heating systems, and methods for storing food and water during freezing temperatures. Homes in these areas should be built to trap heat, using natural building materials that provide insulation. Heating options such as wood stoves or solar heat can help maintain warmth.
- **Hot Climates:** In hotter regions, you'll need strong ventilation and water storage systems. Cooling solutions like passive solar design, ventilation, and shaded areas are essential to avoid overheating. Additionally, water storage and irrigation systems are crucial to prevent drought-related issues. Hot climates demand effective strategies for keeping cool while conserving water.

Expert Tip: Choose building materials and designs that are specifically suited to your chosen climate. This will help mitigate weather-related challenges and ensure your home remains comfortable and functional throughout the year.

Geography

The geography of your land will directly influence your ability to generate renewable energy and access water.

- **Solar Power:** If you reside in a region with abundant sunlight, solar power is an excellent energy option. However, in mountainous or forested regions, access to direct sunlight may be limited, which would require adjustments in energy planning, such as using wind or biomass energy sources.
- **Water Access:** In desert areas or regions with limited natural water sources, advanced water collection methods such as rainwater harvesting or greywater systems will be critical. In regions with abundant water, simple wells and natural water systems can provide more straightforward solutions.

Expert Tip: Tailor your food, water, and energy systems to the specific geography of your land. If you have abundant sunlight, solar panels are an excellent choice. If water is scarce, prioritize advanced water collection and storage techniques. Flexibility in your planning is key to adapting to the geographical limitations of your location.

Self-Sufficiency

The ability to provide for yourself and your family is the foundation of off-grid living. This includes growing food, sourcing water, and generating energy.

- **Food Production:** Your ability to grow food will be determined by the quality of your soil and the available space. Raised beds, permaculture designs, and even aquaponics can all be valuable methods for maximizing food production on your land.
- **Water Supply:** Ensure you have reliable water systems in place. Whether it's a well, a spring, or a rainwater harvesting system, water is the most critical resource in off-grid living. Build redundancy into your water system to ensure you never run dry, especially in areas prone to drought.
- **Energy Systems:** Reliable energy sources are essential for heating, cooling, and cooking. Depending on your geography, solar, wind, or biomass may be the best fit. Backup systems are critical to ensure you always have power when one source fails.

Expert Tip: Always have a backup system for your essential needs—whether it's a secondary water storage tank, a backup generator, or a manual energy solution. Redundancy ensures that if one system fails, you're never left without crucial resources. The location you choose for your off-grid home is arguably the most important decision you'll make. It will influence everything—from the resources you have access to, to the challenges you'll face in becoming self-sufficient. Take your time, thoroughly research potential sites, and visit them multiple times before making your decision.

2. Guidelines to Follow When Building Your Off-Grid Home

Introduction

In the previous book, we explored how to find the right location for your off-grid life—a crucial first step that sets the foundation for everything that follows. Now that you've chosen the perfect site, it's time to take the next step: building your off-grid home. This stage is about transforming the land you've selected into a haven that supports your self-sufficient lifestyle. The location you've chosen influences every decision moving forward, from the type of shelter you build to the materials you use, ensuring that your home is in harmony with its surroundings.

Building your off-grid home is more than just constructing a shelter. It's about creating a sustainable, practical space that aligns with your values and lifestyle. This home will be the heart of your off-grid existence, where you can live comfortably and independently, in tune with nature.

Whether you opt for a yurt, a small cabin, or another design, your off-grid home should offer durability, comfort, and efficiency across all seasons. Each decision—whether about materials, insulation, or layout—impacts the functionality of your home, ensuring it serves you well and minimizes reliance on outside resources.

This section provides clear, practical steps to help you construct a durable, functional home without needing expert building skills. We'll guide you through foundational decisions, from laying the base to insulating for different weather conditions, making the process straightforward and manageable.

By following these guidelines, you'll create a home that is not only practical but also reflects your dedication to sustainable living. Whether you're starting small with room to expand or building a structure designed for long-term use, this guide will empower you to shape a living space that suits your needs and aspirations.

You'll find expert advice on materials, design, and how to make use of local or recycled resources, making sure your home is both budget-friendly and eco-friendly. So, let's dive into the next stage of your off-grid journey—building a home that will be the cornerstone of your self-reliant life. Your path to true independence starts here.

Essential Materials and Tools for Building Your Off-Grid Home

Building your off-grid home begins with carefully selecting the right materials and tools. While your design might vary depending on location, climate, and personal preference, the essential materials and tools remain consistent across all off-grid projects. The goal is to ensure that your home is **durable, cost-effective**, and **practical** to build and maintain. Let's dive deeper into the materials and tools you'll need, and why they're crucial for long-term success.

Materials

- **Wood**: Wood is one of the most versatile materials you'll use in constructing your off-grid home. It's ideal for framing, finishing, and even insulation in some cases. Locally sourced wood not only reduces transportation costs but also aligns with sustainable building practices. Consider using **hardwoods** for framing due to their strength, and **softwoods** for paneling and finishing, as they are easier to work with. Additionally, reclaimed or salvaged wood can offer a rustic aesthetic while being more environmentally friendly.

Tip: Always ensure the wood you choose is treated or naturally resistant to pests and weathering, particularly if you're in a humid or wet climate.

- **Insulation**: Insulation is crucial for temperature regulation, whether you're preparing for freezing winters or scorching summers. Traditional foam insulation is effective but can be costly and less eco-friendly. **Sustainable options** such as straw bales, wool, or recycled denim provide excellent insulation while supporting off-grid sustainability. Proper insulation will lower your heating and cooling needs, saving energy in the long term.

Tip: Consider a layered approach to insulation. Combine materials like wool or straw with a vapor barrier to improve performance in different weather conditions.

- **Roofing**: Your roof is your home's first defense against the elements, so durability is key. **Metal sheets** are a popular option for their strength and water resistance, making them ideal for regions with heavy rain or snow. Alternatively, **shingles** or even a thick **tarp** can be used for temporary or cost-effective solutions. Ensure the roofing material you select can withstand wind, rain, and sun exposure over time.

Tip: If possible, choose a reflective roofing material to help regulate indoor temperature, especially in hotter climates. For cold regions, focus on adding additional weatherproofing layers.

- **Nails/Screws**: It's easy to underestimate the importance of quality fasteners. A variety of **nails, screws, and bolts** will be necessary to assemble everything from the frame to doors and windows. Use **galvanized nails or screws** in high-humidity areas to prevent rust. Investing in good quality fasteners ensures that your structure remains sturdy and resistant to shifting over time.

Tip: Keep a range of sizes and types available—sheet metal screws for roofing, long bolts for framing, and smaller nails for paneling. You'll need a diverse toolkit to manage various tasks efficiently.

Tools

- **Hammer**: A strong hammer is essential for framing, roofing, and any general construction. While a simple tool, using one with a **comfortable grip** and balanced weight will make a big difference during long building sessions. Opt for a **claw hammer** to easily remove misplaced nails as well.

Tip: A **framing hammer** with a longer handle provides greater force, making it easier to drive nails through heavy timbers.

- **Saw**: A saw is essential for cutting lumber to the right size, and having both **manual and powered saws** is ideal. While a hand saw gives you control for detailed cuts, a **circular saw** or **table saw** speeds up the process, especially for large projects. Choose a saw with **adjustable blades** for precision.

Tip: Keep your blades sharp and invest in a saw with an ergonomic grip. Dull blades not only slow you down but can lead to inaccurate cuts.

- **Drill**: A reliable drill is indispensable for drilling holes and driving screws. Opt for a **cordless drill** with multiple battery packs for flexibility, especially if you don't yet have a fully installed power source. The drill should come with various bits to handle wood, metal, and other materials.

Tip: A **high-torque drill** can handle more challenging tasks, such as driving large screws into hardwood or working with metal.

- **Level**: Ensuring your structure is level is essential for both safety and longevity. A **spirit level** will help you keep your walls, foundation, and roof properly aligned. It's an affordable tool, but one that's essential for ensuring your structure's stability.

Tip: Use a **laser level** for larger builds, as it will help you maintain consistency across distances, particularly when leveling floors or rooflines.

Use Recycled and Locally Sourced Materials

Whenever possible, opt for recycled or locally sourced materials. This not only helps you **cut down on costs** but also minimizes your environmental impact. Recycled wood, for instance, can be just as sturdy as new lumber while offering character and sustainability. Similarly, materials salvaged from construction sites or demolition projects can often be repurposed for framing, roofing, or even insulation.

By using local resources, you support your community and reduce the need for transportation, which can be a major advantage when building off-grid. Plus, locally sourced materials are often better suited to your specific climate and environment, as they've already weathered similar conditions.

The foundation of your off-grid home begins with the **right materials and tools**. Take the time to gather everything you need before starting construction. A well-planned approach not only ensures a smoother building process but also increases the durability and comfort of your home for years to come.

Step-by-Step Construction Guide for Your Off-Grid Home

Building an off-grid home is a rewarding challenge that requires a clear approach and practical steps. Every decision you make will impact the comfort, durability, and sustainability of your home. Let's walk through the essential steps, with clear instructions on how to bring your off-grid home to life.

Step 1: Laying a Simple Foundation

Your foundation is the backbone of your off-grid home. It ensures stability and protects the structure from environmental factors like moisture or ground shifting.

- **Cinder Blocks or Wood Planks?** If you're working on a tight budget or building in an area with challenging terrain, cinder blocks are a great option. They're durable, easy to use, and elevate the home, allowing airflow underneath to prevent moisture build-up. Lay them at each corner and midpoints, ensuring the ground is level before placement.

Wood planks can also be used for a raised platform. Treated wood is essential here to prevent rot or damage over time. Wooden planks offer more flexibility in uneven ground conditions.

- **Pro Tip:** After placing your foundation blocks or planks, always double-check the level. This ensures your structure is stable and that everything from walls to windows fits perfectly later on.

Step 2: Building the Frame

Your frame will support the entire structure, so it's important to get this step right.

Choosing Your Materials

- **Wood** is often the best choice due to its flexibility, availability, and ease of use. If you're in an area with severe weather, you might consider **metal poles** for added strength and durability, but they can be harder to work with.
    - **How to Frame It**: Start by building your walls one by one, ensuring that all angles are square. You'll want to make sure the wall height is consistent across the structure. Use heavy-duty screws or bolts at every connection point for long-term durability. After the walls, frame the roof.
    - **Pro Tip:** Reinforce Your Corners

Corners and joints are where your frame is most vulnerable. Ensure they are tightly connected and reinforced to handle wind and movement. This will make your home far more resilient.

Step 3: Insulating the Walls and Roof

Insulation is crucial, whether you're in a hot or cold climate. This step ensures your home is comfortable and energy-efficient.

- **Choosing the Right Insulation**

If you're in a colder area, consider using **straw bales** or **foam boards**. Both offer excellent insulation properties, with straw bales being a sustainable option. Foam boards are lighter and easier to handle. In hotter climates, you can still use these materials but focus on creating airflow as well.

- **Installing Insulation**

  When insulating walls, ensure that the material fits snugly between the frame without any gaps. Gaps will allow air to leak in, making your heating or cooling efforts less efficient. For the roof, consider using double layers if you are in an area prone to extreme temperatures.

  - **Pro Tip: Don't Forget the Vapor Barrier**

    Always add a vapor barrier to prevent moisture from collecting in your walls and insulation. This simple layer keeps mold and rot from developing, protecting the structure long-term.

Step 4: Installing the Roof

Your roof is essential for protecting your home from rain, snow, and sun, so it needs to be durable and properly installed.

- **Roofing Options**

  If you're building a temporary or budget home, a heavy-duty **tarp** can serve as a roof for the short term. However, for a more permanent home, consider using **metal sheets** or **shingles**. Metal roofs are highly durable, weather-resistant, and relatively low maintenance. Shingles are a more traditional option but may need more upkeep depending on the material used.

- **Proper Installation**

  Ensure your roof has a slope or pitch to direct water away and prevent pooling. Install the roofing materials securely, starting from the bottom and working your way up to create overlap, which will stop water from leaking in.

  - **Pro Tip: Secure Your Roof in High-Wind Areas**

    If you're in a region with high winds, use hurricane straps or extra screws to secure your roof tightly to the frame. This extra step could save your roof during strong storms.

Step 5: Installing Doors and Windows

Doors and windows do more than just provide access and light—they play a significant role in insulation and airflow management.

- **Choosing Prefabricated or Salvaged Materials**

  If you want a quick installation, go with prefabricated doors and windows, which are typically well-insulated and come in standard sizes. Salvaged materials can give your home character and save costs, but you'll need to ensure they're properly sealed and sized for your structure.

- **Proper Sealing for Insulation**

  Use weatherstripping around the edges of your doors and windows to prevent drafts. A tight seal will not only improve your home's energy efficiency but also keep out moisture and pests.

  - **Pro Tip: Maximize Natural Light**

    Place windows strategically on different sides of your home to bring in natural light and promote airflow. This reduces the need for artificial lighting and cooling systems during the day.

By following these steps, you'll create a sturdy, efficient, and comfortable off-grid home that can withstand the elements and provide long-term liveability. Each decision you make, from foundation materials to window placement, will shape your home's durability and energy efficiency. Even the best-built off-grid homes need maintenance. Schedule regular checks for insulation wear, structural integrity, and potential leaks. By staying proactive, you'll increase the longevity of your home while saving on expensive repairs down the road

Weatherproofing Your Off-Grid Home

Creating a durable off-grid home requires careful attention to weatherproofing. Whether you're preparing for cold winters, hot summers, or extreme weather conditions, how you insulate and protect your home from the elements will significantly impact your comfort and energy efficiency.

Cold Weather: Insulate Well and Seal Gaps

In cold climates, proper insulation and sealing are critical to keep the warmth in and the cold out.

- **Choose the Right Insulation**: For cold weather, opt for dense materials like foam boards, fiberglass, or even natural alternatives like straw bales. These materials provide high thermal resistance, helping maintain warmth inside your home.
  - **Pro Tip**: Layer your insulation. If you're working with limited space, consider combining foam board with natural materials like wool for added efficiency.
- **Seal Gaps Thoroughly**: Cold air has a sneaky way of entering your home through cracks and gaps. Be sure to seal all potential entry points, including around doors, windows, and between joints in the walls and roof.
  - **Materials for Sealing**: Use high-quality caulking or silicone to seal smaller gaps. For larger gaps, expanding foam is an effective solution. Ensure windows and doors are properly weather-stripped to prevent drafts.
- **Install a Wood Stove**: A simple wood stove provides more than just heat; it reinforces your self-reliance and independence.
- as wood can often be sourced locally. Place the stove centrally for even heat distribution, and ensure the chimney is well-insulated to avoid heat loss.
  - **Pro Tip**: Install a heat reflector behind your stove to maximize heat radiation into the room rather than losing it to the walls.

Hot Weather: Ventilation and Cooling Solutions

In hot climates, keeping your off-grid home cool is just as important as insulating against cold weather. The key is to create airflow and shade to minimize heat buildup inside.

- **Ventilation is Key**: Proper ventilation is essential for keeping your home cool in hot weather. Install windows that can open on opposite sides of the structure to promote cross-ventilation. Roof vents are also a great way to let hot air escape, especially in the peak of summer.
  - **Pro Tip**: Use solar-powered fans to increase airflow in areas with low wind. This low-energy solution works great for moving hot air out without relying on grid power.
- **Reflective Roofing Materials**: If you live in a region prone to high temperatures, consider using reflective roofing materials like metal or white-painted surfaces. These materials reflect sunlight rather than absorbing it, keeping your home cooler throughout the day.
- **Strategic Shade**: Plant trees or install pergolas to provide natural shade around your home. This reduces direct sunlight and helps maintain cooler temperatures indoors.
  - **Pro Tip**: Focus on planting fast-growing trees or using climbing plants like vines around your home to create quick shade. This approach can reduce indoor temperatures by several degrees.

Easy Maintenance and Durability Tips

Maintaining your off-grid home is essential to ensure its longevity. A little regular attention can prevent larger issues down the road.

Regular Inspections

Inspect your home at least twice a year—once before winter and once before summer. This helps you stay ahead of any potential issues related to seasonal changes.

- **What to Look For**: Check for leaks in the roof, damage to insulation, cracks in the walls, or loose connections in your structure. Pay close attention to the areas where different materials meet, such as where walls meet the foundation or roof.
  - **Pro Tip**: Create a checklist for each inspection to ensure nothing gets overlooked. Over time, you'll know where the most common problem areas are, making your inspections quicker and more effective.

Quick Fixes for Common Problems

Being prepared for minor repairs can save you a lot of hassle. Here are some common problems and their quick fixes:

- **Leaky Roof**: Use a tarp patch or sealant for immediate repairs. For long-term solutions, replace damaged shingles or metal panels.
- **Drafty Windows or Doors**: Apply weatherstripping to the edges of windows and doors. You can also use silicone caulk to seal any gaps that have appeared over time.
- **Worn Insulation**: Over time, insulation can degrade or settle, creating gaps where cold air can enter or heat can escape. Check for these gaps and refill or replace insulation as needed.

Pro Tip: Plan for Seasonal Adjustments

- In colder months, make sure to inspect your home before the first snow. Reinforce your insulation and check that your heating system (wood stove or otherwise) is ready to go.
- In hotter months, ensure that your ventilation is optimized and that all seals remain intact to avoid trapping excessive heat inside the house.

Pro Tips for Efficient Shelter Building

When it comes to building your off-grid home, efficiency and practicality are key. The process doesn't need to be overwhelming if you follow some basic principles and build smart. Below are a few expert tips to help guide your construction, ensuring that your home is not only functional but also cost-effective and adaptable to your changing needs.

Tip 1: Start Small and Expand Later

One of the most effective strategies in off-grid homebuilding is to start small. Building a compact structure will allow you to focus on getting the essentials right—solid foundation, insulation, and durability. Once your initial shelter is in place and functioning well, you can expand as your resources and skills grow.

- **Why Start Small?**: A smaller home is easier and faster to build, meaning you can move in and start living off-grid sooner. It also allows you to minimize upfront costs and learn from the building process before committing to a larger project.
- **Future Expansion**: Design your home with expansion in mind. Build a solid foundation and frame that can support future additions like more rooms or storage spaces. It's always easier to add on later than to downsize a home that's too big for your current needs.
- **Pro Tip**: Focus on building the rooms or spaces you'll use the most, like a kitchen, living area, and bedroom. You can always add extra features—like a workshop or storage shed—later.

Tip 2: Focus on Good Insulation for Comfort in All Seasons

Effective insulation is a crucial component of any off-grid home, regardless of your location. It helps maintain warmth during the winter and keeps your home cool in the summer, significantly cutting down the energy required for heating and cooling.

- **Material Choices**: You don't have to rely on expensive commercial products to insulate your home effectively. Straw bales, recycled paper, and even natural wool are excellent, eco-friendly alternatives to traditional foam insulation. These materials are not only sustainable but also provide great thermal resistance.
- **Seal Every Gap**: Insulation isn't just about the materials between your walls—it's also about sealing every crack and gap. Drafts can make a well-insulated home feel cold in winter or hot in summer. Use weatherstripping, caulk, or expanding foam to close up all those tiny gaps that can let heat or cool air escape.
- **Pro Tip**: Invest in double-pane windows or insulated doors to enhance your home's energy efficiency. It's a larger upfront investment but will save you energy and resources over time.

Tip 3: Use Local Materials to Save Money and Speed Up the Process

One of the best ways to make your off-grid home more sustainable—and to save on costs—is by using materials that are readily available in your local environment. This approach can significantly reduce transportation costs, time, and even your environmental impact.

- **Sourcing Locally**: Look for local suppliers of wood, stone, and even reclaimed building materials. Using what's naturally available not only reduces your construction costs but also ensures that your home fits naturally into the surrounding environment.
- **Recycled Materials**: Salvaged materials from demolition sites, scrap yards, or even Craigslist can be perfect for building an off-grid home. Reclaimed wood, old windows, and repurposed metal can give your home character while cutting costs.
- **Pro Tip**: Always inspect reclaimed materials for structural integrity before using them. Make sure they're free from rot, pests, or damage to ensure your home's durability.

Conclusion

Building an off-grid home requires planning, resourcefulness, and adaptability. By starting small, focusing on insulation, and using local or recycled materials, you can create a cost-effective, durable, and comfortable space. Remember, off-grid living is about self-reliance and sustainability, and your home should reflect those principles.

Adapt your build to your environment, continually assess what your needs are, and make adjustments as you gain experience. Building an off-grid home isn't just about the final structure—it's about the journey of learning and refining as you go, creating a home that perfectly suits your lifestyle and environment. Building an off-grid home is more than just completing the build—it's an ongoing experience of gaining knowledge, making adjustments, and evolving throughout the journey.

3. Off-Grid Water Collection and Purification for Sustainable Living

Now that you've established your off-grid home and created a solid foundation for sustainable living, the next critical step is securing a reliable, clean water supply. Without water, none of your other preparations will matter—whether it's for drinking, cooking, cleaning, or growing your own food, water is your lifeline. In this guide, we'll break down the most practical, step-by-step strategies for collecting and purifying water. By the end, you'll know exactly how to build a self-sufficient water system that supports all your off-grid needs.

Water: More Than Just for Drinking

Water's role in your off-grid life goes far beyond quenching thirst. Whether you're off-grid permanently or preparing for an emergency, water is essential for every aspect of your daily routine. Let's look at the different ways you'll rely on water and how each of these uses requires a different level of purification.

Drinking Water: Your Highest Priority

When it comes to survival, clean drinking water is non-negotiable. Waterborne diseases can quickly turn a well-prepared off-grid setup into a life-threatening situation. Your drinking water must be the purest water you have, free of bacteria, viruses, and harmful chemicals. Depending on your source, you may need to filter, boil, or chemically treat the water before it's safe to drink.

Pro Tip: Always prioritize the purification of drinking water. Even if your other systems fail, having safe water to drink will keep you going.

Washing and Cleaning: Less Purified, But Still Safe

Water for washing dishes, clothes, and your body doesn't need to be as highly purified as drinking water, but it should still be free from harmful contaminants. While you may not need to filter out every microorganism, you'll still want water that's free from toxins, pollutants, and large debris. Basic filtration methods can often make water suitable for these tasks.

Pro Tip: Set up a secondary filtration system for your cleaning water to save on resources. It doesn't need to be as advanced as your drinking water purification, but it will keep things sanitary.

Gardening and Irrigation: Untreated Water Sources

If you're growing your own food, your plants don't need purified water. In fact, rainwater or water from natural sources like streams or ponds is often ideal for irrigation. However, you'll still want to ensure that any contaminants in the water won't harm your soil or plants over time, so consider the quality of the water source before using it extensively.

Pro Tip: Collect rainwater for your garden. It's free, sustainable, and plants thrive on it. Just ensure your collection methods don't introduce chemicals or debris into the water.

Key Tip: Different Water Uses, Different Purification Levels

Understanding that not all water needs to be treated the same way is crucial for managing your off-grid water supply effectively. Drinking water requires the highest level of purification, while cleaning and irrigation water can tolerate more impurities. By adjusting your purification process to match the intended use, you can conserve resources and ensure you always have the right kind of water for the task at hand.

Collecting Water: From Roofs to Reservoirs

Creating a reliable water supply is crucial for any off-grid setup. Whether you're relying on rainwater, groundwater, or surface water, each method comes with its own unique challenges and best practices. Let's explore the step-by-step process of collecting water using these natural sources, ensuring you have a solid foundation to build your off-grid water system.

Rainwater Harvesting: A Free, Renewable Resource

Rainwater harvesting is one of the most accessible and cost-effective methods for collecting water. It's renewable and relatively simple to set up, but for it to function properly, you need to follow a clear, structured approach.

Step 1: Choose Your Collection Area

Your roof will likely be your primary collection surface, so it's crucial to make sure it's appropriate for water harvesting. Metal or slate roofs are ideal because they don't leach harmful chemicals into the water like some asphalt shingles or treated wood might.

- **Inspect the Roof:** Ensure there are no loose or broken tiles, as they can lead to contamination or inefficient water flow.
- **Smooth Surface:** The smoother the surface, the more efficiently water will flow into your collection system.

Step 2: Install Gutters and Downspouts

Install a proper gutter system along the edge of your roof to channel water into downspouts.

- **Slope Correctly:** Your gutters should be sloped at 1/16th of an inch per foot towards the downspouts to ensure efficient water flow.
- **Gutter Screens or Guards:** Add screens to your gutters to filter out leaves and large debris. This reduces the risk of blockages and keeps your collected water cleaner.

Step 3: Set Up a First-Flush Diverter

This critical device prevents the first few gallons of rain from entering your storage tanks. The initial rain often washes dirt, leaves, bird droppings, and other debris off your roof. A first-flush diverter works by discarding this contaminated water, ensuring that only cleaner water reaches your tanks.

- **Installation:** The diverter should be positioned between the downspout and the inlet to your storage tank. It needs to have an outlet to discharge the dirty water automatically before switching to your storage system.

Step 4: Use Food-Grade Storage Tanks

For potable water, your storage tanks must be food-grade and BPA-free. Common materials include polyethylene or stainless steel. These tanks ensure that the water remains safe for consumption.

- **Sizing Your Tank:** Estimate your water usage and rainfall patterns. As a rule of thumb, for every 1 inch of rain on a 1,000-square-foot roof, you can collect around 600 gallons of water.
- **Placement:** Store the tanks in a shaded area or underground to prevent algae growth. Cover the tanks tightly to keep pests, dirt, and sunlight out.

Pro Tip: Clean your gutters and tanks at least twice a year. Sediment and dirt can build up over time, leading to contamination. Regular maintenance ensures your water remains safe and usable.

Wells and Groundwater: A Sustainable Long-Term Source

Drilling a well can be an effective solution for long-term water needs, but it requires careful planning and precise installation to ensure a sustainable, safe water supply.

Step 1: Site Selection

Selecting the ideal location for your well is vital. It must be placed far from potential contaminants, including septic systems, animal pens, or chemical storage areas.

- **Distance Requirements:** Ideally, place the well at least 100 feet away from any septic systems or sources of contamination. Higher distances may be necessary if your soil is sandy or porous, as contaminants can travel farther in these conditions.
- **Geological Survey:** Conduct a geological survey or hire a professional to ensure you're drilling into a reliable water table that can supply your needs consistently.

Step 2: Drilling the Well

Depending on the depth of the water table, you'll either dig a shallow well (less than 25 feet) or a deep well (more than 25 feet).

- **Manual Drilling:** If the water table is shallow, you can manually dig the well using a hand auger or posthole digger. For deeper wells, consider renting or purchasing a motorized auger.
- **Professional Drilling:** For deeper wells (over 50 feet), it's generally best to hire a professional driller. They'll use a rotary or cable tool drill rig to reach the aquifer. This ensures the well is properly sealed and avoids collapse.

Step 3: Install a Pump

Once the well is drilled, install either a manual or solar-powered pump to draw water.

- **Manual Pumps:** Great for shallow wells, manual hand pumps can bring water up to the surface without relying on external power.
- **Solar Pumps:** For deeper wells, solar pumps are ideal as they use renewable energy. They can draw water from depths up to 300 feet or more, depending on the model.

Step 4: Water Testing and Safety

Before using the water, it's essential to test it for contaminants like bacteria, nitrates, and heavy metals.

- **Testing Frequency:** Test your well water at least once a year, and always after heavy rains or environmental changes that could affect the groundwater.
- **Treatment:** If contaminants are found, consider treating the water with filters, UV purification, or chemical treatments.

Expert Tip: Install a secure well cap to keep insects, debris, and small animals out of the well. This ensures the water supply remains clean and uncontaminated.

Surface Water: Using Streams and Rivers

Surface water from streams, rivers, or ponds can be a useful resource for non-drinking needs, such as irrigation, cleaning, or even livestock.

Step 1: Collecting Surface Water

Use a pump system to draw water from the stream or river. You can install a simple siphon system or a solar-powered pump for easy, ongoing access.

- **Piping and Pumps:** Use durable, UV-resistant piping to transport water from the source to your storage system. Solar-powered pumps are ideal for off-grid setups, as they eliminate the need for electrical connections.

Step 2: Basic Filtration for Non-Potable Water

Even for non-drinking purposes, it's important to filter out large debris like leaves, twigs, and sediment.

- **Gravel or Mesh Filters:** Set up a basic filter using gravel, sand, and mesh screens. This removes large particles and prevents your storage system from clogging or becoming contaminated with organic material.

Step 3: Contamination Prevention

Place barriers around your intake point to prevent debris and animals from contaminating your water supply.

- **Fencing:** Erect a small fence or screen around the intake area to prevent animals from drinking directly from the collection point or disturbing the water source.

Key Tip: Always monitor upstream activities. Agricultural runoff, industrial pollutants, or heavy rains can introduce contaminants to the water source. Regularly inspect your collection system and ensure it's clean and safe.

Purification: Making Water Safe to Use

In an off-grid situation, ensuring the safety of your water is crucial. Whether you're using water for drinking, cooking, or cleaning, proper purification techniques are essential to avoid health risks. There are multiple methods to purify water effectively, each suited for different scenarios. Below, we'll break down how to filter and treat water to make it safe for your off-grid needs.

Filtration for Potable Water

Filtration is your first defense against physical contaminants in water, such as sediment, debris, and some microorganisms. However, filtration alone does not make water completely safe for drinking—it must be combined with disinfection methods to eliminate pathogens.

Gravity-Fed Filters

Gravity-fed filters, such as the Berkey filter, are highly efficient and popular for off-grid living. These filters use gravity to push water through a filter medium that removes bacteria, protozoa, and in some cases, viruses.

How to Use a Gravity-Fed Filter:
1. **Fill the upper chamber** with untreated water.
2. **Wait for filtration**, allowing gravity to pull water through the filter element into the lower chamber.
3. Collect purified water from the spout.

Key Advantages:
- Long-lasting filter elements that can handle thousands of gallons before replacement.
- Does not require electricity or manual pumping.
- Ideal for both daily use and emergency situations.

Portable Filters

For mobile or on-the-go situations, portable filters like the **Sawyer Mini** or **LifeStraw** are practical. These compact devices can filter up to 100,000 gallons of water, removing bacteria and protozoa, and are highly durable.

How to Use Portable Filters:
1. Attach the filter to a bottle or hydration system.
2. Suck through the filter or squeeze the water out into a separate container.
3. **Repeat as needed**, ensuring the filter remains unclogged by backflushing if required (Sawyer Mini only).

DIY Filters

For non-potable water, you can build a DIY filter using materials like sand, charcoal, and gravel. This method is useful for filtering larger debris and sediment.

How to Build a DIY Filter
1. **Layer a container** with gravel at the bottom, followed by a layer of activated charcoal, and finally sand at the top.
2. **Pour water slowly through the layers**, allowing each layer to trap different-sized particles.
3. **Collect the filtered water** in a separate container. Keep in mind that this water still needs to be disinfected before drinking.

Expert Tip: Filtration removes visible contaminants, but it doesn't eliminate viruses, bacteria, or chemicals. For safe drinking water, always combine filtration with boiling, chlorination, or other purification methods.

Chemical Treatment for Potable Water

Chemical treatments provide a fast and effective way to disinfect water, especially when filtration alone isn't enough. This method is especially useful in emergencies or for larger quantities of water.

Chlorination
Chlorination is a tried-and-true method for treating water. Unscented household bleach (with sodium hypochlorite as the active ingredient) can be used to kill bacteria and viruses.

How to Chlorinate Water:
1. Add **8 drops of unscented bleach** per gallon of clear water (16 drops for cloudy water).
2. **Stir the water thoroughly**, ensuring even distribution of the bleach.
3. Let the water **sit for 30 minutes**. After this time, it should smell slightly of chlorine.
4. **If the chlorine smell is absent**, repeat the process with the same dosage.

Caution: Be mindful of using too much bleach, as it can be harmful. Always store bleach in a cool, dark place to maintain its effectiveness.

Iodine or Chlorine Dioxide Tablets
These tablets are compact and portable, making them perfect for backpacking or emergency kits.

How to Use Tablets:
1. Drop **one tablet per liter** of clear water (adjust if water is cloudy).
2. **Wait 30 minutes** for iodine tablets or follow the specific instructions for chlorine dioxide.

3. **Shake the container** to ensure thorough mixing.

Pro Tip: Chemical treatments can leave an aftertaste, particularly with iodine. For an improved taste, add a vitamin C tablet after the disinfection process is complete.

Boiling Water: Simple and Effective

Boiling is one of the simplest and most reliable ways to disinfect water. It kills bacteria, viruses, and protozoa, but does not remove chemicals or heavy metals, so it's best used with filtered water.

Boiling Water: Step-by-Step
1. **Collect water** and filter it if possible to remove sediment.
2. Place the water in a pot and bring it to a **rolling boil**.
3. **Maintain the boil for 1 minute** (3 minutes if you're above 6,500 feet in elevation).
4. Let the water **cool** naturally before use.

Why It Works: Boiling destroys harmful pathogens that can cause diseases like cholera, dysentery, and giardia. It's a no-fail method when other purification tools aren't available.

Key Tip: Always filter your water before boiling to remove particles. Boiling alone doesn't improve water clarity or taste.

Choosing the Right Purification Method

Selecting the right water purification method depends on the resources available and the intended use of the water. For daily drinking water in an off-grid home, **gravity-fed filters** combined with **boiling** or **chlorination** provide a long-term, low-maintenance solution. For emergencies or mobile use, **portable filters** and **chemical treatments** are ideal.

Step-by-Step Example for Safe Drinking Water:
1. **Start by filtering** water using a gravity-fed or portable filter to remove sediment and large particles.
2. **Boil the water** for 1-3 minutes or add chlorine bleach for a fast disinfection process.
3. If on the move, carry **portable purification tablets** for quick access to safe water.

Pro Tip: Regularly maintain your filters and purification systems. Over time, filters can clog, and stored chemical treatments lose their potency. Always have backup purification methods on hand, especially in an off-grid environment where water safety is paramount.

By mastering these water purification techniques, you'll ensure that your off-grid water supply is safe, no matter the source. Having a reliable, tested water system in place will give you peace of mind, allowing you to focus on other aspects of sustainable living.

Conclusion: Securing a Reliable Water Supply for Off-Grid Living

Water is the lifeblood of your off-grid homestead, and by mastering the art of collection and purification, you've taken a huge step toward true self-sufficiency. Whether it's rainwater gently flowing from your roof into well-placed tanks, or clean groundwater drawn up from a carefully drilled well, you've now laid the foundation for a reliable, sustainable water supply.

But as you've seen, water is more than just something to drink—it's the force that drives your entire off-grid life. From nourishing your garden and livestock to cleaning and cooking, understanding the different uses and purification methods has empowered you to maximize every drop. With the right strategies in place, you've not only secured your immediate needs but also set yourself up for long-term success.

Next, we'll dive into the essential skills of water storage and distribution—key components that will help you manage your supply efficiently. From safeguarding your water during dry seasons to ensuring it's available where and when you need it, you'll learn how to create a seamless, dependable water system. With each new step, you're building toward a resilient, self-sustaining future. Keep moving forward, and watch your off-grid home flourish.

4. Water Storage and Distribution: Efficient Solutions for Long-Term Resilience

After learning how to collect and purify water from natural sources like rainwater, wells, and streams in the previous guide, it's time to take the next step in securing your off-grid water system: proper storage and distribution. While having a reliable way to collect and purify water is essential, it's just as important to ensure you can safely store that water for long-term use and efficiently distribute it where it's needed most.

Water storage is one of the most crucial components of off-grid living. Without a dependable and clean supply, survival becomes challenging. Even with access to water sources like rainwater, wells, or rivers, storing water ensures you're prepared for periods of drought, emergencies, or system failures. Whether it's for drinking, cleaning, or gardening, having water reserves will give you peace of mind and resilience.

In this guide, we'll cover how to store both potable (drinkable) and non-potable water for long-term use. You'll learn how to select the right containers, treat your water to keep it safe, and establish a rotation system to maintain freshness. Additionally, we'll delve into water distribution strategies, ensuring that your stored water can be delivered efficiently throughout your off-grid home, from the kitchen to the garden. With these systems in place, you'll be equipped to manage your water resources with confidence and independence.

Long-Term Water Storage: Protecting Your Supply

When and Why You Should Store Water

Storing water is essential in several scenarios:

1. **Droughts or Water Shortages:** Rainwater or well water may not always be available, particularly during dry seasons.
2. **System Failures:** Off-grid systems like solar pumps can break down. Storing water ensures you have a backup.
3. **Natural Disasters:** Events like floods or fires may contaminate water sources. Having stored water guarantees your access to clean water.
4. **Emergency Situations:** If you become sick or injured, or if there's a supply chain disruption, stored water ensures self-reliance.

Now, let's dive into how to effectively store water for both potable and non-potable uses.

Potable Water Storage

Potable water is your primary concern because it's what you'll drink, cook with, and use for hygiene. Ensuring it remains clean and safe over time requires careful planning and execution.

Step 1: Choosing the Right Containers

The container you choose for potable water storage is critical. Always opt for **food-grade, BPA-free containers** to prevent leaching chemicals. Containers should be clearly labeled as safe for potable use.

- **Plastic Food-Grade Barrels:** Light, easy to move, and resistant to rust.
- **Stainless Steel Tanks:** Durable and UV-resistant, stainless steel containers protect water from light, which can encourage algae growth.

Pro Tip: Choose opaque or UV-resistant containers to prevent sunlight from penetrating the water and causing algae or bacterial growth.

Step 2: Where to Store Your Water

Water needs to be stored in a **cool, dark place**, such as a basement, shed, or underground storage. Sunlight and heat can degrade both the water and the container.

- **Temperature control** is key: Extreme heat accelerates bacteria growth, while freezing temperatures can crack containers.
- **Elevation matters:** Keep containers off the ground to prevent contamination from dirt, chemicals, or rodents.

Step 3: Treating Water for Long-Term Storage

Even if your water source is clean, treat your stored water to prevent microbial growth over time. Here are the most reliable treatment methods:

- **Chlorination:** Add 8 drops of unscented household bleach per gallon of water, stir thoroughly, and let it sit for 30 minutes before sealing the container.
- **Commercial Water Preservers:** Products like **Sodium Hypochlorite** can extend the shelf life of water for up to five years.

Pro Tip: Only use distilled or filtered water for long-term storage. Tap water often contains impurities that can degrade over time.

Step 4: Sealing and Rotating Your Water Supply

Once your containers are filled and treated, seal them tightly to prevent contamination. Even with treatment, water should be **rotated every six months** to ensure freshness, unless you've used a commercial preserver.

- **Label your containers** with the fill date and method of treatment so you can track when it's time for a change.
- **Inspect the water** every few months by checking for discoloration, odor, or cloudiness.

Storing Non-Potable Water

Non-potable water is essential for non-drinking purposes like cleaning, washing, or irrigation. The storage requirements for non-potable water are more flexible but still need attention to avoid contamination and spoilage.

Step 1: Use Larger, Durable Tanks

Since non-potable water is used in larger quantities, you can store it in **high-capacity tanks** like 500-gallon barrels or cisterns.

- **Above-ground plastic or metal tanks** are a common choice. These should be durable enough to handle outdoor exposure.
- **Underground cisterns** are another great option for non-potable water, as they're naturally insulated from temperature changes.

Pro Tip: For non-drinking water, it's not necessary to use food-grade containers. However, ensure that the tanks are still sealed well to avoid contamination from dirt, insects, or animals.

Step 2: Protecting Non-Potable Water from Contamination

Even though this water won't be consumed, you still need to protect it from contamination. Make sure all tanks have secure, tight-fitting lids to keep debris and animals out.

- **Mesh or fine screens** can be used to cover openings while still allowing rainwater collection.
- **Keep tanks shaded** or painted with a UV-resistant coating to avoid algae growth.

Step 3: Installing Pumps for Easy Access

Non-potable water tanks should be fitted with manual or solar-powered pumps for easy access, especially if the tanks are large or situated in a remote area.

- **Manual hand pumps** are simple and reliable in emergencies.
- **Solar-powered pumps** are excellent for off-grid systems, offering energy-efficient access to stored water.

Pro Tip: Consider having a backup pump for emergencies, especially if the non-potable water is critical for everyday tasks like irrigation or cleaning.

Maintenance and Monitoring

Maintaining your water storage systems ensures your supply is always ready when you need it. Here's a simple checklist:

For Potable Water:

- **Check seals** on all containers every 3-6 months to make sure they're airtight.
- **Inspect water quality:** Look for discoloration, strange odors, or sediment.
- **Replace water** every six months unless treated with a preserver, in that case, stick to the manufacturer's rotation guidelines.

For Non-Potable Water:

- **Flush tanks yearly** to remove sediment or debris that may have accumulated at the bottom.
- **Check spigots, hoses, and pumps** regularly for leaks or blockages to ensure smooth operation.
- **Clean filters or screens** to keep the system free of larger contaminants.

When to Use Stored Water

Understanding when and how to rely on your stored water is essential. Use your stored potable water for:

- **Emergency drinking water** during natural disasters, water shortages, or system breakdowns.
- **Cooking and food preparation** when other water sources are contaminated or unavailable.
- **Basic hygiene** (washing hands, brushing teeth) in situations where well or surface water isn't safe.

Use your stored non-potable water for:

- **Irrigation** when rain is scarce or your primary water collection system is down.
- **Cleaning and laundry** to conserve potable water.
- **Flushing toilets** in case of a plumbing failure.

Expert Tip: Save your potable water by using non-potable water whenever you can for non-drinking tasks.

Storing water correctly is about more than just filling barrels; it's about creating a reliable, long-term water management system. By selecting the right containers, treating water effectively, and maintaining your storage setup, you'll ensure your off-grid lifestyle is resilient to disruptions in your water supply.

Water Distribution: Efficiently Managing Your Water Supply

When living off-grid, it's not just about collecting and purifying water—it's equally important to manage how water is distributed throughout your home and property. A well-designed water distribution system ensures that water flows where it's needed for drinking, cooking, cleaning, irrigation, and other essential tasks, without waste or unnecessary effort. In this section, we'll break down the key strategies for building an efficient off-grid water distribution network.

Understanding Your Water Needs

Before setting up a water distribution system, you need to evaluate your daily water needs. This helps you plan the size and scope of your distribution system, ensuring you have enough capacity for all your off-grid activities.

Average Water Use Breakdown:

- **Drinking and Cooking:** 1-3 gallons per person per day.
- **Washing and Cleaning:** 10-20 gallons per person per day (can be reduced with efficient systems).
- **Gardening:** Dependent on climate, plant types, and irrigation methods—estimate at least 1-2 gallons per square foot weekly during growing season.

Tip: For a sustainable system, design your distribution network based on peak demand during dry seasons.

Designing Your Off-Grid Water Distribution Network

A reliable distribution system transports water from your collection or storage tanks to various points around your property, including your kitchen, bathroom, and garden. There are several methods for setting this up, based on factors like terrain, climate, and the size of your home or homestead.

Gravity-Fed Systems: Simple and Energy-Efficient

Gravity-fed water systems are one of the most effective and low-maintenance options for off-grid living. By positioning your water storage tanks at a higher elevation than the points of use, gravity will naturally move water through pipes without the need for pumps or external energy.

How to Set Up a Gravity-Fed System:

1. **Elevate Your Storage Tanks:** Place tanks on a raised platform, hill, or tower. The higher the tank, the more water pressure you'll get.
2. **Install Piping:** Use durable, freeze-resistant piping (like PVC or polyethylene) to connect the tank to various points around your property (sink, shower, irrigation, etc.).
3. **Control Flow with Valves:** Install valves at key points to control the flow and allow you to shut off water to specific areas when not in use.
4. **Calculate Pressure Needs:** Ensure your tank is elevated enough to generate the required pressure. Every foot of elevation provides approximately 0.43 PSI (pounds per square inch) of water pressure.

Pro Tip: If you live in a flat area, you can still use gravity-fed systems by elevating water tanks on platforms or towers. Alternatively, build a small hillside reservoir if your property allows.

Pump-Based Systems: Flexibility with Solar or Manual Pumps

If gravity-fed systems are not feasible, or if you need higher pressure, a pump-based water distribution system is the solution. Solar-powered pumps are ideal for off-grid settings, as they use renewable energy to distribute water without the need for traditional electricity.

Steps for Setting Up a Pump-Based System:

1. **Choose a Pump:** For well water or water stored at ground level, select a solar-powered pump or a manual hand pump. Solar pumps are efficient for continuous use, while manual pumps are good backups.
2. **Install a Pump Controller:** This device helps regulate the flow of water and ensures the pump doesn't run dry. It also prevents the system from overloading.

3. **Pipe Installation:** As with gravity-fed systems, connect your pump to distribution pipes, ensuring all connections are watertight to prevent leaks.
4. **Install Backup Power:** For critical water needs, have a manual pump or backup power source, like a small battery or generator, to ensure access to water if your primary system fails.

Expert Tip: Solar-powered pumps work well for deep wells or distant water sources. Ensure you have solar panels positioned for optimal sunlight throughout the day for reliable water pumping.

Zoning Your Water Distribution: Efficiency and Conservation

Dividing your water distribution network into zones allows you to prioritize water delivery to areas with the highest need, ensuring efficiency and minimizing waste. For example, you might have one zone for your home's drinking and washing water, another for the garden, and a third for livestock.

Setting Up Water Zones:

1. **Map Out Zones:** Designate areas for drinking water, cleaning, irrigation, and livestock. Keep the most critical zones (like potable water) closest to the source or tanks.
2. **Install Shutoff Valves:** Include shutoff valves in each zone so you can control where water is flowing at any time. This also helps during maintenance or repairs.
3. **Prioritize Water Flow:** Ensure water for essential tasks like drinking and cooking is always available, while less critical uses, like irrigation, can be adjusted or paused during water shortages.

Tip: Use drip irrigation systems in the garden to reduce water waste. They provide water directly to the roots, reducing both evaporation and runoff.

Mastering Water for Off-Grid Living

In your journey toward off-grid independence, securing a reliable water supply is one of the most critical steps. In the previous guide, we covered the foundational aspects of water collection and purification—whether from rain, wells, or streams, you've learned how to gather water safely and ensure it's clean for use. That was the essential first step in building a resilient off-grid water system.

Now, with this book, you've taken the next step: understanding how to store that water long-term and distribute it efficiently throughout your property. From storing potable water in food-grade containers to protecting non-potable water for gardening and cleaning, you've learned how to safeguard your water reserves in case of emergencies, droughts, or system failures. You've also explored the practical strategies for getting that water where it's needed most, through simple gravity-fed systems or more robust solar-powered pumps.

Together, these two guides give you a complete, sustainable approach to water management—starting with how to collect and purify water, and then ensuring it's stored and distributed effectively. With these skills, you can now confidently manage one of the most vital resources in your off-grid life, giving you the freedom and peace of mind to focus on other aspects of self-reliant living. Keep refining your systems, and you'll have a water supply that is as resilient as the lifestyle you're building.

5. Off-Grid Sanitation Systems: Managing Waste for a Healthy Homestead

The Vital Role of Sanitation in Off-Grid Living

As you navigate the journey of off-grid living, managing your water supply is just the beginning. Sanitation is one of the most critical aspects of off-grid living. Without access to modern sewage systems or municipal waste management, it's essential to implement proper sanitation methods to protect both your health and the environment. In an off-grid setting, managing waste effectively not only helps prevent the spread of disease but also supports the sustainability of your entire lifestyle.

Poor sanitation can lead to contaminated water sources, illness, and a breakdown in your off-grid system. By adopting safe, eco-friendly waste management practices, you can avoid these risks while promoting long-term health and sustainability. Water safety is a particular concern—improper waste disposal can seep into groundwater or nearby streams, affecting your drinking water supply. Effective sanitation practices are key to maintaining a healthy, self-reliant way of life.

Core Waste Management Strategies: Choosing the Right System

When living off-grid, managing human waste is one of the most critical elements for maintaining health and hygiene. Without access to modern sewage or waste systems, you must take responsibility for creating a sustainable, eco-friendly solution that suits your environment. Whether you're living in a forest, desert, or remote homestead, choosing the right waste management system ensures that you can stay healthy and avoid contaminating the environment. Below, we explore three reliable and safe methods for handling human waste in an off-grid setting.

Composting Toilets: Turning Waste into a Resource

Overview

A composting toilet is an excellent choice for off-grid living due to its simplicity and sustainability. This system doesn't require water, making it ideal for dry environments or places where water is scarce. It turns human waste into usable compost over time, helping to close the nutrient cycle in an eco-friendly way. The best part? It's easy to build and maintain with basic materials, and the compost can later be used to fertilize non-edible plants.

Key Features

- **Waterless and eco-friendly:** Requires no plumbing or water supply, making it perfect for off-grid environments.
- **Turns waste into usable compost:** Over time, the system naturally breaks down waste into compost that can enrich the soil.
- **Low-maintenance if properly ventilated:** With the right setup, composting toilets are straightforward to maintain and don't produce bad odors.

How to Build a Composting Toilet (Step-by-Step Guide)

1. **Create the Base:**

Build a sturdy wooden or plastic box that will house the waste bucket. Make sure it's solid enough to support the weight of the person using it, and top it with a standard toilet seat for comfort.

2. **Add a Covering System:**

Every time you use the toilet, sprinkle a layer of cover material (such as sawdust, peat moss, or straw) over the waste. This step is crucial as it helps to absorb moisture and control odors. Always keep a bucket of covering material next to the toilet for easy access.

3. **Install Ventilation:**

To further reduce odors, install a ventilation pipe that runs from the waste bucket to the outside. This allows gases to escape and promotes airflow, which is critical for the decomposition process.

4. **Composting:**

Once the bucket is full, transfer the contents to a composting bin or designated compost pile outside. The waste will break down naturally over 6-12 months, transforming into nutrient-rich compost. Remember, this compost is best used for non-edible plants to avoid health risks.

Pro Tips for Efficient Composting

- **Use enough cover material:** Always apply a generous amount of sawdust or other covering material after each use. This minimizes odors and helps keep moisture levels balanced.
- **Monitor temperatures:** For the compost to be safe and effective, the pile should reach temperatures of at least 130°F (54°C) for several days. This helps kill harmful pathogens.
- **Location is key:** Keep your composting bin or pile well away from water sources to prevent any risk of contamination.

Pit Toilets (Outhouses): Simple and Reliable

Overview

A pit toilet, or outhouse, is the simplest form of off-grid waste management. It involves digging a deep pit and covering the waste with soil after each use. This option works best in rural or remote areas where the ground is stable and there's no risk of groundwater contamination. While not as eco-friendly as a composting toilet, it's an efficient solution for those needing a straightforward setup.

Construction Steps

1. **Dig a Pit:**

The pit should be at least 6-8 feet deep to handle waste for an extended period. Make sure it's dug at least 100 feet away from any water sources (wells, streams, or ponds) to prevent contamination.

2. **Build a Shelter:**

Construct a simple wooden or plastic structure over the pit for privacy. You can add a door, ventilation, and a seat for comfort. Make sure the structure is weatherproof and stable.

3. **Waste Management:**

After each use, cover the waste with a layer of soil to help control odors and reduce the attraction of insects. This method helps to keep the area cleaner and more sanitary.

Maintenance

- **Regularly add soil:** Each time you use the pit toilet, add a scoop of soil to cover the waste. This not only helps control smells but also discourages insects.
- **Monitor pit levels:** Once the pit fills up (ideally leaving 1-2 feet of space from the top), cover it completely with soil and dig a new pit in a different location.

Pro Tips for Pit Toilets

- **Choose high ground:** Place your pit toilet on elevated land to avoid flooding during heavy rains. Water can carry waste into nearby water sources or your living area if not managed correctly.
- **Consider natural insect deterrents:** Adding lime or ash to the pit can help reduce odors and deter insects from breeding.

Septic Systems: Long-Term Waste Solutions

Overview

A septic system is a more advanced option for off-grid waste management, suitable for homesteads with access to water. Unlike composting or pit toilets, a septic system uses water to flush waste into an underground tank, where solids and liquids are separated. The system then filters the wastewater through a leach field, returning it safely to the environment. Septic systems are ideal for larger homes or families but require more installation work upfront.

Steps to Set Up a Septic System

1. **Choose a Safe Location:**

The septic tank should be installed at least 100 feet from water sources to avoid contamination. The leach field must be placed in an area with good drainage to allow filtered wastewater to seep into the soil safely.

2. **Excavate the Area:**

You'll need to dig trenches for both the septic tank and the leach field. The depth of the trenches will depend on the size of the tank and your soil conditions, but they should be deep enough to ensure that wastewater doesn't pool on the surface.

3. **Install the Tank:**

Place the septic tank in the trench, ensuring it's level and properly supported. Connect PVC pipes from your home's plumbing to the tank's inlet, and another pipe from the tank's outlet to the leach field.

4. **Create the Leach Field:**

In the leach field, lay perforated pipes over a bed of gravel. The pipes will disperse the filtered wastewater into the surrounding soil. Cover the pipes with geotextile fabric to prevent soil from clogging the system, then backfill the trenches with earth.

Maintenance Tips for Septic Systems

- **Monitor tank levels:** Septic tanks need to be pumped out periodically to prevent overflow or blockages. Depending on the size of the system and the number of users, you may need to pump the tank every 3-5 years.
- **Be cautious about what you flush:** Septic systems can be damaged by non-biodegradable items like plastic, paper towels, or chemicals. Only flush biodegradable waste to keep your system running smoothly.

Sustaining Sanitation Off the Grid Sanitation is the backbone of off-grid living. With the right systems in place—whether it's composting toilets, pit latrines, or a full septic setup—you'll protect your health and the environment. By integrating water filtration, greywater reuse, and emergency solutions, you create a sustainable and resilient homestead.

6. Water and Waste Management: Filtration, Greywater, and Emergency Solutions

Introduction: Mastering Water and Waste Management for Sustainable Living

In the previous part, we explored how to build a healthy, waste-free environment through composting toilets, pit latrines, and septic systems. These solutions are essential in safeguarding both your health and the environment. However, maintaining a truly self-sufficient homestead extends beyond just managing waste. Equally important is how you handle water—both for daily use and in emergencies. Water is at the heart of sustainable living, and managing it efficiently ensures that your off-grid system remains resilient, no matter the challenges.

In this guide we dive deeper into the critical elements of water management. Whether it's building a reliable water filtration system to secure clean water for sanitation and cooking, or reusing greywater to optimize resources, every drop counts when living off-grid. Furthermore, we'll cover practical emergency strategies to ensure you're prepared for the unexpected—from setting up makeshift latrines to purifying water on the go. By mastering these skills, you'll be well-equipped to maintain hygiene, prevent contamination, and protect your health during any scenario.

This guide will help you turn challenges into opportunities, transforming waste and water into sustainable resources that support your off-grid life. Let's take the next step in building a truly independent homestead, where both water and waste are managed with efficiency, safety, and care.

Safe Water Management: Filtration and Greywater Systems

Water is life. When living off-grid, the management of water is as critical as the management of waste. Clean water is essential not only for drinking but also for sanitation and hygiene. Failing to handle water properly can lead to contamination, putting your health at risk and potentially polluting your environment. Therefore, having a reliable system for filtering water and managing greywater is essential to sustainable off-grid living. Below, we'll explore two key components of off-grid water management: water filtration and greywater reuse.

Building a Simple Water Filtration System

In an off-grid setting, ensuring access to clean water is paramount. While you may have a natural water source such as a river, well, or rain catchment system, that water is not guaranteed to be free of contaminants like dirt, debris, or pathogens. Building a basic filtration system with readily available materials can give you an effective first step toward clean water for general use.

Materials You'll Need:

- **Large container or barrel**: Acts as the body of your filtration system.
- **Gravel**: The first filtration layer to trap large particles.
- **Sand**: A finer layer that filters smaller debris.
- **Activated charcoal**: A crucial layer for absorbing toxins and impurities.
- **Fine mesh or cloth**: For capturing larger debris before water enters the filtration layers.

How to Build Your Filtration System:

1. **Layer the Filtration Materials:**
   - **Gravel Layer**: Begin by placing a thick layer of coarse gravel at the bottom of your container. This layer captures larger debris like leaves, twigs, or larger dirt particles.
   - **Sand Layer**: Add a layer of fine sand on top of the gravel. The sand will filter out smaller particles such as silt or sediment, improving the clarity of the water.

- Activated Charcoal Layer: The top layer should be activated charcoal. This is the most important filtration layer as it removes chemicals, toxins, and pathogens that might be present in the water.

2. **Install a Mesh Filter:**
   - Secure a fine mesh cloth or similar material over the mouth of the container. This additional layer helps prevent large debris like leaves or insects from entering the filtration system, keeping it cleaner for longer use.

3. **Filter the Water:**
   - Pour untreated water through the system, allowing it to slowly filter through the layers of gravel, sand, and activated charcoal. The water that collects at the bottom will be filtered and much cleaner than when it entered the system.

Important Notes:

- While this filtration system is effective for removing physical impurities and many toxins, **it doesn't guarantee that the water is safe for drinking**. To make it potable, you will need to **boil the water** for at least one minute or **use water purification tablets**.
- This water filtration method is highly effective for producing water suitable for cleaning, irrigation, and general non-drinking use.

Greywater Reuse: Sustainability in Action

In an off-grid environment, greywater—wastewater from sinks, showers, and washing—is a valuable resource that should not go to waste. Properly reusing greywater for irrigation or other non-potable purposes helps you conserve your fresh water supply, contributing to a more sustainable and resource-efficient off-grid lifestyle. However, it's important to handle greywater safely to avoid contamination of your living space or nearby water sources.

Steps for Reusing Greywater Safely:

1. **Install a Greywater Collection System:**
   - Begin by setting up a simple piping or tubing system to direct greywater from areas like sinks, showers, or laundry machines into a dedicated **holding tank** or irrigation area. PVC piping works well for this purpose and is affordable.
   - Ensure that your collection system is well-sealed and flows directly into a filtration area to prevent leaks or contamination around your home.

2. **Create a Basic Greywater Filtration System:**
   - Just like with drinking water, greywater needs to be filtered before reuse. You can use a similar method by layering **gravel**, **sand**, and **mesh** in a barrel or tank.
   - This system will remove larger debris, soap scum, and organic matter from the water, making it safer for reuse in your garden or landscaping.
   - It's crucial to use **biodegradable, non-toxic soaps** in your washing and cleaning to avoid introducing harmful chemicals into the greywater system.

3. **Use Greywater for Irrigating Non-Edible Plants:**
   - Once filtered, greywater can be safely used to irrigate **non-edible plants** like trees, shrubs, and ornamental gardens. Avoid using greywater directly on fruits, vegetables, or herbs to minimize the risk of contamination.
   - By diverting greywater to non-edible plants, you reduce the strain on your freshwater sources and create a more efficient water-use cycle on your homestead.

Best Practices for Greywater Reuse:

- **Separate greywater from blackwater** (sewage): Never mix greywater with blackwater from toilets or other hazardous waste systems. Greywater is relatively clean and can be reused if handled properly.
- **Maintain regular filtration**: Clean out your greywater filtration system regularly to prevent clogging from soap residue or debris. Regular upkeep will prolong the lifespan of the system and improve the quality of the filtered water.
- **Check local regulations**: In some areas, there may be specific rules or recommendations for greywater use. Always make sure your system is compliant with local guidelines, especially if you're close to natural water sources.

Effective water management is foundational to off-grid living. By implementing a basic filtration system, you'll maintain a steady flow of cleaner water for sanitation, cooking, and irrigation. Meanwhile, reusing greywater reduces waste and conserves precious resources, making your off-grid lifestyle more sustainable.

It's important to remember that water from these systems still needs to be purified for drinking, but by following these practical steps, you're well on your way to maintaining a safe, efficient water system for all your other needs.

These strategies are essential building blocks for creating a self-reliant off-grid home, minimizing environmental impact, and ensuring long-term health and sustainability for you and your family.

Emergency Sanitation: Being Prepared for the Unexpected

Living off-grid often means preparing for the unpredictable, especially when it comes to sanitation. Natural disasters, system failures, or even supply shortages can disrupt your usual waste management routines. In these moments, having a solid plan for emergency sanitation ensures that you maintain hygiene, prevent contamination, and protect your health—even when the situation gets tough.

Here, we'll break down the critical steps and methods for setting up temporary sanitation solutions during emergencies. These methods are designed to be simple, effective, and adaptable, using minimal resources while prioritizing safety.

Makeshift Latrines: A Temporary Solution

When your regular sanitation system is compromised, makeshift latrines can provide an effective short-term solution for managing human waste. Setting up a temporary latrine requires minimal tools and can be done quickly, but it's essential to follow a few key guidelines for safety and hygiene.

How to Set Up a Makeshift Trench Latrine:

1. **Choose a Safe Location:**
   - **Distance from water sources**: Always ensure the latrine is at least 100 feet away from any water sources, including rivers, lakes, and wells. This prevents waste from contaminating your drinking water supply.
   - **Downwind placement**: Position the latrine downwind from your living area to minimize odors and keep your home environment clean and comfortable.
   - **Avoid low-lying areas**: Pick a location on higher ground to prevent runoff and flooding, which can carry waste into nearby water sources during rain.

2. **Dig the Trench:**
   o The trench should be **at least 2 feet deep** to ensure that waste is safely buried, reducing the risk of contamination and exposure.
   o If possible, dig a trench long enough to accommodate multiple uses. This way, you can cover waste with soil after each use and move along the trench as needed.
3. **Cover Waste After Each Use:**
   o After every use, cover the waste with **soil or ash**. This helps control odors, reduces flies and pests, and promotes natural decomposition.
   o If you have access to biodegradable materials like leaves or sawdust, sprinkle some over the waste before covering it with soil. This will aid in decomposition and help minimize smells.
4. **Create a Simple Seat (Optional):**
   o For comfort, you can place a sturdy wooden plank or a bucket with a toilet seat over the trench. This setup makes it easier to use the latrine and keeps the surrounding area cleaner.
   o Ensure the seat is stable and secure to prevent any accidents.

Maintenance Tips:

- **Regularly monitor the trench** for any signs of erosion or contamination risks.
- Once the trench is filled to about 1 foot below the surface, **completely cover it with soil** and dig a new trench if needed.
- Always keep a shovel and cover materials nearby for easy maintenance.

Quick Water Sanitation Methods: Clean Water in Emergencies

Clean water is just as critical as waste management during emergencies. Whether your usual water filtration system has failed or your clean water supply has been compromised, knowing how to quickly and effectively sanitize water is essential for staying healthy.

Here are three reliable methods for making water safe to use in an off-grid emergency:

1. **Boiling Water: The Tried-and-True Method**

Boiling water is one of the easiest and most efficient methods to kill pathogens like bacteria, viruses, and parasites, making it safe for drinking and cooking.

Steps to Boil Water for Purification:

   o **Heat the water**: Bring the water to a **rolling boil**—this means bubbles should continuously rise to the surface.
   o **Boil for at least 1 minute**: At higher altitudes (above 6,500 feet), boil the water for **at least 3 minutes** to ensure all pathogens are killed.
   o **Cool and store**: Let the water cool naturally before transferring it to clean containers for storage.

Pro Tip: Always use clean utensils and containers when handling boiled water to avoid recontamination.

2. **Bleach Treatment: A Quick Chemical Solution**

If boiling isn't feasible, you can sanitize water with household bleach. This method is effective for quickly treating small amounts of water when fuel or heat sources are unavailable.

How to Use Bleach to Sanitize Water:

   o Use **unscented household bleach** that contains 5.25% to 8.25% sodium hypochlorite.
   o Add 8 drops of bleach per gallon for clear water, or 16 drops for cloudy water.

o   Stir thoroughly and let it stand for at least 30 minutes. The water should have a mild chlorine smell—this indicates it's properly treated.

Note: If the water doesn't have a slight chlorine smell after treatment, repeat the process and wait an additional 15 minutes.

3. **Water Purification Tablets: Compact and Effective**

Water purification tablets are a convenient, portable solution for disinfecting water in emergency situations. These tablets are particularly handy for when you're on the move or don't have the means to boil water or use bleach.

Using Water Purification Tablets:

o   Adhere to the manufacturer's directions: Every brand provides specific guidelines on how many tablets to use per liter or gallon of water.

o   Most tablets require about **30 minutes to 4 hours** to fully disinfect the water, depending on the contamination level and the brand's formulation.

Pro Tip: Always carry a small supply of water purification tablets in your emergency kit or bug-out bag—they're lightweight and can be lifesaving in a crisis.

In this guide, you've learned how to take control of both areas, from building reliable water filtration systems to safely reusing greywater and preparing for emergency sanitation. These skills not only conserve valuable resources but also ensure that your homestead remains clean, safe, and sustainable.

Effective water management encompasses all aspects of daily life, including cooking, cleaning, and irrigation. By creating efficient filtration systems and reusing greywater, you can maximize your resources and reduce waste. With a deeper understanding of these processes, you'll be able to provide for your household while also protecting the environment that supports your off-grid lifestyle.

In addition, having emergency sanitation plans in place prepares you for unexpected challenges. Whether it's setting up makeshift latrines or quickly purifying water in a crisis, these strategies will allow you to respond effectively and maintain hygiene in any situation.

With these tools in hand, you're now equipped to manage water and waste in a way that supports long-term health and sustainability. Continue building on these foundations, and you'll have a homestead that's not only self-reliant but also ready to thrive, no matter what the future holds.

7. Guidelines to Follow When Building Your Solar Power System

After having covered the essentials of water and sanitation, it's time to shift focus to energy, starting with solar power. Solar energy provides a clean, reliable solution, freeing you from the grid and harnessing the sun's power. Whether you're deep in the wilderness or out in open land, solar power will sustain your off-grid lifestyle with ease and independence.

Introduction to Solar Power for Off-Grid Living

Benefits of Solar Power

Solar power is one of the most effective and reliable energy sources for off-grid living. Here's why it stands out as the go-to solution:

- **Environmentally Friendly and Renewable**: Solar energy harnesses power directly from the sun, a natural and inexhaustible source of energy. By relying on solar power, you minimize your environmental footprint, avoid using fossil fuels, and contribute to reducing greenhouse gas emissions. This makes solar energy a clean, sustainable choice for those who want to live in harmony with nature.
- **Low-Maintenance and Highly Reliable**: Once installed, solar power systems need very little upkeep since the panels themselves have no moving parts, making them durable and long-lasting. With occasional cleaning and regular check-ups on components like batteries and inverters, a well-installed system can operate for decades. This reliability is crucial in off-grid scenarios, where energy needs must be met consistently without relying on external power grids.
- **Reduces Dependence on Traditional Power Grids**: Going off-grid with solar power means gaining full control over your energy production. In rural or remote areas where grid access is limited or non-existent, solar energy provides an independent power source, freeing you from electricity outages and rising utility costs.

How Solar Power Works

Understanding how solar energy converts into usable electricity is essential for optimizing your system.

- **Basic Concepts: Turning Sunlight into Power:** Solar panels, also known as photovoltaic panels, harness sunlight and convert it into direct current (DC) electricity. This process occurs when photons (light particles) hit the solar cells, knocking electrons loose and generating a flow of electricity. This is the core principle behind solar energy production, and the efficiency of this conversion depends on the quality of the panels and the amount of sunlight they receive.
- **DC (Direct Current) vs. AC (Alternating Current) Power:**
  - Solar panels produce DC power, which flows in one direction and is typically used to charge batteries. However, most household appliances operate on alternating current (AC) power, which alternates direction in a flow and is supplied by traditional grids.
  - In off-grid solar systems, an **inverter** is used to transform the DC energy produced by the solar panels and stored in batteries into AC electricity, enabling it to power everyday appliances such as lighting, refrigerators, and other essential devices.

- **The Role of Key Components:**

- o **Solar Panels**: These are the first point of contact between the sun's rays and your energy system. High-quality solar panels ensure maximum efficiency in capturing sunlight and converting it into electricity.
- o **Charge Controllers**: This device manages the electrical current between the solar panels and the battery bank, preventing overcharging and making sure the batteries are protected and charged efficiently.
- o **Batteries**: Off-grid systems rely heavily on batteries to reserve extra energy produced during the day, ensuring power is available at night or when sunlight is limited. Batteries are the backbone of a stable off-grid energy system.
- o **Inverters**: As mentioned, inverters play a key role by transforming the DC energy stored in batteries into AC electricity, making it compatible with standard household appliances and devices in your home.

Why Solar Power is Ideal for Off-Grid Living

When you live off-grid, every resource counts. Solar power provides the perfect solution for ensuring energy independence and reducing reliance on external systems.

- **Ensures Energy Independence and Resilience**: By investing in a solar power system, you take control of your energy supply. This resilience is crucial in remote or disaster-prone areas where power outages or lack of infrastructure can become serious obstacles. With a properly sized solar power system, you can produce enough electricity to meet your needs year-round, regardless of the local grid's condition or availability.

- **Adaptable to Various Climates and Locations**: Solar energy systems can be customized to work effectively in a broad spectrum of climates. Whether you live in a sunny desert or a cloudy, temperate region, solar panels can be sized and positioned to maximize output based on local weather patterns and sunlight availability. Advances in solar technology have made it possible to generate substantial power even in less-than-ideal conditions.

- **Reduces Carbon Footprint, Promoting Sustainability**: Using solar power as your primary energy source significantly reduces your environmental impact. Opting for off-grid solar power significantly reduces your carbon footprint and helps conserve natural resources. Over the life of your solar system, the reduction in greenhouse gases is comparable to planting hundreds of trees or removing several cars from the road.

Reducing Your Carbon Footprint: Building a Sustainable Off-Grid Lifestyle

One of the most compelling reasons to adopt solar power for your off-grid living is the significant reduction in your carbon footprint. By relying on renewable solar energy instead of fossil fuels, you directly contribute to lowering greenhouse gas emissions. This not only supports environmental preservation but also guarantees your energy needs are met without placing additional pressure on the planet's finite resources. In a world increasingly affected by climate change, every step toward sustainability matters. By integrating solar energy into your off-grid setup, you'll be making an impact while gaining the long-term benefits of energy independence.

Planning Your Solar Power Setup

A successful solar power system starts with proper planning. The key is understanding your energy needs and designing a system that meets them efficiently. This section will guide you through assessing your requirements, prioritizing essential devices, and sizing your system accordingly.

1. Assessing Your Energy Needs

Before investing in solar equipment, it's crucial to determine exactly how much energy your household consumes daily. This involves calculating the power requirements for every appliance and device you plan to use in your off-grid home. Here's how you can do it step by step:

Step-by-Step: Calculating Power Requirements

1. **List Every Device:** Start by listing all the devices you will power with your solar system—lights, refrigerator, water pump, stove, heater, and any other appliance.
2. **Estimate Wattage:** Look for the wattage rating on each device. If it's not provided, you can typically locate this information in the product manual or by doing a quick online search.
3. **Calculate Daily Usage:** Multiply the wattage of each device by the number of hours it will be used daily. This will give you the total watt-hours (Wh) consumed per device each day.
    o   Example:
        ▪ A 100-watt lightbulb used for 5 hours per day = 500 watt-hours.
        ▪ A 1,500-watt space heater used for 3 hours per day = 4,500 watt-hours.
4. **Calculate Peak Energy Usage:** Some appliances use more power during specific times (such as heating during the night). Identify your peak usage periods to ensure your system can handle these loads.
    o   **Tip:** It's essential to account for peak power consumption, as it helps prevent system overloads.
5. **Total Daily Energy Usage:** Sum up the watt-hours for all devices. This gives you the total energy requirement your system must meet on a daily basis.

2. Prioritizing Essential Energy Needs

When designing an off-grid system, it's wise to prioritize which devices are essential for your lifestyle and which are optional. By focusing on powering only the most critical appliances, you can reduce energy consumption and save on system costs.

Steps for Prioritization:

*   **Identify Non-Essential Devices:** These might include luxury appliances like TVs, gaming consoles, or extra lights. Decide which devices you can comfortably live without to lower your energy load.
*   **Focus on Essentials:** Items such as lighting, refrigeration, and water pumps should take priority. Ensure that your system can support these even during periods of low sunlight.
    o   **Pro Tip:** Energy-efficient appliances can dramatically reduce your overall power requirements. For example, switching to LED lighting or choosing an Energy Star-rated fridge can cut down your energy consumption significantly.

3. Sizing the Solar Power System

Now that you have a clear idea of your energy needs, it's time to size your solar system. This involves choosing the right solar panels, battery storage, charge controllers, and inverters to match your requirements.

A. Solar Panels

Solar panels form the core of your off-grid energy system. The quantity and size of these panels

you need depend on the total daily watt-hour consumption, geographic location, and available sunlight.

Key Considerations:

- **Wattage and Efficiency Ratings:** Solar panels come with different wattage outputs and efficiency ratings. Higher wattage panels can produce more power, but might be larger or more expensive.
- Formula for Panel Calculation:
  - Daily energy usage (in watt-hours) ÷ average sunlight hours per day = total panel wattage required.
  - **Example:** If your daily energy consumption is 6,000 Wh and your location receives 5 hours of sunlight per day, you'll need at least 1,200 watts of solar panels (6,000 Wh ÷ 5 hours).
- **Geographic Location:** The amount of sunlight available varies by location and season. Use online solar calculators or consult local data to estimate how much solar power you can generate based on your region's sunlight availability.
  - **Tip:** In areas with low sunlight, consider increasing your panel size to compensate.

B. Battery Storage

Batteries store the solar energy you generate to provide power when sunlight is limited, like at night or on overcast days. Sizing your battery bank correctly is critical to ensure you have enough energy stored for uninterrupted use.

Types of Batteries:

- **Lead-Acid Batteries:** These are typically less expensive, though they tend to have a shorter lifespan and demand more upkeep.
- **AGM (Absorbent Glass Mat) Batteries:** Offer better efficiency and maintenance-free operation but are more expensive.
- **Lithium-Ion Batteries:** The most efficient and longest-lasting option, though they come with a higher upfront cost.

Determining Battery Bank Size:

1. **Calculate Nighttime Usage:** Identify how much energy you'll need when there's no sunlight. For example, if you use 3,000 Wh of energy at night, your battery bank must store at least that much.
2. **Depth of Discharge (DoD):** This refers to how much of the battery's capacity can be used without damaging it. Most batteries operate best at 50% DoD, meaning you'll need twice the storage capacity.
   - **Example:** If your nighttime usage is 3,000 Wh and you choose a battery with a 50% DoD, you'll need a 6,000 Wh battery bank.
3. **Battery Lifespan:** Consider how often you will cycle through your batteries and how long they'll last. Lithium-ion batteries tend to last longer and provide more charge cycles than traditional lead-acid batteries.

C. Charge Controllers

A charge controller manages the energy transfer between your solar panels and battery bank, ensuring the batteries are not overcharged and remain protected..

Types of Charge Controllers:

- **PWM (Pulse Width Modulation):** A more affordable option but less efficient, especially for larger systems.
- **MPPT (Maximum Power Point Tracking):** More efficient and can extract more power from the same solar panel setup, making it the ideal choice for most off-grid systems.

D. Inverters

Inverters transform the direct current (DC) from your batteries into alternating current (AC), making it compatible with the majority of household appliances.

Choosing the Right Inverter:

1. **Sizing the Inverter:** Ensure the inverter matches your peak energy needs. If your appliances draw 3,000 watts at peak times, you'll need an inverter rated for at least that much.
2. **Pure Sine Wave vs. Modified Sine Wave:** Pure sine wave inverters deliver clean, consistent power ideal for sensitive electronics, while modified sine wave inverters are cheaper but may not work as well for certain devices.
3. **Surge Protection:** Inverters should have built-in surge protection to handle power spikes when larger appliances (like refrigerators or pumps) start up.

Designing an efficient solar power system for off-grid living requires thoughtful planning and a solid grasp of your energy requirements. By adhering to these guidelines, you can ensure your system is properly sized to meet your requirements and provides reliable, renewable energy for years to come.

Pro Tip: As you build your system, prioritize energy efficiency wherever possible. Every watt saved through smarter energy use translates into a smaller, more cost-effective solar setup.

With the right approach, solar power can provide a sustainable, independent energy solution that allows you to thrive in your off-grid lifestyle, free from the constraints of traditional energy systems.

Budgeting and Cost Analysis for Your Off-Grid Solar Power System

When planning an off-grid solar power system, budgeting is an essential part of the process. You need to understand the initial investment, long-term savings, and available financing options. Building a solar power system might seem costly at first, but the long-term benefits will pay off. Let's break down the budget and explore ways to make the most of your investment.

1. Initial Investment

The initial costs of setting up a solar power system vary depending on the size and complexity of your installation. Here's how to approach this step:

Breaking Down the Costs:

- **Solar Panels:** The largest upfront cost. Panels are priced based on their wattage and efficiency. Higher efficiency panels might cost more but produce more energy in the same footprint.
- **Batteries:** Essential for storing energy for use when the sun isn't shining. Lithium-ion batteries tend to be more expensive but last longer and are more efficient than lead-acid options.
- **Inverters:** Convert the DC energy from your panels and batteries into usable AC power for your home. Pure sine wave inverters are recommended for sensitive electronics but are more expensive than modified sine wave inverters.
- **Wiring and Mounting Materials:** Include high-quality cables, mounting racks for the panels (roof or ground), and any weatherproofing needed to protect your equipment from the elements.

Pro Tip: When comparing prices, remember that higher-quality components will last longer and require less maintenance over time, making them a more cost-effective option over time.

Comparing Solar Panel Brands and Types:

- **Monocrystalline Panels:** More expensive but highly efficient and space-saving. Ideal if you have limited roof or ground space.

- **Polycrystalline Panels:** Lower cost but slightly less efficient. Great for larger installations where space isn't a concern.
- **Thin Film Panels:** Generally cheaper but less efficient. Best suited for low-power needs or flexible installation surfaces.

2. Long-term Savings

While the upfront costs of solar power can be high, the savings over time make it an excellent long-term investment.

Estimating Payback Time: Calculate your payback time by dividing the initial cost of your system by the amount of money saved on energy bills each year. For instance, if your system costs $10,000 and you save $1,500 annually on electricity, your payback period is about 6.7 years.

- **Tip:** Keep in mind that energy prices are expected to rise, so your savings will likely increase over time, reducing the payback period.

Long-term Maintenance Savings: Solar systems require minimal maintenance compared to traditional generators, which have ongoing fuel and service costs. A well-maintained solar setup can last 25-30 years with few additional expenses.

- **Battery Maintenance:** Modern lithium-ion batteries tend to last longer (10-15 years) compared to lead-acid batteries, reducing replacement costs in the long run.
- **Inverter Replacement:** Inverters typically need replacing every 10-15 years, so factor that into your long-term budget.

3. Options for Financing and Government Incentives

Financing options and government incentives can significantly reduce your upfront costs. Be sure to explore all available resources.

Tax Credits and Rebates:

- **Federal Tax Credits:** In the U.S., the federal government offers a tax credit (ITC) for solar installations, which enables you to deduct a percentage of the system cost from your taxes. Be sure to check the current percentage, as it may vary from year to year.
- **State and Local Incentives:** Many states and municipalities offer additional tax credits, rebates, or grants for solar installations. These vary by location, so check with your local government or utility provider.

Pro Tip: Combine federal and local incentives to maximize your savings. Many homeowners end up saving 30-50% on their solar installations through these programs.

Financing Options:

- **Solar Loans:** Many banks and lenders offer loans specifically for solar installations. These loans typically offer competitive interest rates and flexible repayment options, allowing you to spread out the initial costs.
- **Leasing or Power Purchase Agreements (PPAs):** Under a lease or PPA, a third-party company installs and maintains the solar system, and you pay for the electricity it generates. This option can reduce or eliminate the upfront costs but doesn't provide ownership benefits.

Step-by-Step Guide to Solar Panel Installation

Once you've budgeted for your system, the next step is installation. Proper placement and installation of your solar panels are critical to maximizing their efficiency. Follow these steps to ensure a successful setup.

1. *Choosing the Best Location for Solar Panels*

The location of your solar panels has a huge impact on their energy production.

Maximizing Sunlight Exposure:

- **South-Facing Orientation:** In most parts of the world, a south-facing array will capture the most sunlight throughout the day.
- **Unobstructed Areas:** Avoid placing panels near trees, chimneys, or other obstructions that might cast shadows on your solar array, as even a small amount of shading can greatly reduce the panels' overall efficiency.

Tilt and Angle Adjustments:

- **Based on Latitude:** Your solar panels should be tilted at an angle roughly equal to your latitude for maximum efficiency. In the summer, you can reduce the tilt to capture more of the high-angle sun, while in the winter, a steeper angle will capture more low-angle sunlight.
- **Seasonal Adjustments:** If you live in an area with distinct seasons, adjusting the angle of your panels can boost their efficiency year-round.

Roof-Mounted vs. Ground-Mounted Systems:

- **Roof-Mounted:** Typically cheaper and more space-efficient. However, installation can be more complex, especially on angled or shaded roofs.
- **Ground-Mounted:** Easier to install and adjust but requires additional space. Ground-mounted systems also allow for better airflow, which can keep the panels cooler and more efficient.

2. Installation Process

Once you've chosen the best location for your panels, it's time to install them. Here's a detailed, step-by-step breakdown to guide you through the process:

Securing the Panels:

- **Tools and Materials Required:** You'll need mounting racks, bolts, a drill, a wrench, and weatherproofing materials.
- Step-by-Step Installation:
    1. Install the mounting racks or brackets, ensuring they are securely attached to the roof or ground.
    2. Attach the panels to the racks with bolts, ensuring they are tightly secured and angled correctly.
    3. Use weatherproofing materials to seal around any roof penetrations to prevent leaks.

Pro Tip: Use a solar pathfinder tool to ensure your panels are in the optimal position, with no shading throughout the day.

Ensuring Panels are Weatherproof:

- **Wind and Snow Loads:** In areas with high winds or heavy snowfall, it's important to use mounting brackets rated for the appropriate loads. Failure to do so could result in panels being damaged or dislodged during extreme weather.
- **Waterproofing:** Seal all joints and roof penetrations to prevent water ingress, which could damage both the panels and your home.

3. Wiring the Solar Panels

Once the panels are mounted, the next step is to wire them properly.

Connecting Panels in Series vs. Parallel:

- **Series:** Increases the system's voltage but keeps the current constant. Ideal for systems with long wiring distances.
- **Parallel:** Increases the system's current while maintaining the voltage. Good for minimizing energy loss in systems with shorter wiring distances.

Guidelines for Safe and Efficient Wiring:

- Use high-quality, weather-resistant cables.
- Ensure all wiring is securely fastened and not exposed to the elements.
- Label your wiring to make troubleshooting easier in the future.

4. Connecting to Charge Controller and Battery Bank

Once your panels are wired, the next step is to connect them to your charge controller and battery bank.

Wiring the Panels to the Charge Controller:

- The charge controller regulates the flow of energy from the panels to the batteries. Connect the positive and negative terminals from your solar array to the controller's input terminals.

Connecting the Charge Controller to the Battery Bank:

- The charge controller should be connected to the battery bank using appropriately sized cables. Depending on your system's voltage, you may wire your batteries in series (to increase voltage) or parallel (to increase capacity).

Pro Tip: Always install a fuse or breaker between the charge controller and the battery bank for safety.

5. Connecting the Inverter

Finally, connect your inverter to transform the DC energy stored in your batteries into functional AC power for your home.

Wiring the Inverter:

- Connect the inverter to the battery bank, ensuring that the cables are sized correctly for the inverter's power rating.
- Connect the inverter's output to your home's electrical system, making sure to include a disconnect switch for safety.

Ensuring Proper Grounding:

- Ground both the inverter and the battery bank to prevent electrical shocks or fire hazards.
- Follow local electrical codes and best practices for grounding solar systems.

Optimizing Solar System Performance

When you're living off-grid, ensuring your solar system runs at peak performance is essential. This section will provide you with detailed, actionable steps to keep your system operating efficiently, prolong the lifespan of your components, and ensure energy independence. Let's break this down step by step.

Maximizing Solar Panel Efficiency

Solar panels are the heart of your off-grid system, and maximizing their efficiency is key to generating the power you need. Here's how to keep your panels working at their best.

1. Regular Cleaning and Maintenance

- **Why it's important:** Dirt, dust, bird droppings, and snow can block sunlight from reaching your panels, drastically reducing their efficiency.
- **Action step:** Clean your panels every few months, or more often if you're in a dusty area. Use a soft brush or squeegee with soapy water to softly rinse the surface and skip any harsh cleaning agents that could damage the panels.
- **Expert Tip:** After cleaning, inspect for visible signs of damage or wear. Catching small issues early will prevent costly repairs down the line.

2. Adjusting Panel Tilt and Orientation

- **Why it matters:** Solar panels are most efficient when they directly face the sun. The angle of the sun changes with the seasons, so adjusting your panel tilt can optimize energy capture.
- **Action step:** In the summer, lower the tilt to around 15-30 degrees, allowing the panels to capture more high-angle sunlight. In the winter, raise the tilt to around 45-60 degrees to catch the low-angle sun.
- **Pro Tip:** Use a solar angle calculator to determine the exact tilt for your location. Automating this process with a solar tracking system can boost efficiency by up to 25%.

3. Installing Monitoring Systems

- **Why you need it:** Monitoring systems provide real-time data on your system's energy production and consumption, helping you catch inefficiencies before they become bigger problems.
- **Action step:** Install a smart monitoring system connected to your charge controller. This allows you to track energy production, panel performance, and battery health. You can monitor data through a mobile app, making it easy to adjust your usage or detect problems even when you're away.
- **Tip:** Some monitoring systems also allow you to set automated alerts for low performance or system malfunctions, giving you peace of mind that your system is always running efficiently.

Monitoring Your System

Keeping an eye on your system's performance will help you understand how much energy you're producing and using. This helps you make smarter decisions about energy consumption and system maintenance.

1. Using Charge Controllers, Meters, and Monitoring Tools

- **Why it's crucial:** Your charge controller is the brain of your system, regulating energy flow from the panels to the batteries. Keeping an eye on this data ensures that everything is functioning as expected.
- **Action step:** Install meters that track voltage, current, and energy storage levels in your system. Monitor these regularly to ensure your panels are generating enough power and that your batteries are storing energy properly.

2. Understanding System Performance Data

- **How it helps:** Knowing how to read your system's performance data can help you optimize its use. Monitor key metrics such as voltage, current, battery charge level, and system efficiency to understand how well your setup is performing.
- **Tip:** Keep track of trends in performance to identify any dips in efficiency. For example, if your energy production drops over time, this could signal that your panels need cleaning or a component is malfunctioning.

3. Implementing Smart Meters

- **Why consider it:** Smart meters automatically adjust energy usage during peak hours, helping to manage power consumption. They can also provide real-time feedback and usage recommendations.
- **Action step:** Install a smart meter that integrates with your inverter and charge controller. This will allow you to automatically optimize your energy consumption based on current system performance and environmental conditions.

Battery Maintenance

Your battery bank is responsible for storing the energy your solar panels generate, and proper maintenance is key to ensuring long-term performance and dependability.

1. Proper Battery Charging and Discharging Practices

- **Why it matters:** Overcharging or deep discharging your batteries can significantly reduce their lifespan.
- **Action step:** Use a charge controller to regulate energy flow to the batteries, ensuring they're never overcharged or excessively drained. Set your charge controller to maintain battery levels between 20% and 80% for optimal performance.
- **Tip:** For lithium-ion batteries, avoid deep discharges below 20% to extend their life. Lead-acid batteries, on the other hand, should not discharge below 50%.

2. Regular Inspections for Corrosion, Leaks, or Damage

- **Why it's necessary:** Battery terminals can corrode over time, reducing efficiency and potentially causing safety hazards.
- **Action step:** Every few months check the battery terminals for any signs of corrosion. If present, clean them using a solution of baking soda and water. Check for any leaks, swelling, or unusual odors, which could indicate a failing battery.

3. Temperature Control and Storage Conditions

- **Why it helps:** Batteries operate most efficiently when kept within an optimal temperature range, usually between 50°F and 85°F (10°C to 30°C).
- **Action step:** Keep your batteries in a well-ventilated area with stable temperatures. Use battery insulation or temperature-controlled environment to prevent batteries from overheating or freezing.

4. Avoiding Overcharging or Deep Discharging

- **Action step:** Set limits on your charge controller to prevent overcharging, and use a battery monitoring system to alert you when your battery levels are too low. Following these practices will dramatically extend your battery life and ensure a reliable power supply.

Safety Considerations and Best Practices

Safety should always come first when handling solar power systems. Here's how to ensure your system is both safe and efficient.

Electrical Grounding

1. Proper Grounding to Prevent Electrical Shocks and Fire Hazards

- **Why it's critical:** Grounding protects your system and home from electrical shocks and reduces the risk of fires caused by electrical faults.
- **Action step:** Ensure that all system components, including panels, inverters, and batteries, are properly grounded using a grounding rod. This creates a safe path for excess electricity to dissipate into the ground.

2. Installing Ground Fault Protection

- **Why it's needed:** Ground fault protection devices detect electrical leaks and automatically shut down the system to prevent accidents.
- **Action step:** Install ground fault circuit interrupters (GFCIs) at key points in your system to protect against electrical faults. These are especially important in high-moisture environments like outdoor installations.

Fire Safety

Solar installations come with specific fire risks, especially when dealing with high-voltage components.

1. Fireproofing Areas Around Solar Installations

- **Why it's important:** Faulty wiring or component failures can lead to fires. Fireproofing the area minimizes damage if something goes wrong.
- **Action step:** Use fire-resistant materials around inverters and batteries. Ensure that any vegetation near ground-mounted panels is cleared to prevent the risk of wildfires.

2. Installing Surge Protectors and Circuit Breakers

- **Why it's necessary:** Power surges from lightning or electrical faults can damage your system and cause fires.
- **Action step:** Install surge protectors at key points in your system, particularly at the inverter and charge controller. Use circuit breakers to automatically cut off power during a surge or short circuit.

3. Steps to Take in Case of System Failure or Electrical Fire

- **Why it's essential:** Knowing how to handle an emergency will keep you safe and protect your system from further damage.
- **Action step:** Have a clear shutdown procedure in place. Ensure that everyone in your household knows how to safely disconnect the system in case of a malfunction. Keep fire extinguishers rated for electrical fires nearby.

Weather Resilience

Extreme weather can pose a threat to your solar power system. Make sure it's prepared to handle everything from heavy snow to high winds.

1. Securing Panels Against High Winds, Snow, or Hail

- **Why it matters:** Windstorms, heavy snow, and hail can damage or dislodge your panels if they're not properly secured.
- **Action step:** Use mounting hardware rated for your local weather conditions. In areas prone to high winds or snow, reinforce mounts and consider adding extra bracing.

2. Protecting Wiring and Components from Water Ingress or Extreme Temperatures

- **Why it's necessary:** Water damage can ruin electrical components, while extreme heat or cold can reduce the efficiency of your panels and batteries.
- **Action step:** Ensure all wiring is sealed with weatherproof connectors. Install conduit to protect wiring from physical damage and water ingress. For extreme temperatures, insulate components or provide adequate ventilation to maintain optimal performance.

Expanding and Scaling Your Solar Power System

As your energy needs grow, expanding your solar power system becomes crucial to maintaining off-grid independence. Whether you're powering additional appliances, adding more occupants, or preparing for changing environmental conditions, scaling your solar setup can keep you in control of your energy needs. Here's a complete guide to expanding and optimizing your system step by step.

Adding Additional Solar Panels

When your energy consumption increases, adding more solar panels can boost your system's capacity. Here's how to do it efficiently:

1. How to Expand Your System as Energy Needs Grow

- **Why it's essential:** Your current setup might be sufficient today, but as your needs evolve, adding extra panels can help accommodate new appliances, tools, or increased household activity.
- **Action Step:** Assess your current energy production and compare it to your growing requirements. Make a list of new appliances or additional energy-consuming activities and calculate the extra wattage you'll need to generate. This will inform the number of new panels you need.

2. Step-by-Step Instructions for Integrating New Panels

- **Step 1: Check compatibility.** Before adding panels, ensure they match your existing system in terms of voltage and current. Panels should have similar specifications to avoid overloading or underutilizing your charge controller and inverter.
- **Step 2: Wiring configuration.** Decide whether to wire your new panels in series or parallel. Wiring in series increases the voltage, while wiring in parallel increases current. Use the configuration that best suits your existing system's needs.
- **Step 3: Connect to charge controller.** Your charge controller must be able to handle the additional energy load from the new panels. If it's near its limit, consider upgrading to a higher-capacity controller.
- **Step 4: Monitor performance.** After integrating new panels, closely monitor your system to ensure it's functioning efficiently. Check the charge controller's display for any overload warnings.

Expert Tip: For larger expansions, consider upgrading your inverter and charge controller in tandem with the panels to ensure optimal system performance.

3. Balancing Panel Output and Ensuring Adequate Battery Storage Capacity

- **Why it's important:** As you add more panels, you also need to expand your battery bank to store the extra energy being produced, especially if you want to ensure 24/7 energy availability.
- **Action Step:** For every kilowatt of additional panel capacity, ensure you have enough battery storage to handle cloudy days and nighttime usage. Monitor how quickly your batteries charge and discharge to determine if your storage needs an upgrade.

Scaling Battery Banks

Expanding your battery bank is critical when you're producing more energy. Here's how to scale it effectively:

1. Adding More Batteries for Increased Energy Storage

- **Why it's necessary:** If you're adding more panels but not enough storage, you risk wasting the extra energy generated. Having additional batteries ensures you can store the excess energy for later use.
- **Action Step:** Choose batteries that are compatible with your existing system (AGM, lead-acid, or lithium-ion). For larger setups, lithium-ion batteries tend to offer better longevity and efficiency.

2. Managing Larger Battery Banks and Balancing the Load

- **Step 1: Wiring configuration.** When adding batteries, decide if you'll wire them in series (to increase voltage) or parallel (to increase capacity). This decision should match your system's voltage and energy storage requirements.
- **Step 2: Charge controller capacity.** Ensure your charge controller can manage the increased battery load. If your controller can't handle the added batteries, it's time to upgrade to one with a higher amp rating.

Pro Tip: Regularly monitor your battery bank's state of charge. Adding a battery management system (BMS) can help automate monitoring, preventing overcharging or discharging.

Combining Solar with Other Renewable Energy Sources

Diversifying your energy sources can add resilience to your off-grid system, ensuring continuous power even during cloudy or low-sunlight periods.

1. Integrating Wind Turbines or Micro-Hydro Systems with Solar

- **Why it matters:** Wind and water turbines can generate power when the sun isn't shining, making your system more reliable across different weather conditions.
- **Action Step:** Assess your geographic location. If you're in an area with steady winds or near a water source, integrating wind or micro-hydro energy can complement your solar system.

Step-by-Step Integration:

- **Step 1: Install the new system.** For wind turbines, install them in a high, unobstructed area. For micro-hydro, ensure you have access to flowing water year-round.
- **Step 2: Connect to your existing setup.** Use a hybrid inverter that can manage both solar and other renewable energy sources. This inverter will prioritize solar but automatically switch to wind or hydro as needed.
- **Step 3: Balance the load.** Make sure your charge controller is capable of handling inputs from multiple sources and that your battery bank can store the additional energy.

2. How to Balance Multiple Energy Sources for Consistent Power Supply

- **Why it's essential:** Each renewable energy source has its strengths and weaknesses. Balancing them ensures you have power when you need it, even if one source underperforms.
- **Action Step:** Use a hybrid charge controller and inverter that can manage multiple sources simultaneously. This ensures that excess energy from wind or hydro complements your solar system, keeping your batteries charged and your household powered.

Troubleshooting and Maintenance

Keeping your system in peak condition requires regular monitoring and maintenance. Here's how to troubleshoot common issues and prevent system failures.

Diagnosing Common Solar System Issues

Even well-maintained systems can experience occasional problems. Here's how to diagnose and fix the most common issues:

1. Identifying and Fixing Common Problems Like Battery Underperformance, Panel Output Drops, or Inverter Malfunctions

- **Battery Underperformance:** If your batteries aren't holding a charge as they should, check for signs of corrosion or aging. A quick cleaning of the terminals might help, but aging batteries will likely need replacing.
- **Panel Output Drops:** If you notice your panels aren't producing as much energy, they may need cleaning, or they could be obstructed by shade. Also, check for wiring issues or damage to the panel surface.
- **Inverter Malfunctions:** If your inverter stops converting DC to AC power, first check the wiring and fuses. If everything looks fine, the inverter may need a reset or replacement.

2. Step-by-Step Troubleshooting for:

- **Battery Storage Issues:** Regularly check the voltage levels to make sure they are within the recommended range for optimal performance. Use a battery tester to determine if a specific battery is underperforming.
- **Charge Controller Malfunctions:** Verify the connections between the controller, panels, and batteries. Ensure the controller settings match your system's specs, and update or reset as needed.
- **Wiring and Connection Faults:** Inspect all wiring for wear, corrosion, or looseness. Tighten any loose connections and replace damaged wires to restore full functionality.

Preventative Maintenance

Routine maintenance helps avoid costly repairs and ensures your system runs efficiently.

1. Routine Checks on Solar Panels, Batteries, and Wiring

- **Action Step:** Perform visual inspections monthly. Check for debris or dirt on panels, inspect wiring for any signs of wear, and look at the battery bank for leaks or corrosion.

2. Tips for Preventing Common Issues Like Corrosion, Overcharging, or Wiring Wear

- **Preventing corrosion:** Routinely clean your battery terminals using a mixture of baking soda and water. Use anti-corrosion sprays to protect the connections.

- **Avoiding overcharging:** Set your charge controller to maintain battery levels between 20% and 80% capacity to extend battery life and prevent overcharging.
- **Wiring wear:** Protect exposed wiring from the elements using weatherproof conduits.

3. Monitoring Tools to Ensure Your System is Operating at Maximum Efficiency

- **Action Step:** Use monitoring tools like smart meters, charge controller displays, or app-based systems to track your solar system's performance in real-time. Set up alerts for low battery levels, panel performance drops, or charge controller issues.

Innovations in Energy Storage

The technology around energy storage is evolving rapidly. Here are some of the most exciting innovations that could enhance your off-grid system.

Tesla Powerwalls and Other Advanced Storage Systems

1. Exploring High-Tech Battery Storage Options Like Tesla Powerwall

- **Why it's revolutionary:** Tesla Powerwalls offer long-lasting, high-efficiency storage with built-in safety features. They integrate seamlessly with solar systems and provide automatic backup power during outages.
- **Action Step:** If you're ready to upgrade, consider a Powerwall to replace or supplement your existing battery bank. The initial investment is higher, but the longevity and performance often pay off in the long run.

2. Pros and Cons of Advanced Battery Systems for Off-Grid Setups

- **Pros:** Higher energy density, longer lifespan, smart management features, and low maintenance.
- **Cons:** High upfront cost, compatibility concerns with older systems, and potential integration challenges.

Hybrid Systems

1. Integrating Advanced Energy Storage Solutions with Traditional Lead-Acid or Lithium-Ion Systems

- **Why it's essential:** A hybrid system lets you combine the affordability of lead-acid batteries with the efficiency of lithium-ion or Tesla Powerwall systems.
- **Action Step:** Start by integrating advanced batteries for critical power usage, while keeping traditional batteries for less essential needs.

2. Exploring Options for Mobile or Portable Solar Storage Solutions

- **Why it matters:** Portable storage solutions, such as foldable solar chargers or compact battery banks, allow you to power tools, small appliances, or mobile devices when on the go.
- **Action Step:** Consider adding a portable power station to your off-grid toolkit for emergencies, travel, or remote work.

Environmental Impact and Sustainability

As you transition to off-grid solar power, understanding its broader environmental impact is essential. Solar energy not only benefits your immediate energy independence but also significantly reduces your carbon footprint and contributes to a more sustainable future. Here's how your solar power system plays a vital role in protecting the environment and how you can manage the lifecycle of your system components responsibly.

Carbon Footprint Reduction

One of the most compelling reasons for adopting solar power is its potential to drastically reduce greenhouse gas emissions. Here's how:

- **How Solar Energy Contributes to Reducing Greenhouse Gas Emissions:**

When you generate electricity using solar panels, you are effectively reducing your reliance on fossil fuels like coal, oil, and natural gas, which are the primary culprits in carbon emissions. Solar panels generate electricity through the photovoltaic effect—no combustion, no emissions. Over the lifespan of your solar system, this translates into a significant reduction in your carbon footprint.

Actionable Tip: Calculate your carbon offset by comparing the amount of electricity you generate from your solar system against what you would have consumed from the grid. Many online tools allow you to measure how much CO_2 you've prevented from entering the atmosphere.

- **Long-Term Environmental Benefits of Off-Grid Solar Power:**

Beyond just reducing emissions, solar power encourages a shift toward sustainability. By opting for renewable energy, you're also contributing to less environmental degradation associated with mining, drilling, and transporting fossil fuels. Additionally, solar power promotes energy efficiency at home, prompting a reduction in energy consumption overall, further lowering environmental impact.

Actionable Tip: Integrate other sustainable practices into your off-grid lifestyle—like rainwater harvesting, composting, and using energy-efficient appliances—to maximize the environmental benefits of your solar system.

Life Cycle of Solar Panels

Like any other technology, solar panels have a finite lifespan, typically ranging from 25 to 30 years. Understanding the production, lifespan, and disposal of your panels can help you make informed decisions about their environmental impact.

- **Understanding the Production, Lifespan, and Recycling of Solar Panels**

Solar panels are made from materials like silicon, glass, and aluminum—most of which can be recycled once they reach the end of their lifespan. While the production of solar panels does have an environmental impact, including energy use and some emissions, this is vastly offset by the clean energy they produce over their lifespan.

After 25-30 years, solar panels may still function, though at reduced efficiency, which makes recycling them a crucial step in their lifecycle. Many manufacturers offer take-back or recycling programs to handle the disposal of old panels responsibly.

Actionable Tip: Research your solar panel manufacturer's recycling program before purchasing. Knowing how to recycle your panels at the end of their life ensures that their environmental impact remains minimal.

- **Best Practices for Disposing of Old Panels and Batteries**

When it becomes necessary to replace your solar panels or batteries, don't simply discard them in a landfill. Old panels can be taken to specialized recycling centers where materials are extracted and reused. Similarly, lead-acid and lithium-ion batteries are made of valuable components that can be extracted and reused through recycling if handled properly.

Actionable Tip: Contact your local e-waste recycling center or your solar manufacturer for panel and battery disposal options. Some regions offer incentives for recycling solar components.

Case Studies and Practical Examples

To give you a clearer idea of how to adapt and implement solar power for off-grid living, here are three practical examples that showcase different setups tailored to unique environments and household needs.

Small Cabin Solar System

If you're living in a small cabin or remote getaway, a compact, cost-effective solar system can provide all the energy you need without overspending.

- **Example Setup:**

A typical small cabin setup might involve a 2kW solar panel system, coupled with a 5-10 kWh battery bank to store energy for evening and cloudy-day use. This setup can easily power basic lighting, a small refrigerator, and a few appliances, making it perfect for weekend getaways or minimalist off-grid living.

Step-by-Step Guide:
  - **Step 1:** Install 6-8 solar panels (around 250W each) on your roof or a ground-mount system. Ensure they're angled correctly for maximum sunlight.
  - **Step 2:** Connect these to a 24V battery system, which offers an ideal balance between power and cost for small setups.
  - **Step 3:** Use a small inverter (2-3 kW) to convert the stored energy to AC power for your appliances.

Pro Tip: Install a small, portable generator as a backup in case of extended cloudy weather.

Family Home Setup

For a medium-sized off-grid family home, your solar power system needs to support a higher energy demand. This example focuses on a system large enough to power the necessities of a full household while ensuring stability during less-than-ideal weather.

- **Example Setup:**
  A family home may require a 5-8 kW system, paired with a 20-30 kWh battery bank. This system is powerful enough to run multiple appliances, charge devices, power heating/cooling systems, and even operate more energy-intensive machines like washing machines.

Step-by-Step Guide:
  - **Step 1:** Install 20-24 solar panels (300W each), ensuring they are positioned in an optimal location for full sunlight exposure year-round.
  - **Step 2:** Use a hybrid inverter that can manage multiple energy sources, like wind or a backup generator, for periods when solar energy production might be low.
  - **Step 3:** Scale your battery bank accordingly, ensuring it can store at least 24 hours of power.

Pro Tip: Monitor the system using a smart meter that tracks energy usage, panel efficiency, and battery levels in real-time to maximize performance.

Solar in Extreme Environments

In extreme climates—whether it's high-altitude locations, harsh deserts, or freezing tundras—your solar system needs to be adapted to withstand severe weather while maintaining efficiency.

- Adapting Solar Power Setups for Extreme Climates
  - **High-Altitude Locations:** At higher elevations, the atmosphere is thinner, meaning solar panels can be more efficient. However, these areas are also prone to colder temperatures and heavy snow. Use rugged, weatherproof panels and install an automatic tilt system to adjust angles for maximum efficiency during seasonal shifts.
  - **Desert Environments:** In hot, arid climates, solar panel efficiency can drop due to overheating. Choose panels with high heat tolerance and ensure they have proper ventilation. Also, regularly clean panels to prevent dust and sand from reducing their efficiency.
  - **Cold, Snowy Regions:** Ensure your solar system is equipped with heating elements to prevent snow from accumulating on the panels. Batteries in these environments also need temperature control, so insulated enclosures or battery warmers are a must.

Step-by-Step Adaptation:

  - **Step 1:** In high-altitude regions, install solar panels with adjustable mounts that can be shifted according to the sun's seasonal position.
  - **Step 2:** For desert environments, use panels that can withstand high temperatures without losing efficiency. Keep them clean using automatic dust-removal systems if possible.
  - **Step 3:** In cold climates, ensure your panels are installed at an angle where snow can slide off easily, and protect your battery storage area with insulation.

Pro Tip: Hybrid systems combining solar and wind energy are especially effective in extreme environments, where sunlight might be unreliable but wind is abundant.

Reaping the Benefits of a Well-Maintained Solar Power System

After building and optimizing your off-grid solar power system, it's essential to recognize the many benefits you've gained and what lies ahead to ensure your energy setup remains efficient, reliable, and sustainable.

Review of Benefits

Your solar power system isn't just a means of generating electricity—it's a foundation for true energy independence and sustainability.

- **Energy Independence**: You've reduced or eliminated reliance on traditional power grids, which not only grants you autonomy but also shields you from rising energy costs and outages.
- **Environmental Sustainability**: By using a renewable resource—sunlight—you are actively reducing your carbon footprint and contributing to a greener planet.
- **Cost Savings**: While the upfront costs may have been significant, you've secured long-term financial savings through lower utility bills and minimal maintenance needs.
- **Resilience**: With proper planning, your system is prepared to handle varying energy demands, weather conditions, and even expand as your needs grow.

Encouragement to Continue Monitoring and Expanding

While your system is designed for the long haul, the key to keeping it running smoothly is continuous monitoring and thoughtful upgrades. Off-grid living is dynamic, and your energy needs may evolve. Therefore, regular assessments will help you fine-tune the system's performance.

- **Ongoing Adjustments**: Keep an eye on your energy production and usage patterns. Seasonal shifts, new appliances, or family growth can affect how much energy you consume. By adjusting your panel angle, maintaining batteries, or adding capacity as needed, you ensure maximum efficiency year-round.

Pro Tip: Use monitoring tools and smart meters to track daily and seasonal energy performance. These can help you identify when your system needs minor tweaks, like adjusting panel orientation or replacing aging components.

- **Scaling for Long-Term Sustainability**: If you foresee an increase in your energy needs—such as adding more appliances, expanding your home, or integrating new technologies—consider scaling your system. Whether it's adding more panels, upgrading your battery bank, or integrating wind or hydro energy sources, your solar setup is highly adaptable.

Pro Tip: Set aside a small budget for future upgrades, as battery and inverter technologies continue to advance. When scaling, consider hybrid systems that combine solar with other renewables for a more robust energy mix.

Final Tips for Longevity

Maintaining your solar power system doesn't need to be overwhelming, but routine attention is key to ensuring it remains reliable for decades to come. Here are some final tips to keep your system in peak condition and prolong its lifespan:

- **Routine Maintenance:**
  o Regularly clean your solar panels to remove debris, dust, or snow that could obstruct sunlight. Aim for a quarterly inspection, but adjust the frequency based on your environment (e.g., deserts may need more frequent cleaning).
  o Inspect wiring, connections, and mounting hardware for signs of wear, corrosion, or damage. Tighten any loose fittings and replace damaged components as needed.
  o Keep an eye on battery health, ensuring they are charged and discharged within recommended levels to prevent degradation.

Pro Tip: Develop a simple maintenance checklist that you can follow each season to avoid overlooking any small but critical tasks.

- **System Expansion**: As your off-grid lifestyle evolves, your energy needs may increase. Expanding your system—whether by adding more panels, upgrading batteries, or integrating complementary energy sources— will help you stay ahead of any potential energy shortfalls.

Pro Tip: Before expanding, conduct a thorough energy audit to pinpoint where efficiency improvements can be made. It's often more cost-effective to reduce consumption (e.g., by using energy-efficient appliances) than to add new capacity.

- **Staying Informed on Technological Advancements**: Solar technology is constantly advancing, especially in the areas of battery storage and energy management. Keep up with the latest innovations—such as more efficient solar panels, longer-lasting batteries, and smart energy systems—that could enhance the performance of your setup.

Pro Tip: Subscribe to renewable energy news, forums, or attend workshops on solar technologies. Being informed will help you make strategic decisions on when to upgrade or how to optimize your system further.

Conclusion

The journey of building and maintaining an off-grid solar power system is rewarding, not only in terms of energy savings but also in the self-reliance it fosters. You're not just generating electricity; you're creating a resilient, eco-friendly lifestyle that can withstand the tests of time, technology, and environmental challenges.

By staying proactive—monitoring your system, performing regular maintenance, and adapting to changes in your energy needs—you can ensure that your off-grid setup continues to provide sustainable, reliable power for years to come. With the freedom and flexibility that solar energy offers, you've taken an important step toward living independently, sustainably, and with peace of mind

8. Wind Power Projects for Off-Grid Energy

In the journey toward true off-grid living, diversifying your energy sources is not just a smart choice—it's essential for long-term sustainability. While solar power provides an incredible foundation, there are limitations, especially in regions with inconsistent sunlight or during the winter months when daylight hours are short. This is where **wind energy** steps in as the perfect complement to your solar setup, ensuring that your energy needs are met 24/7, regardless of the season or weather conditions.

Why Wind Energy?

Wind energy is a reliable, sustainable power source that works when solar energy can't. On those cloudy days or long winter nights when your solar panels aren't producing sufficient electricity, a wind turbine can keep your batteries charged and your home powered. Wind doesn't follow the sun's schedule—it's often strongest during the night and in bad weather, which makes it an excellent backup or even primary energy source for areas where wind is abundant.

Wind energy isn't just about filling the gaps left by solar; it's also about resilience and energy security. By combining wind with your existing solar system, you create a hybrid power setup that dramatically reduces your dependence on any one source. Whether you're living in an area with strong seasonal winds or just need a reliable backup, wind power offers a practical and cost-effective solution for off-grid living.

Benefits of Wind Power

One of the main reasons wind energy is such a popular choice for off-grid living is its **renewable and low-maintenance** nature. Once your wind turbine is set up and running, it requires minimal upkeep, letting you concentrate on other areas of self-sufficiency. Unlike fossil fuel generators that need regular refueling and maintenance, a wind turbine works tirelessly, converting the natural power of the wind into electricity.

Wind energy is incredibly effective in diverse climates. Whether you're in a coastal region, high-altitude areas, or open plains, wind can provide consistent power where solar might struggle. It can easily work alongside other renewable energy sources, like solar, to form a hybrid power grid that keeps your home or off-grid setup powered at all times.

- **Renewable**: Wind is a never-ending resource. You'll never run out of it, and it costs nothing to harness.
- **Low-Maintenance**: Compared to other energy sources, wind turbines need relatively little maintenance once installed.
- **Effective in Various Climates**: Coastal areas, high-altitude locations, and plains often have excellent wind potential, making turbines highly effective.
- **Hybrid Power Potential**: Wind can work hand-in-hand with solar or other renewable systems, giving you a versatile and reliable energy setup.

Basic Concepts of Wind Energy

Understanding how wind turbines work is essential for anyone looking to add wind power to their off-grid energy system. At its core, a wind turbine is designed to convert **kinetic energy from the wind** into electricity. When the wind turns the turbine blades, the mechanical energy is transferred to a generator, which converts it into electrical energy for storage or used directly in your home.

The key components of a wind turbine include:

- **Blades**: These capture the wind's kinetic energy and transfer it to the rotor.
- **Generator**: Transforms the mechanical energy generated by the spinning blades into electricity.
- **Tower**: Elevates the blades to an optimal height where wind speeds are stronger and more consistent.

- **Inverter**: Converts the electricity generated from direct current (DC) to alternating current (AC) for use in your home.

Another important factor to consider is **wind consistency**. Wind energy generation relies on having a steady supply of wind. While solar is somewhat predictable—following the day/night cycle—wind is less predictable and can vary depending on your location, time of year, and even the time of day. That said, wind is often most abundant during times when solar energy is not, making the two an ideal pairing for consistent off-grid power.

Wind consistency is key to reliable energy production. Areas with consistent wind speeds above 5 mph are typically ideal for wind turbines, though higher wind speeds are even better. When planning your wind power system, understanding how the wind moves through your area at different times of the year is crucial to optimizing your turbine's placement and ensuring maximum energy production.

Key Tips for Success:
- **Blending Wind and Solar**: A hybrid energy system maximizes efficiency by utilizing solar power during the day and wind power at night or during overcast conditions.
- **Choosing the Right Location**: Elevate your wind turbine to an optimal height (generally 30 feet or more) to avoid turbulence and capture stronger winds.
- **Invest in Monitoring Tools**: Set up tools to track wind speeds and energy output to ensure your system is performing efficiently and identify any potential issues early.

Planning Your Wind Power Setup

When planning to incorporate wind power into your off-grid system, careful preparation and understanding of your environment are critical to ensuring the success and efficiency of your setup. This section will walk you through every essential aspect of assessing your wind resources, choosing the right location, and determining the size and scope of your wind turbine project. Whether you're combining wind with other energy sources like solar or using it as your primary source of power, these steps will help you establish a resilient and reliable energy solution.

Assessing Your Wind Resources

Before you dive into setting up a wind power system, it's essential to evaluate the wind resources at your location. Wind turbines require consistent and adequate wind speeds to produce energy efficiently. Understanding the wind conditions around your home will be your first step toward making an informed decision.

Measuring Wind Speeds

Wind speed is the most critical factor in determining whether a wind turbine is viable for your off-grid setup. Consistent wind speeds of **5 mph (8 km/h)** or higher are generally considered the minimum requirement for effective power generation, though speeds of **10-15 mph (16-24 km/h)** are ideal for maximizing energy output. Here's how you can measure and evaluate wind speeds at your location:

- **Anemometers**: These handheld devices can help you measure wind speeds over time. Set up an anemometer in the area where you plan to install your turbine and track wind speeds for a week or more to get an accurate reading of your conditions.
- **Wind Maps & Apps**: Utilize online wind maps or dedicated apps to assess average wind speeds in your area. These tools can give you a broader understanding of seasonal wind patterns and help you make informed decisions on turbine placement.
- **On-Site Testing**: For the most accurate results, testing wind speeds at different heights and times of day can assist you in identifying the optimal possible location and height for your turbine.

Choosing the Right Location for Your Turbine

Location plays a pivotal role in ensuring your turbine generates the maximum possible energy. Even with the right wind speeds, poor placement can reduce the effectiveness of your system. Here's what to consider:

- **Elevation**: The higher your wind turbine, the stronger and more consistent the wind will be. A general rule is to place your turbine at least **30 feet above** any nearby obstacles like trees, buildings, or other structures that could block or disrupt airflow.
- **Obstacles and Wind Direction**: Avoid areas with frequent wind obstructions like dense trees, hills, or large buildings. These obstacles create **turbulence**, which can negatively affect the efficiency of your turbine.
- **Turbulence Zones**: Make sure to place your turbine in a location with clear, unobstructed wind flow. Turbulence caused by nearby structures or uneven terrain can significantly reduce energy output. Placing the turbine far from turbulent zones and higher above the ground improves performance.

Hybrid Considerations

If you're planning to create a **hybrid energy system** that combines solar and wind power, it's crucial to understand how the two sources complement each other. Wind turbines are often most productive during the night and in stormy or overcast weather, when solar panels may not generate much power. By leveraging both, you can ensure consistent energy production:

- **Complementary Energy Production**: Wind often blows strongest when sunlight is minimal, such as at night or during cloudy days, making wind an excellent partner for solar energy.
- **Balanced Energy Storage**: Combining solar and wind also helps reduce the strain on your battery storage. Wind can keep batteries charged when solar isn't an option, providing a continuous flow of energy to meet your daily needs.

Sizing Your Wind Power System

Once you've assessed your wind resources and chosen the best location, the next step is to size your wind power system. This ensures that your turbine produces enough energy to meet your off-grid needs while considering your budget and space limitations.

Calculating Energy Needs

The first task in sizing your system is to calculate your **daily energy consumption**. This will give you a clear idea of how much power you'll need to generate through wind energy alone or in combination with other energy sources like solar.

- **List Your Appliances**: Make a list of all the appliances and devices you plan to power using wind energy. Include essential items like lights, refrigerators, heaters, and communication devices.
- **Energy Usage**: Calculate the **wattage** of each device and how many hours per day you use them. Multiply the wattage by the hours of usage to get your daily energy consumption in **watt-hours (Wh)**.

Once you have this total, you can begin selecting a wind turbine with enough capacity to meet your needs.

Balancing Wind Power with Other Energy Sources

If you're using wind energy as part of a hybrid system, you'll need to balance the power generated by your turbine with that of your solar panels or other energy sources. The goal is to ensure that both systems provide a steady and reliable flow of energy, even during times of low production.

- **Energy Diversification**: Use wind to supplement solar energy during periods of low sunlight, and vice versa. This creates a robust and resilient off-grid system that can handle fluctuations in weather and energy demand.

Estimating Output

Your turbine's energy output depends on both its size and the wind speeds at your location. Here's how to estimate the power generation potential of your wind turbine:

- **Turbine Capacity**: Turbines are typically rated in **kilowatts (kW)**. A 1 kW turbine can produce 1,000 watts of electricity in optimal wind conditions. The larger the turbine, the more power it can generate.
- **Wind Speed Impact**: Turbine output increases significantly with higher wind speeds. For instance, doubling the wind speed can result in **eight times more energy production**. Use online calculators or manufacturer data to estimate how much energy your specific turbine can produce based on local wind conditions.
- **Formula for Energy Output**: Most wind turbines have efficiency ratings that account for varying wind speeds and other factors. Use this formula to calculate daily energy production:

$$\text{Energy Output (kWh/day)} = \text{Turbine Capacity (kW)} \times \text{Average Wind Speed Factor}$$

Budgeting for Your Wind System

Cost is a key aspect to take into account when planning your wind power system. While the initial investment may seem steep, the long-term savings and energy independence can make it worthwhile. Here's how to budget for your project:

- **Turbine Costs**: Wind turbine prices vary depending on size and type. Expect to pay between $1,500 and $10,000 for most off-grid turbines, depending on your energy needs.
- **Installation Costs**: If you're not installing the turbine yourself, factor in the cost of labor, which can range from $500 to $5,000 depending on the complexity of the project.
- **Long-Term Savings**: Compare the upfront investment with the long-term savings on energy costs. A well-installed turbine can pay for itself within **5 to 10 years**, depending on wind availability and energy consumption.

By carefully planning and sizing your wind power system, you can ensure you generate enough energy to live off the grid with confidence, while also maximizing the return on your investment.

Step-by-Step Guide to Building and Installing a Wind Turbine

Selecting the Right Wind Turbine

The key to a successful wind power setup is selecting the turbine that aligns with your location and energy requirements. Knowing the various types of turbines and how to size them correctly ensures you're investing in a system that will work efficiently in your specific conditions.

Types of Wind Turbines

Wind turbines generally come in two main designs: **horizontal-axis** and **vertical-axis**. Each has its own strengths and weaknesses depending on location, wind consistency, and terrain.

- **Horizontal-Axis Turbines**: These are the most common type of wind turbine, characterized by a propeller-like design. They work best in areas with consistent, steady winds and can produce significant amounts of power if properly placed.
  - **Benefits**: High efficiency, proven technology, large-scale power generation.
  - **Drawbacks**: Requires unobstructed, consistent wind flow; needs higher towers for best performance.
- **Vertical-Axis Turbines**: This type of turbine is less common but can be advantageous in areas with unpredictable or turbulent winds. Its compact design allows it to operate closer to the ground and in tighter spaces.

- o **Benefits**: Performs well in turbulent or changing wind directions, operates at lower altitudes, and is easier to maintain.
- o **Drawbacks**: Generally less efficient than horizontal-axis turbines and generates less power.

The ideal option for your off-grid system will depend on your wind conditions, available space, and energy requirements.

Sizing the Turbine

Selecting the right turbine capacity is critical to meet your household's energy consumption. Follow these steps to determine the correct size:

1. **Calculate Your Energy Requirements**: Add up the power consumption of the appliances and devices you intend to run with wind energy. Multiply their wattage by the number of hours you plan to use them each day to calculate your total energy consumption in watt-hours (Wh).
2. **Consider Wind Speeds**: Turbine efficiency is tied directly to local wind speeds. A higher wind speed means more energy production. Use online wind maps or anemometer readings to find your area's average wind speeds and adjust your calculations accordingly.
3. **Choose the Right Turbine Capacity**: Wind turbines are typically rated in **kilowatts (kW)**. A small, off-grid household might need a 1–5 kW turbine, while a larger home could require a system rated between 5–10 kW. Match the turbine size to your calculated energy needs while accounting for wind consistency at your location.
4. **Factor in Location and Consistency**: If your wind speeds vary, you may need a larger turbine to compensate for lower energy output during calm periods. Consistency in wind speed is key—intermittent, low winds may require integrating solar or other energy sources to fill gaps.

Building Your Wind Turbine

Once you've selected the right turbine, the next step is to gather materials and start the building process. Whether you choose a DIY approach or opt for a pre-built kit, careful assembly and installation are crucial to maximize your system's efficiency and longevity.

Materials and Tools Needed

You'll need several components to assemble your wind turbine. Here's a breakdown of the essential materials:

- **Blades**: Typically made of lightweight, durable materials such as fiberglass or plastic.
- **Generator**: Converts the mechanical energy of the spinning blades into electricity.
- **Tower**: Elevates the turbine to capture stronger, more consistent winds.
- **Charge Controller**: Regulates the energy flowing into your battery bank to prevent overcharging.
- **Inverter**: Transforms the DC (direct current) stored in batteries into AC (alternating current) for household appliances.
- **Batteries**: Save the energy produced by the turbine for use when wind speeds are low.

Tools you will need include wrenches, screwdrivers, a level, climbing gear (if working on high towers), and electrical tools for wiring.

Assembling the Turbine

Follow these steps to assemble your wind turbine:

1. **Install the Blades**: Begin by attaching the blades to the turbine hub. Ensure the blades are balanced and securely fastened to prevent excessive wear or damage during operation.
2. **Mount the Generator**: The generator is the heart of your turbine. Attach it to the turbine shaft and connect it to the blades. Make sure everything is tightly secured and well-lubricated to reduce friction and wear.

3. **Test Rotation**: Before installing the tower, test the turbine to ensure the blades rotate freely and generate power. Rotate it manually or use light winds to check for any resistance or issues.

Installing the Tower

Turbine height is essential to maximize wind capture and minimize turbulence caused by buildings, trees, or terrain. Follow these guidelines to ensure proper tower installation.

1. **Choosing the Right Height**: Aim for at least **30 feet** above any obstacles within a **300-foot radius**. The higher the tower, the more stable and consistent the wind will be.
2. **Securing the Tower**: Whether you're using a guyed, freestanding, or tilt-up tower, it must be securely anchored to the ground. Use concrete footings or earth anchors to ensure stability, especially in high winds.
3. **Reinforcement for Extreme Weather**: Add extra bracing and ensure all bolts and anchors are tight to protect the tower and turbine from strong storms, snow, or freezing conditions.

Wiring and Connecting the System

After assembling and installing your wind turbine, it's time to wire the system to your energy storage and conversion components.

Wiring the Wind Turbine

Proper wiring ensures efficient and safe energy flow from the turbine to your off-grid energy system. Follow these steps:

1. **Connecting to the Charge Controller**: The charge controller manages the flow of energy from the turbine to the battery bank, ensuring batteries are charged efficiently while preventing overcharging or damage. Connect the turbine's output cables to the charge controller following the manufacturer's wiring guide.
2. **Storing Energy in Batteries**: Once the charge controller is connected, wire it to your battery bank. Ensure the battery storage is sufficient for your energy needs. Use appropriately sized cables to handle the current flow without overheating.
3. **Grounding**: Proper grounding is essential to protect your system from lightning strikes and electrical surges. Ground the turbine, tower, and electrical components following local regulations.

Using an Inverter

The inverter transforms the DC electricity stored in your batteries into AC electricity, making it suitable for powering your household appliances.

- **Select the Right Inverter**: Select an inverter with enough capacity to match your daily energy consumption. For example, if your household uses **3 kWh/day**, select an inverter with at least that output capacity.
- **Wire the Inverter**: Attach the inverter to the battery bank, making sure the positive and negative terminals are correctly aligned. Follow all safety protocols, and consult the inverter's manual for specific instructions.

Hybrid System Considerations

A hybrid system combines wind power with solar or other renewable energy sources to ensure consistent energy production, even when one source is underperforming.

Combining Wind with Solar Power

When designing a hybrid system, the goal is to balance energy production from both sources. Wind can often generate power when solar panels are less effective, like during the night or when it's cloudy.

- **Energy Flow Management**: Use charge controllers to direct power from both sources into your battery bank. A hybrid inverter or a dedicated energy management system can automatically balance the input from solar and wind to ensure efficient energy storage and use.

Energy Management

For optimal efficiency, set up a system to **prioritize energy use and storage**. Monitor your system's performance regularly and adjust based on seasonal variations in wind and sunlight.

- **Monitoring Tools**: Use meters and software to track how much energy each source is producing and how much is being consumed. This helps identify inefficiencies and allows for adjustments in energy use.

By following these steps, you can successfully build and install a wind turbine as part of your off-grid energy system, ensuring a steady and dependable source of power for your independent living setup.

Maintaining and Optimizing Your Wind Turbine

A well-maintained wind turbine ensures consistent power generation, maximizes efficiency, and prolongs the system's lifespan. Regular maintenance and optimization are key to a long-term, reliable energy solution in off-grid living. This guide breaks down the essential steps to keep your wind turbine in top condition, even under changing weather conditions and evolving energy needs.

Routine Maintenance

Your wind turbine, like any mechanical system, needs regular checkups to ensure it remains functional and efficient. Here's how to approach maintenance with a practical, step-by-step approach.

Inspecting the Turbine Blades and Tower
1. **Regular Visual Checks**: Inspect the blades and tower monthly. Inspect for any indication of wear, cracks, chips, or warping in the blades. These issues, if unchecked, can reduce efficiency and even lead to system failure.
2. **Blade Alignment and Balance**: Ensure that the blades are properly aligned and balanced. Misaligned or unbalanced blades put strain on the system and reduce energy output. If you notice any wobbling or unusual vibrations, it may be a sign that the blades need adjustment or replacement.
3. **Check for Tower Stability**: Inspect the tower for structural integrity. Over time, weather and environmental factors can loosen bolts or weaken the structure. Tighten any loose bolts and ensure the tower remains firmly anchored.
4. **Monitor Wear Points**: Look for areas on the tower and rotor where metal components meet. Over time, friction may cause wear. Apply grease or lubricant to moving parts to minimize friction, prolong the life of components, and reduce noise.

Cleaning and Lubrication
1. **Cleaning the Blades**: Dust, dirt, and grime can accumulate on the turbine blades, decreasing their aerodynamic efficiency. Clean them every few months, or more frequently if you live in a dusty or coastal area, using a soft cloth and water. Avoid harsh chemicals as they may damage the blade material.
2. **Lubricating Moving Parts**: Periodically lubricate the moving parts of your turbine—especially the rotor, bearings, and yaw mechanism (which allows the turbine to rotate towards the wind). A lack of lubrication can cause friction, heat buildup, and mechanical failures.

Monitoring System Efficiency

1. **Use Energy Meters**: Install energy output meters to monitor the power your turbine is producing. Tracking this data over time can aid in detecting inefficiencies or emerging problems before they turn into bigger challenges.
2. **Watch for Signs of Trouble**: Sudden drops in energy output, abnormal noises, or vibrations are indicators that something is wrong. Investigate immediately—small issues can become costly repairs if left unresolved.
3. **Perform Load Tests**: Regularly test the system's load-bearing capacity to ensure your turbine can handle peak energy demands. This step ensures you're getting the most energy possible from your setup.

Seasonal Adjustments

Weather conditions can greatly impact the performance of your wind turbine. Seasonal adjustments and preparations are necessary to keep your system running efficiently all year long.

Optimizing for Different Weather Conditions

1. **Winterization**: In colder climates, freezing temperatures, ice, and snow can interfere with turbine operations. Ensure all moving parts are well-lubricated with a cold-weather grease that won't freeze. Install **anti-icing systems** if necessary to prevent ice buildup on blades.
2. **High Wind Conditions**: Storms and high winds can overwork your turbine or even damage it. Most modern turbines have a cut-out speed—when winds reach dangerous speeds, the turbine shuts down to protect itself. Regularly check and adjust these settings if your turbine allows it. Additionally, secure the tower more firmly in preparation for extreme winds.
3. **Preparing for Storms**: If you expect a major storm or hurricane, consider manually shutting down your turbine to avoid potential damage. Lock the blades and secure the tower with additional tie-downs or anchors.

Troubleshooting Common Problems

Even with regular maintenance, issues may arise that require troubleshooting. Here are some common problems and how to address them.

Power Fluctuations

Power fluctuations are a frequent issue in off-grid wind energy systems. This could be caused by variable wind speeds, improper turbine placement, or electrical problems.

1. **Check Wind Speeds**: Ensure that your turbine is in an optimal location where wind speeds remain consistent. Use an anemometer to measure local wind speeds and compare them to the turbine's rated output. If wind speeds are too low or inconsistent, you may need to adjust the height of the tower or its location.
2. **Review Wiring Connections**: Loose or corroded electrical connections can cause fluctuations in energy output. Inspect all wiring from the turbine to the charge controller and battery bank, and tighten or replace connections as needed.
3. **Balance Energy Sources**: In hybrid systems, fluctuations can occur when wind and solar energy sources are not properly balanced. Use a **hybrid charge controller** to manage the flow of energy from both sources, ensuring a steady supply.

Mechanical Issues

Wind turbines are mechanical devices, and like any machinery, they can experience wear and tear.

1. **Blades Not Spinning**: If the blades stop spinning, the problem could be mechanical or electrical. First, check for physical obstructions like debris in the rotor or damage to the blades. If all appears well, inspect the bearings and rotor shaft for signs of wear or failure.
2. **Noises and Vibrations**: Abnormal noises or vibrations can indicate a variety of problems, from loose components to misalignment of the blades. Tighten any loose parts and rebalance the blades. Excessive vibration can also damage the tower, so act quickly if you notice this issue.
3. **Lubrication**: Lack of lubrication is a common cause of mechanical failure. Ensure all moving parts are well-lubricated, and replace bearings or other components that are worn out.

Electrical Problems

Electrical issues, if left unchecked, can cause more serious damage to your system.

1. **Wiring Failures**: Check for any frayed or damaged wires, as well as loose connections. Replace worn wiring immediately to prevent power loss or shorts.
2. **Charge Controller Malfunctions**: If your charge controller is not functioning properly, it could either overcharge your batteries or fail to store power. Inspect the controller's connections and settings to ensure it is correctly regulating the flow of power.
3. **Inverter Issues**: If your inverter is failing to convert DC power to AC, first check that it's properly connected to the battery bank. If the wiring is correct but you're still experiencing issues, the inverter itself may need repair or replacement.

By following this practical maintenance and troubleshooting steps, you'll ensure that your wind turbine remains efficient, reliable, and optimized for long-term off-grid living. Regular checkups, seasonal adjustments, and prompt troubleshooting will maximize your system's lifespan and power output, ensuring a continuous supply of renewable energy no matter the conditions.

Innovations in Wind Energy Storage

Advancements in wind energy storage have revolutionized off-grid living by enhancing the efficiency, reliability, and sustainability of energy systems. In this section, we'll dive into the latest storage technologies, hybrid systems, and portable energy solutions that complement wind power and provide energy independence.

Tesla Powerwalls and Advanced Storage Systems

One of the most groundbreaking innovations in energy storage is the **Tesla Powerwall**. Designed for both residential and off-grid applications, the Powerwall is a rechargeable lithium-ion battery engineered to capture and store excess energy generated by your wind turbine.

- Advantages:
  - **Efficient Energy Storage**: Tesla Powerwalls offer high energy density, meaning they can store more power in a smaller space. This is essential for off-grid setups where space is often limited.
  - **Seamless Integration**: These systems are designed to integrate easily with renewable energy sources like solar and wind, storing surplus energy for later use and releasing it when needed.
  - **Smart Energy Management**: Equipped with advanced software, the Powerwall can intelligently manage energy distribution, ensuring power is available during peak consumption periods or during times when wind speeds are low.

- Disadvantages:
  - **Cost**: One of the primary drawbacks of high-tech systems like the Tesla Powerwall is the upfront investment. Although prices have dropped, the initial cost is still significant, which might not be ideal for every budget.
  - **Dependency on Technology**: As these systems rely on advanced software and firmware updates, you must be comfortable managing digital systems and ensuring your setup remains up to date.

Other Advanced Storage Systems

In addition to Tesla, other companies provide **lithium-ion battery** solutions and **flow battery** systems, which offer longer lifecycles and more efficient energy storage. When deciding which system to use, compare factors such as battery life, capacity, and the ease of integration with your wind power system.

Hybrid Energy Systems: Integrating Solar and Wind Power Storage

Hybrid energy systems—those that combine both solar and wind power—are ideal for off-grid living, as they ensure a more **balanced** and **reliable energy supply**. Each source has its strengths, and by combining them, you can take advantage of the complementary nature of solar and wind.

- **Solar-Wind Synergy**: Solar power tends to be more reliable during daylight hours and in sunnier months, while wind power excels during stormy weather or at night when winds tend to pick up. A hybrid system can ensure that you have consistent energy available at all times.
- **Energy Flow Management**: To efficiently manage energy from both sources, you need a **hybrid charge controller**. This device intelligently directs energy from both solar panels and wind turbines to your battery bank, optimizing charging cycles and preventing overcharging.
- **Balancing Power Generation and Storage**: With a hybrid system, you may need to expand your battery storage to accommodate the increased energy generation. This will allow you to store more energy during periods of excess production and tap into it during cloudy or calm days.

Expert Tip: A properly configured hybrid system can eliminate the need for backup generators, minimizing dependence on fossil fuels and offering a more sustainable, reliable energy alternative.

Mobile or Portable Solar Storage Solutions

For off-grid living or those on the move, **portable solar storage solutions** offer flexibility and mobility. These systems can be used to **supplement your wind turbine** setup or serve as a backup when weather conditions aren't favorable for wind energy production.

- **Portable Solar Panels with Battery Storage**: Lightweight and foldable, these panels are ideal for camping or moving between locations. They often come with integrated battery storage, which allows you to capture solar energy during the day and store it for use at night.
- **Mobile Power Stations**: For more substantial energy needs, consider **mobile power stations**—portable, large-capacity batteries designed to store and distribute energy. These systems are perfect for emergencies or for powering essential devices when away from your primary off-grid setup.

Special Consideration: When selecting portable systems, look for models that can integrate with your wind system. Some mobile solutions offer hybrid compatibility, allowing you to use both solar and wind to recharge the portable battery.

Case Studies and Practical Examples

Understanding how these technologies work in real-world scenarios can help you apply them effectively to your own off-grid lifestyle. Below are case studies and practical examples of wind power systems designed for different living situations.

Small Cabin Wind Power System

For those living in **small off-grid cabins**, a modest wind power system can be the perfect solution. This case study outlines how a homeowner installed a budget-friendly wind turbine system to power essential appliances and lighting.

- System Overview:
    - **Wind Turbine Size**: A 1-2 kW wind turbine.
    - **Battery Bank**: A small bank of deep-cycle batteries for energy storage.
    - **Controller and Inverter**: A simple charge controller and inverter to convert stored DC power to AC.
- **Key Challenges**: The cabin was located in a wooded area, which caused turbulence. To overcome this, the tower was extended to a height of 35 feet, well above the tree line. The owner also installed **guy wires** for extra stability during storms.
- **Results**: The system provided steady power for critical needs like lighting, a small refrigerator, and a water pump. The addition of a portable solar panel for backup ensured the system remained functional during low-wind periods.

Family Home Setup

This case study highlights the installation of a **medium-sized wind turbine** system for a full off-grid family home, integrated with solar power for hybrid energy production.

- System Overview:
    - **Wind Turbine Size**: A 5-10 kW turbine to generate enough power for a household with multiple appliances.
    - **Hybrid Setup**: Combined with a 3 kW solar array to balance energy production between sunny and windy days.
    - **Advanced Storage**: A Tesla Powerwall battery was installed for optimal energy storage and distribution.
- **Key Challenges**: The household required a large energy storage solution due to the varying energy demands throughout the day. Additionally, the location experienced seasonal shifts in both solar and wind resources, making the hybrid system essential.
- **Results**: The family achieved nearly complete energy independence by minimizing dependence on the grid by over 90%. The Tesla Powerwall provided uninterrupted energy supply during the night and on cloudy or calm days.

Wind Power in Extreme Environments

For those living in **extreme climates**, wind power can be adapted to ensure reliable performance. This example showcases a wind turbine system designed for **high-altitude** living in a mountainous region.

- System Overview:
    - **Wind Turbine Size**: A 3 kW turbine optimized for strong, consistent winds at high altitudes.
    - **Durability Modifications**: The turbine blades were reinforced with **composite materials** to withstand extreme winds, and the tower was anchored to bedrock to prevent toppling during storms.

- **Challenges**: Extreme weather conditions, such as strong winds, snow, and ice, made the system prone to damage. However, with regular maintenance and seasonal adjustments (such as adding anti-icing systems), the turbine remained operational throughout the year.
- **Results**: The system produced more than enough power for heating, lighting, and essential appliances, even during harsh winters. The owner used a small backup generator only during the most severe storms, further enhancing energy independence.

The Importance of Wind Energy for Off-Grid Living

Wind energy is not just a tool; it's a pathway to long-term **energy independence**, sustainability, and security for your off-grid lifestyle. By integrating wind power into your off-grid setup, you are taking control of your energy needs and building a resilient system that can withstand the unpredictable nature of modern living.

Commitment to Maintenance and Optimization

One of the key factors in making your wind energy system thrive is ongoing **commitment** to its **maintenance** and **optimization**. Regular inspections and adjustments ensure your wind turbine operates efficiently and consistently, providing dependable

energy year-round.

- **Routine Inspections**: Make it a habit to check for wear, damage, and alignment in your turbine blades, tower, and connections. Minor issues can escalate if ignored, but when caught early, they are easy to resolve and maintain system efficiency.
- **Seasonal Adjustments**: Your wind turbine system will require slight tweaks throughout the year, particularly as seasons shift. This might mean adjusting the blade pitch or tightening guy wires to accommodate changing weather conditions, wind speeds, or storm events.
- **Energy Output Monitoring**: Installing monitoring tools helps you track your system's performance, allowing you to quickly identify and solve any drop in efficiency. By keeping an eye on energy data, you'll have a better understanding of your wind turbine's output and when to make proactive adjustments.

Staying committed to maintaining and optimizing your wind power system means you'll continue to benefit from clean, sustainable energy for many years.

Sustainable Energy Solutions for Off-Grid Independence

Wind energy provides more than just power—it offers **sustainability** and **freedom**. In a world increasingly reliant on external systems, having your own renewable energy source guarantees that your power is truly yours, irrespective of grid failures or fossil fuel shortages.

- **Energy Independence**: With wind energy, you break free from dependence on traditional utilities. Your energy becomes a product of your environment, harnessing the natural power of the wind to keep your home running, even when external power grids fail.
- **Sustainability**: Wind energy is one of the most environmentally friendly power sources available. It doesn't rely on burning fuels, which means it contributes to a cleaner planet and reduces your overall carbon footprint. By using wind power, you are actively participating in the shift toward renewable energy solutions that benefit both the planet and future generations.
- **Resilience in Extreme Conditions**: Whether you live in a region prone to extreme weather or remote locations, wind energy systems are adaptable and reliable. They can be customized to suit various environmental challenges, from desert landscapes to high-altitude regions. This versatility ensures you can maintain energy security no matter where you are.

Final Thoughts on Long-Term Resilience

Your decision to incorporate wind power into your off-grid lifestyle is an investment not only in your present but also in your future. It reflects a proactive approach to living independently and sustainably, reducing your reliance on outside systems while increasing your ability to weather challenges—whether environmental, economic, or societal.

Take pride in what you've built. You're not just constructing a wind turbine or setting up renewable energy systems; you're securing **long-term resilience** for yourself and your loved ones. This system is your key to maintaining a self-sufficient, off-grid lifestyle—one where your energy needs are met reliably, sustainably, and independently.

By continuing to **monitor, optimize, and expand** your system as needed, you'll ensure that your wind energy setup evolves alongside your needs. And remember, the more you understand and engage with your system, the more empowered you'll be to troubleshoot, innovate, and refine it. Embrace the power of wind energy and enjoy the freedom, sustainability, and resilience it brings to your off-grid lifestyle.

9. Exploring Biomass Energy Solutions

Introduction to Biomass Energy for Off-Grid Living

As you continue to expand your off-grid living capabilities, integrating various renewable energy sources, it's essential to consider biomass energy. If you've already explored solar and wind power solutions, biomass is a perfect complement that adds another layer of sustainability and self-reliance to your energy mix. Like solar panels that capture the sun's rays and wind turbines that harness the breeze, biomass energy taps into the natural resources around you—wood, agricultural residues, animal waste, and even food scraps—to provide reliable heating and cooking solutions.

Why Biomass Energy?

Biomass is a practical and renewable energy source, ideal for those living off the grid. It provides a consistent supply of heat for cooking and warmth, all while using materials that might otherwise go to waste. Whether you're heating your off-grid home during winter or cooking meals for your family, biomass can significantly reduce your dependency on fossil fuels and lower your overall costs.

Benefits:

- **Cost-Effective:** Biomass is an economical option because it relies on materials you can often gather for free—logs from fallen trees, agricultural waste from your garden, or animal by-products from livestock.
- **Reduces Waste:** Utilizing organic waste for energy allows you to turn potential waste products into a functional fuel source.
- **Reliable Heating and Cooking:** Biomass provides a steady, reliable form of energy that you can use year-round, regardless of sun or wind availability.
- **Energy Independence:** By tapping into readily available resources, you can reduce your reliance on external fuel sources, making your off-grid system more self-sufficient.

Environmental Impact:

- Biomass promotes the sustainable use of natural resources, closing the loop in your energy system. Rather than discarding organic matter, you repurpose it for energy, creating a circular system that reduces the environmental footprint of your off-grid living.

Integration with Other Energy Sources:

- Biomass is a great partner for solar and wind energy. On days when the sun isn't shining or the wind isn't blowing, biomass can be your fallback, ensuring you never run short of power. Together, these energy sources create a balanced and efficient off-grid system, allowing you to tailor your energy use to the conditions at hand.

Types of Biomass Sources

When it comes to biomass energy, a variety of materials can be used, all of which are likely readily available in an off-grid setting. Here are the most common sources you can harness:

- **Wood:** Logs, branches, wood chips, and sawdust from your surroundings can serve as fuel for biomass stoves and heaters.
- **Agricultural Residues:** Corn husks, straw, and leaves from your garden or nearby farms can easily be repurposed into fuel.

- **Animal Waste:** Manure from livestock, such as chickens or cows, can be converted into energy through composting and other biomass systems.
- **Food Waste:** Even kitchen scraps, such as vegetable peelings or food leftovers, can be turned into fuel, further reducing waste and maximizing your resources.

Planning Your Biomass Energy System

To ensure your biomass energy setup is both efficient and sustainable, careful planning is crucial. You'll need to choose the right biomass sources based on your environment and energy needs, while also considering how to balance biomass with other renewable resources like solar and wind power.

Choosing the Right Biomass Source

Local Resource Selection:

The key to a successful biomass energy system lies in sourcing materials that are abundant and easily accessible in your area. Identify what's available—whether it's wood from nearby forests, agricultural waste from your garden, or manure from livestock. The more local and sustainable your resources, the easier it will be to maintain your system.

Seasonal Considerations:

Your biomass energy needs will fluctuate throughout the year, so it's essential to plan for seasonal availability of resources. For example, you might gather wood during the fall to prepare for winter heating, or stockpile agricultural waste during harvest season for use throughout the year.

Energy Needs and Biomass Supply

Before setting up your biomass system, take a close look at how much energy you consume for cooking, heating, and other daily needs. Calculate how much biomass you'll need to maintain consistent energy output, ensuring you have enough material to last through colder months when heating demand is higher.

Balancing Biomass with Other Energy Sources:

Biomass is a great addition to a diversified energy strategy. Pair it with solar and wind systems to create a hybrid approach. For example, during sunny summer months, you might rely more on solar energy for cooking and lighting, while biomass takes over in the colder, windier months when heating is the priority.

Sustainability Practices

When gathering biomass materials, it's important to do so in a way that doesn't harm your environment. Harvesting wood, agricultural waste, and animal by-products should be done sustainably, ensuring that your biomass energy system is in harmony with the natural ecosystem. By rotating resources and not overharvesting, you can create a continuous supply of energy without depleting your environment.

This approach, combined with solar and wind power solutions, will help you develop a resilient and self-sufficient off-grid energy system that serves your needs year-round, regardless of environmental conditions.

Building a Small-Scale Biomass Energy System

Transitioning from solar and wind energy, biomass energy brings a powerful, sustainable addition to your off-grid living system. It offers the flexibility to use local, natural resources to meet your energy needs for cooking and heating, even in situations where the sun and wind are less reliable. With a step-by-step approach, this guide will help you create an efficient and safe biomass energy system that complements your existing solar or wind power setup.

DIY Biomass Stove for Cooking

A biomass stove can serve as a reliable, low-cost solution for cooking, turning wood, agricultural waste, or other biomass into heat for preparing meals. Here's how to build an efficient stove:

Materials Needed:
- Steel drums or metal barrels (preferably heat-resistant)
- Metal pipes for air intake and exhaust
- Fire bricks to line the stove
- Simple tools: hammer, nails, drill, and cutting tools

Step-by-Step Build Guide:
1. **Constructing the Combustion Chamber:**

Begin by shaping the steel drum into a combustion chamber. The size should be large enough to hold a reasonable amount of fuel but compact enough to ensure efficient heat retention. Line the inside with fire bricks to protect the metal from extreme heat.

2. **Installing Proper Air Intake and Exhaust for Airflow:**

Airflow is crucial for ensuring the fire burns efficiently. Drill holes in the lower section for the intake and attach metal pipes to guide air into the combustion chamber. Similarly, attach an exhaust pipe at the top to release smoke and gases, directing them away from the cooking area.

3. **Safety Tips:**

Always ensure that your stove is safely positioned, away from flammable materials, and has proper ventilation to avoid carbon monoxide buildup. Use fireproof materials for surrounding the stove to prevent accidents.

Using the Biomass Stove:
- **Lighting and Maintaining an Efficient Fire:**

Start with dry biomass material like wood chips or agricultural waste. Once lit, control airflow through the intake to regulate the fire's strength.

- **Heat Control:**

Manage your cooking temperature by adjusting the air intake. Allow more airflow for high heat when boiling or frying, and reduce airflow for simmering.

DIY Biomass Heating System for Your Shelter

A well-designed biomass heating system can keep your shelter warm, even in the coldest seasons. Here's how to build a biomass heater using the highly efficient **rocket mass heater design**:

Designing a DIY Biomass Heater:
1. Using a Rocket Mass Heater Design:

A rocket mass heater efficiently burns biomass and stores heat in a thermal mass like stone or clay. This design allows it to retain heat for extended periods, reducing the amount of fuel needed to maintain warmth.

Step-by-Step Build Guide:

1. **Constructing the Burn Chamber and Heat Riser:**

The burn chamber should be made from durable steel or fireproof materials. Build it in a vertical position with a heat riser (a hollow insulated tube) that helps intensify the combustion process, ensuring maximum fuel efficiency.

2. **Installing Heat-Exchange Pipes:**

Run heat-exchange pipes from the burn chamber through your shelter to distribute warmth. Lay these pipes under seating areas or along walls to radiate the captured heat throughout the space.

Optimizing Efficiency:

- **Fuel Efficiency Tips:**

To minimize fuel consumption, use dry, seasoned wood and regulate airflow for efficient combustion. A well-insulated heat riser ensures less heat loss.

- **Combining with Solar or Wind Heating Systems:**

On milder days, solar heating can complement the biomass heater, reducing the need for constant fire maintenance. Use the biomass heater primarily during cold nights or overcast days when solar isn't effective.

Storing and Managing Biomass Fuel

To ensure a consistent fuel supply for cooking and heating, you'll need a proper storage solution to keep biomass materials dry and accessible.

Building a Biomass Storage Solution:

1. **Creating Covered, Dry Storage:**

Build a simple shelter or repurpose containers to keep your wood, plant matter, or other biomass materials dry. Moisture will hinder combustion efficiency and create more smoke, so prioritize dryness.

2. **Simple Storage Techniques:**

Use pallets or shelves to store biomass off the ground. Cover the top with a tarp or build a small roof structure to prevent rain or snow from soaking the materials.

Managing Biomass Supply:

- **Rotating and Stockpiling Fuel:**

Keep a regular cycle of fresh biomass and rotate older materials for use. Stockpile fuel in advance, especially before winter when you'll need more for heating.

- **Long-Term Storage:**

For long-term storage, ensure that your biomass is well-ventilated to prevent mold or decay. Stack materials loosely to allow air to circulate and keep the fuel dry.

Maximizing Fuel Efficiency and Reducing Waste

Making the most of your biomass resources is key to sustaining your off-grid energy needs without exhausting supplies.

Using Agricultural Waste:

- **Incorporating By-Products Like Corn Husks or Straw:**

Plant residues like corn husks and straw are excellent biomass sources. Break down these materials into smaller pieces for easier burning in your stove or heater.

Recycling Animal Waste:

- **Safely Using Manure and Organic Waste:**

Livestock manure, when dried and processed, can be an additional source of biomass fuel. Use simple composting techniques to turn organic waste into energy.

Composting Techniques:

- **Turning Organic Waste into Energy:**

Convert kitchen scraps or yard waste into usable biomass fuel by composting them. Once decomposed and dried, these materials can fuel your stove or heater, reducing your overall waste.

Maximizing Biomass Energy Output:

To further enhance your biomass energy system, consider integrating the latest innovations. Modern methods like catalytic converters help maximize combustion efficiency, reducing smoke and increasing heat production. These innovations ensure that your system operates cleaner and requires less fuel for the same output.

Troubleshooting and Maintenance for Biomass Systems

When operating a biomass system, you'll eventually encounter challenges that need troubleshooting and routine maintenance to ensure optimal performance. Addressing these issues promptly will not only extend the lifespan of your system but also improve fuel efficiency and safety.

Common Issues and Solutions:

- **Smoke Buildup:**

Smoke buildup is often a sign of inefficient combustion, typically caused by poor airflow, wet biomass, or an improperly constructed combustion chamber. To resolve this:

1. **Check the Airflow**: Ensure that the air intake and exhaust vents are unobstructed. Proper airflow is key to maintaining clean combustion. If necessary, widen the vents or reposition your system to allow better ventilation.
2. **Use Dry Biomass**: Wet or damp materials won't burn efficiently. Make sure your biomass is thoroughly dried and stored in a dry location.
3. **Improve Combustion Chamber Design**: If the chamber isn't retaining heat efficiently, consider rebuilding or reinforcing it with fire bricks for better heat insulation and retention.

- **Heat Loss:**

If your biomass system is losing heat, especially in colder climates, this usually points to insulation issues. Heat loss can be reduced by:

1. **Insulating the Combustion Chamber**: Reinforce your system with proper insulation materials such as ceramic fiber or fire-resistant bricks.
2. **Check for Leaks**: Ensure there are no gaps where heat could be escaping. Seal off any cracks or joints where the air might leak.
3. **Enhance Heat Retention**: If you're using a rocket mass heater, ensure the heat-exchange pipes are correctly installed, circulating warmth throughout the space efficiently.

Routine Maintenance:

Regular maintenance will prevent the buildup of problems over time. Set a schedule for the following tasks:

- **Clean the Combustion Chamber**: Ashes and soot can accumulate, leading to inefficient combustion. Clean out the chamber regularly to maintain optimal airflow and heat production.
- **Inspect Exhaust Pipes and Airways**: Ensure there are no blockages or cracks in the exhaust system. Regular inspection can prevent dangerous buildups of smoke or toxic gases.
- **Check for Wear and Tear**: Over time, high temperatures can weaken certain parts of the biomass system. Inspect your stove or heater for signs of cracking, rust, or loose components, and repair or replace them as needed.

Safety Inspections:

Safety is paramount in any off-grid setup. Make sure you:

- **Inspect Exhausts and Ventilation Regularly**: Poorly ventilated biomass systems can lead to smoke buildup and carbon monoxide poisoning. Check airways frequently and ensure exhaust vents are clear.
- **Install Smoke and Carbon Monoxide Detectors**: In enclosed spaces, always have detectors installed to alert you in case of hazardous gas buildup.

Expanding and Upgrading Your Biomass System

Once you've successfully built and maintained your basic biomass system, you may find that your energy needs grow or that technology presents new opportunities. Here's how to take your setup to the next level.

Upgrading from Basic to Advanced Systems:

As your off-grid living evolves, your biomass system can adapt to your growing energy needs. You can:

- **Enhance Your Current System**: By adding additional components like a catalytic converter, you can increase the efficiency of biomass combustion, reducing waste and increasing energy output.
- **Invest in Larger Capacity**: If you find your small-scale system isn't providing enough heat or energy, consider upgrading to a larger biomass system that can power an entire off-grid home. Use larger heat risers and burn chambers to accommodate more fuel and generate more heat.

Hybrid Systems:

Biomass works excellently in tandem with other renewable energy sources. Consider integrating biomass into a hybrid energy system with solar and wind to:

- **Maximize Energy Efficiency**: A hybrid system ensures that you're always drawing on the best energy source available, whether it's sunny, windy, or you're burning biomass.
- **Utilize Tesla Powerwalls**: Store excess energy generated by your biomass system in a Tesla Powerwall or other advanced energy storage systems, which can provide backup power when other sources like solar or wind aren't producing enough.

Scaling Up:

If your off-grid setup becomes larger or expands to serve more people (such as in a homestead or small community), scaling your biomass system might be the solution:

- **Larger Community Systems**: Set up neighborhood-scale biomass systems that can provide energy to several homes. These larger systems are designed to handle more significant loads of biomass and distribute heat and energy to multiple buildings.
- **Economies of Scale**: Larger systems tend to be more fuel-efficient because they retain and distribute heat more effectively. You can optimize these setups to reduce energy waste.

Innovations in Biomass Energy Storage

To take full advantage of your biomass system, incorporating advanced energy storage technologies can provide you with more consistent power output and increased efficiency. Whether you're integrating biomass with solar and wind or looking for portable solutions, innovations in energy storage will help you get the most out of your off-grid setup.

Tesla Powerwalls and Advanced Storage Systems

One of the most cutting-edge energy storage options available is the Tesla Powerwall, designed to store renewable energy for use when the system isn't generating enough power. Here's how it fits into an off-grid biomass system:

- **Exploring Modern High-Tech Storage Options**: Tesla Powerwalls and similar systems store excess energy produced by your biomass stove or heater, which can then be used when needed. These high-tech solutions provide a reliable energy backup, ensuring your home is never without power, even if biomass is not being actively burned.
- **Advantages**: Powerwalls offer a seamless way to store energy and provide uninterrupted power. They can handle energy storage for both short-term needs and extended periods without the need for manual intervention. Moreover, they reduce waste by efficiently capturing unused energy from biomass systems.
- **Disadvantages**: While Tesla Powerwalls offer top-of-the-line performance, their high cost may be prohibitive for some off-grid enthusiasts. Additionally, their reliance on advanced technology can make repairs more complex in remote locations.
- **Off-Grid Applications**: For off-grid living, Tesla Powerwalls can integrate with other renewable energy systems—like solar and wind—creating a hybrid setup that provides consistent, reliable energy across various sources.

Hybrid Energy Systems

Biomass works best when used in tandem with other energy sources. A hybrid system combining biomass, solar, and wind ensures a diversified energy approach that reduces dependence on any single source.

- **Combining Biomass with Solar and Wind**: Hybrid systems use multiple sources of renewable energy to maintain a reliable energy supply. Even during periods when the sun isn't shining or the wind isn't blowing, biomass can serve as a dependable alternative for heating and cooking. This balanced energy approach enables you store solar energy collected during the day while generating biomass energy at night, for example.

- **Maximizing Energy Efficiency**: Hybrid setups are the best way to capture energy whenever it's available and use it when it's most needed. This method increases overall system efficiency, especially in regions with unpredictable weather patterns or seasonal shifts.
- **Mobile and Portable Biomass Solutions**: For those living a mobile off-grid lifestyle, portable biomass systems offer a flexible solution. Small, easy-to-assemble biomass stoves or heaters can be transported to new locations and used with local biomass resources, ensuring energy independence on the move.

Case Studies and Practical Examples

Understanding how others have successfully implemented biomass systems in real-world situations can inspire and guide you through your off-grid journey. These case studies showcase diverse setups in different environments, providing valuable insights into challenges and solutions.

Small Cabin Biomass System

A small, off-grid cabin can benefit significantly from a biomass energy system that provides reliable heat and energy during colder months. Let's look at a real-world example:

- **Challenges**: One challenge often faced by small cabins is ensuring enough fuel is available to maintain warmth during long winters. In this scenario, gathering and properly storing biomass in advance is critical. Additionally, smoke buildup can be an issue if ventilation isn't managed effectively.
- **Solutions**: Installing a rocket mass heater with a well-insulated burn chamber and exhaust system can help retain heat for long periods while using minimal fuel. Regular chimney maintenance and a well-designed airflow system also prevent smoke buildup, ensuring safe and efficient operation.

Family Home Biomass Setup

For larger households, biomass systems can offer a consistent heat source throughout the home. In this case study, we explore how a medium-sized off-grid family home integrates a biomass system with solar and wind power.

- **Integration with Other Renewable Sources**: The family's biomass system is paired with a solar power setup, allowing them to generate electricity during the day while using biomass for heating and cooking. During colder or cloudier days, the biomass system becomes the primary heat source, reducing dependence on solar energy.
- **Optimizing Efficiency**: By using a rocket mass heater, the family is able to maximize heat retention, ensuring their home stays warm while minimizing the need to continuously feed the fire. Solar power is stored in Tesla Powerwalls to ensure a backup energy source when biomass isn't being used.

Biomass in Extreme Environments

In extreme environments, whether it's deserts or frigid climates, adapting your biomass system is crucial to ensuring efficient performance and safety.

- **Adapting for Desert Climates**: In dry, desert climates, sourcing biomass materials like wood and plant matter may be more challenging. However, using agricultural residues like straw and husks can provide a reliable source of fuel. In such environments, the system's air intake needs to be carefully managed to prevent overheating, and proper insulation is required to retain heat during cold desert nights.
- **Handling Cold Climates**: For those living in extreme cold, the primary challenge is keeping the system running efficiently in freezing temperatures. Insulating pipes and the combustion chamber will help retain heat, and regular maintenance is necessary to ensure the system doesn't freeze or lose efficiency. Properly storing dry biomass fuel indoors can also help ensure it burns efficiently during long, cold winters.

Innovating within your biomass system, from incorporating Tesla Powerwalls to adapting for extreme climates, can make your off-grid life both sustainable and efficient. By integrating hybrid energy systems and learning from real-world examples, you're equipped to optimize the performance of your biomass system, ensuring that it meets your energy needs while minimizing waste. Keep refining and expanding your system as your off-grid journey evolves, and enjoy the independence and sustainability that biomass energy provides.

Conclusion: Long-Term Benefits of Biomass Energy

As you conclude your journey into off-grid biomass energy, it's important to take a moment to reflect on the transformative power of this renewable resource. Biomass offers a practical solution that is both sustainable and cost-effective for those seeking energy independence, allowing you to break free from the reliance on fossil fuels. Here's why integrating biomass into your off-grid lifestyle is a smart, long-term decision:

Environmental, Cost, and Energy Independence Advantages

Biomass energy stands out for its ability to reduce waste, cut costs, and minimize your environmental footprint. By converting organic materials like wood, agricultural residues, and even food waste into energy, you're not only powering your home but also contributing to a more sustainable planet. This closed-loop system ensures that what nature provides is used efficiently and responsibly. Biomass reduces greenhouse gas emissions, providing a cleaner and more sustainable option compared to traditional fuel sources, all while utilizing materials you might otherwise discard.

From a financial standpoint, biomass is an incredibly cost-effective energy source. Once your system is in place, the fuel—whether it's wood, plant matter, or manure—is either free or very inexpensive. This can lead to substantial reductions in your energy bills, offering long-term financial savings. Unlike other renewable energy systems that rely on unpredictable factors like sunlight or wind, biomass provides a steady and reliable source of power.

Most importantly, biomass empowers you with energy independence. As part of a diversified energy system that may include solar or wind, biomass fills in the gaps, ensuring that your off-grid living is resilient and reliable. When solar and wind power are unavailable, biomass keeps your household warm and functional, regardless of external conditions.

Sustainability and Off-Grid Living

Biomass energy systems are not just about the present—they're a forward-thinking solution that can carry you into the future. As you continue refining and expanding your system, you'll discover new ways to increase efficiency and sustainability. Whether it's upgrading your stove, incorporating advanced energy storage solutions like Tesla Powerwalls, or expanding your system to serve a community or neighborhood, biomass energy is scalable and adaptable to your growing needs.

Sustainability is at the heart of off-grid living, and biomass plays a central role in that mission. By harvesting and utilizing renewable resources, you're living in harmony with the environment, creating a self-sustaining energy cycle that reduces your impact on the planet. It's a system that rewards foresight and careful management, ensuring that you can continue to thrive off-grid for decades to come.

10. Hybrid Energy Systems: Maximizing Off-Grid Efficiency

Introduction to Hybrid Energy Systems

When you're living off the grid, one of the most significant hurdles is creating a reliable energy source that can handle your daily needs—whether sunlight is abundant and the wind is steady, or neither is happening. In our previous books, you've already explored how to harness solar, wind, and biomass energy. These systems work well individually, but when combined, they can create a powerhouse of energy for your off-grid lifestyle. This is where hybrid energy systems come into play.

What is a Hybrid Energy System?

A **hybrid energy system** integrates multiple renewable energy options including solar, wind, and biomass—into a single, cohesive setup. It also incorporates battery storage and, in many cases, a generator as a backup. The beauty of a hybrid system is its flexibility and reliability. By combining different energy sources, you can reduce your dependence on any one resource and optimize power generation across a variety of conditions.

Imagine this scenario: During the day, your solar panels are working at full capacity. At night, your wind turbine picks up the slack as the breeze blows across your homestead. If it's a calm, cloudy day, you can turn to your biomass heater or generator to meet your energy needs. This multi-source approach ensures you have a consistent, reliable energy flow, no matter what nature throws your way.

Why Hybrid Systems Are More Reliable

Hybrid systems are more reliable than standalone energy solutions because they combine multiple sources of energy generation. Solar power might be abundant during the summer, but during the winter, shorter daylight hours and more overcast days might significantly reduce your solar output. Wind energy can be more consistent, but if there's no wind, a generator or biomass system can supplement your power needs.

The redundancy built into hybrid systems also means you'll never be left without energy. If one system goes down or is underperforming due to weather, another can step in. This kind of setup is key to a sustainable, resilient off-grid energy strategy.

Why Go Hybrid?

When you're off the grid, relying on a single energy source can be risky. Integrating multiple energy sources allows you to diversify your power generation, ensuring that you have the ability to adapt to changing weather and energy demands.

Key Benefits:
1. **Energy Security**: With solar, wind, biomass, and backup generators working together, your system is far more secure than relying on a single power source. If one element is not working efficiently, the others can pick up the slack.
2. **Efficiency**: Hybrid systems can be designed to optimize energy capture throughout the day and night, across different seasons, and in varying weather conditions.
3. **Long-Term Savings:** Although the upfront investment may seem higher, the long-term savings from lower energy costs and reduced reliance on fossil fuels make it a financially sound decision.
4. **Environmental Sustainability**: Hybrid systems maximize the use of renewable resources, making your energy consumption far more sustainable.

Key Considerations:

- **Climate**: Hybrid systems work best when designed around the specific climate and geography of your location. If your area experiences long winters with little sunlight, wind and biomass might be more critical than solar.
- **Location**: The location of your home plays a huge role in determining which energy sources to prioritize. Coastal areas may be more suited to wind power, while areas with abundant woodlands may favor biomass.
- **Energy Needs**: Your system must be designed to meet your household's daily energy consumption, including periods when one or more energy sources may be unavailable.

Energy Sources in Hybrid Systems

Now, let's break down the various energy sources you'll be working with in a hybrid system and how they integrate to create a reliable, off-grid energy network.

Solar Energy

Solar energy is often the foundation of most off-grid setups because it's relatively easy to harness and maintain. Solar panels produce electricity throughout the day, and with battery storage, you can reserve this energy for use during the night or on overcast days.

Solar Panel Efficiency: When designing a hybrid system, you must carefully consider solar panel efficiency. Look at the efficiency rating of your panels and make sure they're installed in a location that gets maximum sun exposure.

- **Panel Placement and Setup**: Placing your solar panels at the optimal angle and avoiding shading will drastically improve their performance. Hybrid systems benefit most from a well-placed solar array, combined with battery storage.
- **Integration with Battery Storage**: Solar power generation alone is not enough; integrating a battery storage system ensures the energy produced is not wasted and can be used when needed. This will be critical for nighttime energy usage.

Wind Power

Wind power adds an important dimension to hybrid systems, especially in areas where winds are consistent.

- **Harnessing Wind Energy**: A small wind turbine can generate energy during periods when the sun isn't shining. The most effective hybrid systems typically use wind energy to supplement solar during night hours or cloudy days.
- **Siting Considerations**: To get the most out of wind power, it's crucial to place your wind turbines where they can catch consistent, strong winds. If your home is situated in a valley, wind may not be as consistent, while coastal or elevated locations tend to provide better wind energy.
- **Integrating Wind with Solar and Other Energy Sources**: Hybrid systems should combine wind and solar seamlessly. For example, during winter months, wind power can often become the primary energy generator, supplementing solar power's reduced output.

Biomass Energy

Biomass offers an excellent backup energy source and is particularly useful in hybrid systems for cooking and heating.

- **Biomass as a Backup**: Biomass systems burn organic material like wood or crop waste to produce energy. It's not just a backup; biomass energy can also handle heating needs when the weather is cold and energy demand is high.

- **Biomass Stoves and Heaters**: These systems are highly effective in hybrid systems, where they can step in when solar and wind fall short, providing you with heat and energy for basic needs.
- **Integration with Solar and Wind**: Biomass systems are ideal for when solar and wind resources are low, such as during winter nights or stormy weather.

Generators

While renewable sources should be your primary energy producers, a generator is an essential element in any hybrid system.

- **Types of Generators**: You can choose from diesel, propane, or manual crank generators, depending on your preferences. Diesel is more commonly available, but propane is a cleaner alternative.
- **Strategic Use**: Generators should be used sparingly in hybrid systems—primarily as a backup during periods of peak energy demand or during extended cloudy and windless periods.

Building a hybrid energy system integrates the best of all energy worlds, ensuring that you're never reliant on a single source for your energy needs. By combining solar, wind, biomass, and generators into a seamless system, you'll ensure energy security, resilience, and long-term sustainability for your off-grid living.

In the next sections, we'll dive deeper into designing these systems, integrating battery storage, and optimizing energy distribution. Each element must work together to ensure you're maximizing efficiency and minimizing waste, setting you up for long-term off-grid success.

Designing Your Hybrid Energy System

Designing an efficient and reliable hybrid energy system is a crucial step for anyone serious about off-grid living. Hybrid systems are the most resilient because they allow you to draw energy from multiple sources—solar, wind, biomass, and backup generators—ensuring that you never rely too heavily on just one. This section will guide you through assessing your energy requirements, designing the system layout, and integrating battery storage to create a robust and efficient hybrid setup.

Assessing Your Energy Needs

The first step in designing your hybrid energy system is to assess your energy consumption. It's important to understand the amount of energy your household uses daily and plan your energy sources accordingly. This ensures that you don't overspend on unnecessary equipment or, worse, underpower your home.

- **Calculating Daily Power Consumption**: Begin by creating an inventory of all appliances and systems you'll be running in your off-grid home, from lighting to heating to refrigeration. Calculate the total power consumption in kilowatt-hours (kWh) for each.
  - **Example**: If your refrigerator uses 1.5 kWh per day and your lights use 0.5 kWh per day, you'll need at least 2 kWh of energy just to cover these essentials.
  - **Tip**: Plan for the worst-case scenario—days when solar power might be low or wind may not blow. This means you need to have backup energy reserves available in your system.
- **Balancing Multiple Energy Sources**: Once you know your daily energy consumption, it's time to balance your power needs between your different energy sources—solar, wind, biomass, and battery storage. Ideally, during sunny days, your solar panels should cover most of your power needs, while at night or on cloudy days, wind turbines and biomass systems should take over. Your battery storage will act as a reserve, capturing surplus energy and supplying it when required.

- o **Off-Peak and Peak Planning**: For example, during the day when solar production is high, you might focus on energy-intensive tasks, like washing clothes or cooking. At night, your energy needs might be lower, but your battery should have stored enough power to run essential systems like lighting and refrigeration.
- **Examples of Energy Usage**:
  - o A small off-grid household might consume 5-10 kWh per day.
  - o A larger family home with more appliances could need upwards of 20-30 kWh daily.

Siting and System Design

Next, you'll need to plan the physical layout of your hybrid system. The location of each component—solar panels, wind turbines, biomass heaters, and battery storage— is crucial in determining the overall efficiency and reliability of your system.

- **Choosing the Best Location for Solar Panels**: Solar panels need direct sunlight for the majority of the day. Ideally, you'll install them facing south (in the northern hemisphere) and free from shading from trees or buildings. Roof-mounted systems work well in most cases, but ground-mounted arrays may allow you more flexibility in optimizing sun exposure.
- **Siting Wind Turbines**: Wind turbines need consistent wind speeds to function properly. They should be installed in open areas, away from obstructions like buildings and trees, and elevated for maximum exposure to the wind. Coastal or hilltop areas are ideal, but if your location doesn't have strong, steady wind, wind energy might play a less prominent role in your system.
- **Integrating Biomass Systems**: Biomass systems should be located close to your living space for easy access to the heat they generate. You'll also need a safe storage area for biomass materials like wood, straw, or agricultural waste. Make sure your biomass system is integrated with the rest of your energy sources to provide backup power and heat during energy shortfalls.
- **Planning for Expansion**: As your energy needs grow over time, you might need to expand your system. Leave room for additional solar panels, batteries, or even wind turbines as your household or community expands.

Integrating Battery Storage into Hybrid Systems

Battery storage is a critical component of any hybrid system. It bridges the gap between when energy is produced and when it's consumed, ensuring you have power even when your energy sources aren't actively generating electricity.

- **The Role of Batteries in Hybrid Systems**: Batteries enable you to store surplus energy produced by solar panels or wind turbines and use it when production is low. Without a battery storage setup, excess energy would be wasted, and you'd have to rely more on backup generators. Batteries help you manage your power output, reduce generator usage, and ensure a continuous power supply.
- Types of Batteries:
  1. **Lead-Acid Batteries:** These are the most cost-effective and commonly utilized in off-grid setups, though they are heavier and have a shorter lifespan compared to other options. They need frequent upkeep.
  2. **Lithium-Ion Batteries:** These are the best option for most off-grid systems. They're lightweight, last longer and need very little upkeep. While they have a higher upfront cost, their efficiency makes them ideal for hybrid setups.

  3. **Nickel-Iron (NiFe) Batteries:** These are extremely durable and can last for decades. However, they're expensive and less efficient compared to lithium-ion. If you're building a system with a focus on long-term reliability, NiFe batteries could be a good option.

Sizing the Battery Bank

Determining the right size for your battery bank depends on your energy consumption and how much energy you need stored for backup.

- **Calculating Storage Capacity**: To calculate how much battery storage you need, take your daily energy consumption and multiply it by the number of days you want the system to run without generating new power (for instance, during cloudy, windless days).
  - **Example**: If your household uses 10 kWh per day and you want three days of backup power, you'll need at least 30 kWh of battery storage.
- **Practical Sizing Examples**: A small hybrid system with 5 kWh daily consumption might need a 10-15 kWh battery bank for sufficient backup, while a larger system using 20 kWh daily might require 40-60 kWh of storage to ensure smooth operation.
- **Peak Needs and Backup**: You should also ensure your battery bank can handle peak loads—times when energy demand is higher than average. This includes running high-energy appliances or charging electric vehicles.

Connecting Batteries in Hybrid Systems

How you connect your batteries in a hybrid system affects both their performance and the system's overall efficiency.

- Series vs. Parallel Connections:
  - **Series connections** increase the voltage of your battery bank. This is useful when your system needs higher voltage to operate efficiently.
  - **Parallel connections** increase the storage capacity without increasing voltage. This is ideal when you need to store more energy for later use.

Most hybrid systems use a combination of both series and parallel connections to balance voltage and capacity.

- **Optimizing Battery Connections**: When connecting your batteries, ensure that they are configured to match the output from your solar panels, wind turbines, and other energy sources. This helps distribute energy evenly across your system.
- **Wiring Safety and Best Practices**: Proper wiring is crucial for ensuring your system functions safely and efficiently. Always use the correct gauge of wire for the current being carried. Overloading a circuit with undersized wires can lead to overheating and system failure. Installing fuses and circuit breakers will also protect your batteries from being damaged by power surges.
  - **Tip**: Label all connections clearly and ensure that your wiring meets local safety codes. This will not only protect your system but also simplify future maintenance.

Designing and integrating a hybrid energy system requires careful planning, but once done right, it provides you with a reliable, resilient, and sustainable off-grid power solution. By calculating your energy needs, siting your systems correctly, and integrating battery storage, you can ensure consistent power regardless of weather conditions. Battery storage is key to making your hybrid system work efficiently, and with proper sizing and connections, your system will offer long-term energy independence.

In the next section, we'll cover energy distribution, managing power loads, and scaling your hybrid system for future growth. Stay tuned for more in-depth insights on how to make your hybrid system even more efficient!

Energy Distribution in Hybrid Systems

In a hybrid off-grid energy system, distribution plays a key role in ensuring that energy generated from various sources—solar, wind, and biomass—is delivered efficiently to power your home. Proper energy distribution is not just about connecting your energy sources to your appliances, but it involves a careful balance of wiring, safety protocols, and effective energy management. This section will cover the specifics of wiring and cable selection for different energy sources, designing a seamless distribution network, and preventing energy loss and overload.

Distribution for Solar, Wind, and Biomass Energy

Each energy source in your hybrid system—solar panels, wind turbines, and biomass systems—has its own specific wiring needs to ensure safe and efficient distribution. Choosing the right type of wiring and cables is critical for transferring energy without loss or damage.

- **Solar Panel Distribution**: Solar panels produce direct current (DC), which needs to be wired into a charge controller and possibly an inverter before reaching your battery bank or home appliances. For solar systems, use high-quality, UV-resistant cables to withstand outdoor conditions. Copper wiring is preferred for its conductivity, but aluminum can be used if cost is an issue. Make sure you select cables with the appropriate gauge based on the system's voltage and current.
    - **Cable Thickness**: The longer the distance between your solar panels and the charge controller, the thicker the cable you'll need to avoid voltage drop. For instance, a 12V system running more than 30 feet may require 8 AWG or thicker cables.
    - **Safety Tip**: Install fuses or circuit breakers between the panels, charge controllers, and batteries to protect the system from short circuits.
- **Wind Turbine Distribution**: Wind turbines, like solar panels, produce DC that needs to be properly wired into your system. The wiring should be capable of handling fluctuating voltages, as wind turbines often produce varying levels of energy depending on wind speed. Use flexible, insulated cables for wiring wind turbines to accommodate movement and protect against wear and tear.
    - **Cable Considerations**: Given the height of wind turbines, the cables may need to run long distances from the tower to the charge controller. Thicker cables (e.g., 6 or 8 AWG) are often required to minimize energy loss over distance.
    - **Grounding**: Ensure that the wind turbine is properly grounded to avoid lightning strikes or electrical surges damaging your system.
- **Biomass Energy Distribution**: Biomass systems generate energy typically used for heat, but if you are converting biomass into electricity using a generator, it will likely produce alternating current (AC). Biomass generators can be directly wired to the electrical system or to battery storage for later use. Use standard AC wiring for distribution, ensuring proper insulation and grounding.
    - **Wiring Consideration**: Generators often have high output, so you'll need heavy-duty cables to handle the higher current load. Ensure that these cables are rated for both indoor and outdoor use if they will be exposed to the elements.

Selecting the Right Cables for Each Source

The choice of cables is essential in preventing energy loss and ensuring the longevity of your hybrid system. Different energy sources have different power outputs, and the cable type and thickness must match these requirements.

- **Length, Thickness, and Insulation:**
    - The longer the distance your energy must travel (e.g., from your solar panels to your battery bank), the thicker the cable should be to prevent voltage drops.

- Thicker cables are better for high-current loads, such as those from wind turbines or biomass generators. Insulated, weather-resistant cables are critical for outdoor use to prevent wear from UV rays, rain, or snow.
- **Safety Protocols:**
  - Always install fuses, circuit breakers, and grounding systems to protect against electrical surges.
  - Label all wires clearly to avoid confusion during maintenance or troubleshooting.
  - Avoid energy overloads by matching the wire gauge with the energy output—using an undersized cable can lead to overheating and potential fire hazards.

Designing an Efficient Distribution Network

A well-planned energy distribution network ensures that power flows efficiently from your energy sources to where it's needed in your home. Proper circuit design helps you avoid common pitfalls such as power drops, inefficiencies, or system overloads.

- **Key Considerations:**
  - **Load Distribution**: Plan your circuits based on load distribution. For instance, keep high-energy appliances (e.g., water heaters, refrigerators) on separate circuits from low-power devices (e.g., LED lights) to prevent overload.
  - **Centralized vs. Decentralized**: Decide whether you want a centralized system with a single distribution hub (e.g., inverter connected to all sources), or decentralized, where each energy source powers specific circuits.
  - **Future-Proofing**: Leave room for future expansion, such as adding more solar panels or a second wind turbine. This way, you won't need to overhaul your entire distribution network if your energy needs grow.
- **Circuit Design for Homes and Appliances:**
  - When wiring appliances, use dedicated circuits for high-load devices like ovens, washing machines, or heaters. These should be powered directly by the inverter or battery bank to avoid dips in performance when multiple devices run simultaneously.
  - For lighting and smaller electronics, a shared circuit with surge protection can manage power distribution without overloading the system.

Managing Power in Hybrid Systems

Managing the power flow in your hybrid system ensures that all components work efficiently together. Charge controllers, inverters, and careful monitoring tools are necessary to balance energy input from multiple sources and ensure you're not overloading or underutilizing your system.

Charge Controllers and Inverters

Charge controllers manage the flow of energy from solar panels or wind turbines to your battery system, protecting it from overcharging and maintaining battery health. In contrast, inverters transform the stored DC energy in your batteries into usable AC power for your household.

- **Selecting Charge Controllers:**
  - Use **PWM (Pulse Width Modulation)** controllers for smaller systems or if budget is a concern. They're affordable but slightly less efficient.

- o **MPPT (Maximum Power Point Tracking)** controllers are best for larger, more efficient hybrid systems. They maximize energy harvested from solar and wind, adapting to changing conditions (e.g., varying sunlight or wind speeds).
- **Inverters:**
  - o Choose an inverter that matches your household's energy demands. A pure sine wave inverter is preferred for sensitive electronics, whereas a modified sine wave inverter offers a more budget-friendly option for basic appliances.
  - o **Tip**: Always choose an inverter rated slightly higher than your peak energy usage to avoid overload.

Power Management Techniques

Managing the energy flow between your sources, storage, and usage points helps to avoid system overload and prolong the life of your components.

- **Energy Monitoring**: Install energy monitoring tools to track how much energy is being generated by each source (solar, wind, biomass) and how much is being used. This helps you identify periods of high demand and allows you to adjust accordingly.
  - o **Tip**: Use smart meters to automatically prioritize which energy source to draw from based on current availability (e.g., using solar during the day, wind at night).
- **Load Distribution**: Distribute power loads evenly across your energy sources to avoid straining any one part of the system. For example, assign lighting and low-power devices to solar panels, while high-demand appliances like refrigerators or water heaters can draw from wind or biomass.

Routine Maintenance and Troubleshooting

Maintaining your hybrid system ensures that all components continue to operate at peak performance. Regular cleaning, battery checks, and system diagnostics can prevent major breakdowns.

Routine Maintenance:

- **Solar Panels**: Clean regularly to remove dust and debris that can block sunlight. Check for any damage or cracks.
- **Wind Turbines**: Inspect moving parts for wear and tear. Lubricate bearings and check for any obstructions that could impact performance.
- **Biomass Systems**: Clean combustion chambers and check fuel storage areas to prevent fire hazards.

Battery Care:

Monitor charge cycles to avoid deep discharges. Regularly inspect connections for corrosion and keep terminals clean. For lead-acid batteries, inspect electrolyte levels and refill with distilled water as required to ensure proper function.

Common Troubleshooting:

- **Low Output**: Check for shading over solar panels or wind turbines not positioned correctly. Faulty wiring can also reduce efficiency.
- **Charge Controller Failures**: Make sure the controller is compatible with the battery bank and other components.
- **Generator Breakdowns**: Check fuel levels and perform regular engine maintenance.

Expanding and Scaling Up Hybrid Systems

Scaling up your hybrid energy system is essential as your energy needs grow or as your community expands. Whether you are upgrading from a basic system or planning for future demand, expanding a hybrid system requires careful planning and consideration to ensure seamless integration of new components, increased efficiency, and sustained reliability.

Upgrading from Basic to Advanced Systems

As your energy consumption increases, so will the need to enhance your hybrid setup. This could involve adding more solar panels, wind turbines, or even integrating an additional energy source like biomass or hydroelectric power. The goal is to maintain reliability and ensure that your system can handle fluctuating energy demands without failure.

- **Scaling Your Energy Sources:**
    - **Solar**: If your current setup is insufficient, consider adding more panels. A key tip is to increase solar panel coverage incrementally to avoid overloading the charge controller or inverter. Ensure that your battery storage is sufficient to store the extra power.
    - **Wind**: If wind energy is part of your system, installing additional turbines or upgrading to more efficient models can help increase energy production during low solar periods. Choose turbines that match the existing system to ensure easy integration.
    - **Biomass and Generators**: Upgrading to larger or more efficient biomass systems and generators provides excellent backup, especially during peak usage or emergencies. Larger generators can handle higher power loads but should be strategically used to avoid excessive fuel consumption.
- **Adding Batteries and Backup Generators:**
    - As·you expand your energy system, adding more battery storage becomes crucial. Larger battery banks ensure that the extra energy produced is stored effectively, offering more flexibility during cloudy days, low-wind periods, or power surges.
    - For generator backup, consider fuel-efficient models that can integrate smoothly with your existing hybrid setup. Diesel or propane generators can power critical appliances during outages or times of low renewable energy production, ensuring redundancy in your system.
- **Advanced System Integration:**
    - Ensure all new components are compatible with your current infrastructure. For example, when adding solar panels or wind turbines, verify that your inverter and charge controller can handle the extra load.
    - **Tip**: When scaling up, always consider upgrading your wiring and distribution network to handle the increased power output. Failure to do so can lead to inefficiencies, power loss, and potential system failures.

Community and Neighborhood Hybrid Systems

A well-planned hybrid system can expand beyond individual use to serve entire communities. Scaling up a hybrid system to a community level requires additional planning, resources, and management, but the benefits are significant—shared resources, increased energy production, and collective resilience.

- **Shared Energy Sources:**
    - **Solar and Wind**: Larger, shared solar farms or wind fields can power entire neighborhoods, offering economies of scale that reduce costs for everyone involved. This involves setting up multiple energy sources strategically placed to maximize output and balance energy needs.
    - **Biomass Systems**: Larger-scale biomass systems, such as shared community stoves or bio-digesters, can be utilized to run heating systems or even produce electricity for communal use. This is especially useful in rural or agricultural communities where biomass materials are abundant.

- **Collective Energy Storage:**
  - Community energy systems need large-scale battery banks capable of storing energy for shared use. This often requires more advanced energy storage options, like lithium-ion batteries, due to their higher capacity and longevity.
  - **Backup Generators for the Community**: Centralized backup generators ensure that power is available for critical systems like healthcare centers, refrigeration, or water pumps during outages. Larger generators must be maintained collectively to avoid fuel shortages and operational issues.
- **Management and Distribution:**
  - Community hybrid systems require centralized management to ensure energy is distributed fairly and efficiently. Smart grids and energy-sharing platforms can monitor and regulate how energy is used, preventing overconsumption by a few users while maintaining access for everyone.
  - **Grid Design**: When scaling up to community-sized systems, the design of the distribution grid becomes even more important. Well-planned circuits and redundant pathways can prevent single points of failure and ensure reliable power delivery across the entire community.

Redundancy and Backup Systems

In any hybrid energy system, redundancy is critical for ensuring uninterrupted power supply. A redundant system is one that has multiple backups, ensuring that even if one component fails, the others can pick up the slack. This is especially important for off-grid living, where access to quick repairs or new components may be limited.

- **Battery Storage Redundancy:**
  - One of the most effective ways to build redundancy into your hybrid system is by increasing your battery capacity. Having more battery banks on standby means that in case of a power surge or system overload, your backup battery will kick in seamlessly.
  - **Tip**: Always maintain backup batteries at a partial charge to prevent degradation and keep them ready for emergency use.
- **Backup Generators:**
  - No hybrid system is complete without a reliable backup generator. For smaller systems, a manual crank generator or a small propane unit may be enough, but for larger systems, especially at the community level, a more robust solution like a diesel generator is essential.
  - **Fuel Storage**: Plan for long-term fuel storage to avoid running out during extended periods of bad weather or system failure. Store your fuel in a dry, cool location and rotate it regularly to prevent it from becoming stale or unusable.
- **Monitoring Backup Systems:**
  - Regularly test your backup systems to ensure they're functioning properly. This includes running the generators periodically, checking battery charge levels, and ensuring the fuel is fresh. Implement a maintenance schedule to prevent any issues before they arise.

Best Practices for Storing Emergency Fuel and Monitoring Backup Systems

Maintaining a consistent fuel supply for your backup generators is essential for long-term off-grid living. In addition to storing enough fuel, you must also have proper systems in place to monitor its usage and ensure that your backup systems are operational when needed.

- **Emergency Fuel Storage:**
  - Store emergency fuel (diesel, propane, or gasoline) in proper containers in well-ventilated, dry areas. Ensure these containers are up to code and not exposed to direct exposure to sunlight or extreme temperature variations, as this can degrade the fuel.

- Rotate stored fuel regularly—use a first-in, first-out system to ensure that the oldest fuel is used first, preventing waste or spoilage. You can also add fuel stabilizers to extend the shelf life of your stored fuel.

- **Fuel Efficiency and Management:**
  - Practice fuel efficiency by limiting generator use to only the most essential appliances or systems during power outages. Reducing unnecessary consumption will aid in conserving fuel and prolonging the lifespan of your generator.

- **Backup System Monitoring:**
  - Use monitoring devices to track the status of your backup batteries and fuel levels. Smart meters can help you see in real-time how much fuel remains and whether your backup systems are performing optimally.
  - Regular inspections of your backup systems—batteries, inverters, and generators—are critical to ensure everything runs smoothly when you need it most.

Building Resilience in Hybrid Systems

By planning for growth and redundancy in your hybrid system, you can create a resilient, sustainable energy solution that serves you for years to come. Whether expanding to meet the demands of a growing household or scaling to power an entire off-grid community, carefully designed hybrid systems can provide consistent, reliable energy, even in the face of uncertainty.

Having backup generators, robust battery banks, and a well-planned fuel storage system ensures that you're prepared for the unexpected. As your needs evolve, so too can your energy system—continuing to support your off-grid lifestyle and providing the power security necessary to thrive.

By carefully managing power distribution, balancing energy loads, and maintaining your hybrid system, you'll benefit from a dependable and eco-friendly off-grid energy solution. Hybrid systems, when properly designed and maintained, offer resilience and flexibility, ensuring that your home remains powered no matter what nature throws your way.

Conclusion: Sustainable Energy Independence

Achieving true energy independence is not just about producing power but building a resilient system that evolves with your needs. A hybrid energy system offers you the flexibility and security to live off-grid sustainably, using the combined strengths of solar, wind, biomass, and battery storage. It empowers you to harness nature's renewable resources, minimizing your reliance on external factors and fossil fuels. The long-term benefits of hybrid systems go beyond just power generation—they provide peace of mind, cost savings, and environmental protection.

Long-Term Benefits of Hybrid Energy Systems

Hybrid systems are designed for longevity and adaptability, which makes them the cornerstone of a successful off-grid lifestyle. Over time, they allow you to tailor your power needs to match your lifestyle, scaling as necessary and integrating new technologies.

- **Resilience and Independence**: A well-designed hybrid system ensures you are prepared for any energy challenge—whether it's a cloudy week, low wind, or limited biomass. With a balance of energy sources and reliable battery storage, you can create a system that offers uninterrupted power. This resilience ensures that even in times of natural disasters or power grid failures, you remain energy-independent.
- **Economic Benefits**: While the initial investment in a hybrid system might be higher, the long-term savings are substantial. By reducing or eliminating dependence on fuel-powered generators or public utilities, you save

money year after year. Moreover, maintenance costs for hybrid systems tend to be lower, especially when using renewable sources that are naturally replenishing.

- **Environmental Impact**: The environmental benefits are profound. By using renewable energy sources like the sun, wind, and biomass, you significantly reduce your carbon footprint. Hybrid systems allow you to make the most of these clean energy sources, helping to advance the worldwide fight against climate change while ensuring that you leave behind a smaller environmental footprint.

Final Thoughts on Hybrid Energy Systems

As you continue to refine and upgrade your hybrid system, always consider your future needs. Energy consumption may increase with additional technologies or changes in lifestyle, and your system should be able to adapt to these demands. Scaling your hybrid energy system requires thoughtful planning but ensures that you'll always have access to a stable and sustainable power supply.

- **Maintenance and Upgrades**: Consistent upkeep is crucial for extending the lifespan of your system. Routine checks on your solar panels, wind turbines, biomass systems, and batteries will ensure that everything is running efficiently. Always keep an eye on new technological advancements in the energy sector. Upgrading to more efficient solar panels, batteries with longer lifespans, or wind turbines that generate more power could significantly enhance the performance of your system.
- **Community Involvement**: If you're part of a larger community or plan to expand your system for neighborhood use, hybrid systems offer scalability. A shared hybrid energy system can power multiple homes, reducing the individual cost burden while ensuring collective energy independence.

Encouragement for the Future

Your journey toward complete energy independence is ongoing, but with a hybrid system in place, you're building a resilient future. Each adjustment, upgrade, and enhancement you make to your system brings you closer to total sustainability. You now have the tools to fine-tune your energy setup and ensure that it remains reliable, efficient, and eco-friendly. With regular improvements, your hybrid system will continue to serve you well for decades.

Your choice to invest in renewable, sustainable energy not only enhances your lifestyle but also plays a vital role in fostering a greener, more sustainable world.

This guide has walked you through every step of building, maintaining, and expanding a hybrid energy system. Whether you're powering a small cabin or an entire community, the principles you've learned here can help you adapt and thrive off-grid. As you refine your system, continue to innovate, seek out new energy solutions, and stay committed to living sustainably. Your hybrid system is a living entity that will grow with you, providing energy independence and peace of mind for the long term.

11. Off-Grid Heating Solutions

The Critical Role of Heating in Off-Grid Living

In off-grid living, heating is not just about comfort—it's about survival. When you're disconnected from modern infrastructure, staying warm becomes a fundamental necessity. Without the conveniences of central heating or electricity, the ability to generate and manage heat efficiently can be the difference between enduring the harsh elements or thriving in them.

Mastering off-grid heating techniques ensures not only your comfort but also your safety. Whether you're battling freezing temperatures, or maintaining protection from the elements, heat is at the core of sustainable living. In this guide, we'll explore essential heating methods that range from traditional fire to modern, eco-friendly solutions like solar and biomass. These techniques are designed to maximize efficiency, conserve resources, and ensure that you remain self-reliant, no matter where you are.

Fire as the Foundation of Off-Grid Heating

The Importance of Fire in Off-Grid Living

Fire has been humankind's primary heating source for thousands of years, and in off-grid living, it remains indispensable. Beyond providing warmth, fire offers psychological comfort and a sense of control in remote environments.

Fire for Warmth and Safety

- **Surviving Cold Temperatures**: Fire is a lifesaver in cold climates. Without a reliable heat source, even mild exposure to cold can lead to hypothermia, a potentially fatal condition. Knowing how to start and maintain a fire is critical for ensuring that your shelter remains warm and safe.
- **Deterring Wildlife**: In wilderness environments, fire acts as a natural deterrent for animals. The light and heat repel most predators, providing peace of mind as you sleep through the night.

Practical Tip: Always gather enough firewood before nightfall to maintain heat throughout the night. Proper planning is essential to ensure continuous warmth.

Fire-Starting Techniques

Starting a fire is an indispensable survival skill, and whether you rely on modern tools or primitive methods, knowing multiple ways to spark a flame ensures you're never without heat.

Modern Methods

- **Lighters and Matches**: These tools are dependable and user-friendly, making them a must-have in any survival kit. However, they must be kept dry, so always store them in waterproof containers.

Pro Tip: Always carry more than one lighter or matchbox in separate waterproof containers. Redundancy ensures you're never left without an easy way to start a fire.

- **Ferro Rods**: A ferrocerium rod, or ferro rod, is a highly effective fire-starting tool, especially in wet or windy conditions. The sparks it produces burn at extremely high temperatures, making it possible to ignite tinder even in difficult weather.

Pro Tip: Pair your ferro rod with high-quality tinder, such as cotton balls soaked in petroleum jelly, to ensure quick and efficient fire-starting.

Primitive Methods
- **Friction Fire (Bow Drill, Hand Drill)**: Primitive fire-starting methods, while requiring more effort and practice, are essential skills for off-grid living. The bow drill is the most efficient of the friction methods, using a bow to rapidly spin a spindle, creating heat and eventually an ember.

Step-by-Step Guide to Bow Drill:
1. Construct a bow from a flexible branch and strong cord.
2. Find a dry spindle and a hearth board.
3. Wrap the string around the spindle and place it into a notch on the hearth board.
4. Use the bow to spin the spindle back and forth rapidly to generate friction.
5. Once an ember forms, transfer it to a tinder bundle and gently blow to ignite a flame.

Pro Tip: Practice this method regularly, as it requires patience and skill. Always carry prepared tinder for quicker results when using friction fire techniques.

- **Flint and Steel**: Striking a piece of steel against flint is an ancient method for starting fires. It's a simple, reliable technique that has stood the test of time.

Pro Tip: Always have flint and steel in your fire kit, along with fine tinder like char cloth, to catch the sparks and ignite your fire quickly.

Efficient Use of Fire for Heating

Once your fire is going, managing it effectively ensures long-lasting warmth while conserving resources. Here's how to make the most of your fire in off-grid living.

Fire Management in Cold Climates
- **Use Seasoned Wood**: Properly dried, seasoned wood burns hotter and generates less smoke, while green or wet wood is inefficient and leads to excessive smoke, wasting valuable fuel.
- **Build Efficient Fires**: Stack wood in a way that maximizes airflow to keep the fire burning efficiently. Use a combination of kindling and larger logs to build a fire that provides immediate heat and sustains warmth over time.

Pro Tip: Keep your fire small and controlled—oversized fires waste fuel and generate more heat than necessary.

- **Indoor Fireplaces**: For indoor heating, wood stoves and fireplaces are excellent options, but safety is paramount. Ensure proper ventilation to avoid the buildup of carbon monoxide, and regularly clean your chimney to prevent creosote accumulation.

Pro Tip: Install carbon monoxide detectors in your home to monitor air quality. Safety should never be compromised when using fire indoors.

By mastering fire-starting and fire management, you'll have a dependable source of heat that can sustain you through any off-grid challenge. Whether using modern tools or relying on ancient techniques, being skilled in the art of fire ensures you're prepared to heat your home and protect yourself—all while remaining self-reliant in the most remote environments.

Wood Stoves: The Heart of Off-Grid Heating

When it comes to reliable, long-term heating solutions in off-grid living, wood stoves are the undisputed champions. Wood stoves stand as a cornerstone of off-grid heating because they offer consistency, independence from electricity, and fuel efficiency.

Why Wood Stoves Are the Most Practical Long-Term Heating Solution

For those living off-grid, wood stoves are indispensable. They are highly efficient, durable, and versatile, making them the most practical heating solution for long-term use. Unlike other heating methods that rely on external energy sources or fuel supplies, wood stoves thrive on renewable resources—wood, which is often readily available in forested or rural areas. This independence from the grid is crucial for maintaining a self-sufficient lifestyle.

Wood stoves are also ideal for regions where winter temperatures plummet. They provide consistent, long-lasting heat, allowing you to maintain warmth in your living space while consuming minimal wood. Their longevity, paired with simple maintenance, ensures that once installed, a wood stove can serve you for decades with proper care.

Overview of Wood Stove Types and Their Uses in Off-Grid Heating

There are several types of wood stoves, each suited to different off-grid living needs:

- **Traditional Wood Stoves**: Classic, highly durable stoves that offer reliable heat output for large spaces.
- **Pellet Stoves**: Efficient and clean-burning, these stoves use compressed wood pellets for fuel, though they require a small amount of electricity.
- **Masonry Stoves**: These stoves store heat in their thermal mass and slowly release it, providing warmth long after the fire has gone out.

Choosing the right stove depends on your heating needs, the size of your space, and how much fuel you can sustainably gather.

Installing and Using a Wood Stove

A properly installed wood stove is both a reliable heating source and a centerpiece of your off-grid home. To ensure maximum efficiency and safety, the installation process must be precise and thoughtful.

1. **Positioning**: Place the stove in a central area to maximize heat distribution throughout the space. Make sure the surrounding area is free from flammable materials.
2. **Ventilation**: Proper ventilation is critical. Install a high-quality chimney or flue to direct smoke and gases outside. This reduces the risk of carbon monoxide buildup and ensures efficient airflow.
3. **Fire Safety Precautions**: Always install the stove on a heat-resistant surface, such as stone or tile. Keep a fire extinguisher nearby, and make sure you have working carbon monoxide detectors.

Efficient Wood Stove Operation

The key to efficient operation is controlling the airflow. Too much air makes the fire burn too hot, consuming wood quickly, while too little air can suffocate the fire or produce dangerous creosote buildup.

- **Airflow Control**: Adjust the stove's dampers to regulate the oxygen supply and maintain steady heat. Start the fire with the damper fully open to allow for a strong burn, then adjust as needed.

- **Steady Heat**: Once your fire is established, maintain a moderate flame by adding small amounts of seasoned wood regularly. This prevents temperature fluctuations and conserves fuel.

Pro Tip: Always stockpile enough seasoned wood before winter arrives. Seasoned wood burns cleaner and hotter, reducing creosote buildup in the chimney.

Wood Stove Maintenance

A well-maintained wood stove will provide decades of reliable service. Routine care ensures the stove operates efficiently and safely.

- **Chimney Cleaning**: Over time, creosote and soot build up in the chimney, increasing the risk of chimney fires. Clean your chimney at least once per season, or more frequently if you use the stove daily.
- **Stove Care**: Regularly inspect the stove's components, such as the door seals, to make sure they are fully airtight. Replace any worn parts immediately to maintain efficiency.
- **Common Issues**: If you notice excessive smoke, poor heat output, or difficulty starting the fire, these are signs of a problem. Often, these issues are related to airflow blockages or creosote buildup.

Pro Tip: Always keep a carbon monoxide detector and fire extinguisher nearby for added safety. Prevention is the best way to ensure a long-lasting and efficient wood stove setup.

Rocket Stoves: High-Efficiency Heating and Cooking

Rocket stoves excel in efficiency due to their unique design, which maximizes airflow to produce higher temperatures with less wood. The stove burns hot and fast, creating a highly concentrated heat source that requires less fuel compared to traditional fires. For off-grid living, where fuel sources might be limited, this efficiency is a major advantage.

Building a Rocket Stove

Building your own rocket stove is straightforward and requires only basic materials that you likely have on hand. Here's a simple guide:

Materials:

- 16 bricks (or empty metal cans if you're improvising)
- A handful of dry sticks or twigs

Steps:

1. **Build the Structure:** Stack the bricks in an **L-shape** to form the stove. This creates a vertical chamber for heat and a horizontal feed for the fuel. The "L" allows you to feed small sticks through the bottom while the vertical section concentrates the heat.
   - If using metal cans, arrange them in the same shape, leaving an opening at the bottom for air and fuel to flow through.
2. **Feed the Fuel:** Start by feeding small, dry twigs into the horizontal chamber. Light the twigs from the bottom, allowing air to flow upward through the vertical stack, which intensifies the heat.

Practical Tip: Always use smaller sticks to fuel your rocket stove. This ensures quicker heat and reduces the need to constantly manage the fire. Avoid overloading the stove with large logs, which can choke the airflow and reduce efficiency.

Once your rocket stove is set up, managing the fire becomes easy. The stove requires very little wood to maintain a strong flame, making it ideal for heating small spaces or cooking food quickly.

Because the rocket stove burns at a high temperature, you can adjust the heat output by controlling how much wood you feed into the stove. Small twigs and branches are sufficient to maintain a steady fire.

Pro Tip: The rocket stove is perfect for situations where you need to conserve wood but still require powerful heat. Its compact size also makes it portable and easy to use in different locations.

Solar Heating: Harnessing the Sun's Energy

For those looking to reduce their reliance on wood and fuel, solar heating offers a sustainable, renewable solution. Solar heating systems use the sun's energy to warm spaces without the need for conventional fuels.

Why Solar Heating Works in Off-Grid Living

Solar heating is particularly valuable in off-grid living because it harnesses a completely renewable resource: sunlight. By incorporating solar heating solutions, you can reduce your dependency on wood and other fuel sources, making your off-grid setup more sustainable and cost-effective in the long term.

Building a Simple Solar Heater

You can create a basic solar heater using readily available materials like glass, aluminium, and insulation. Here's a quick guide:

1. **Materials**: Gather reflective materials like aluminium foil and glass to capture and focus sunlight.
2. **Structure**: Build a flat box with an angled surface to catch sunlight, lining the interior with reflective materials to amplify the heat.
3. **Positioning**: Place the heater in a sunny spot and adjust the angle to capture the most sunlight throughout the day.

Pro Tip: Solar heaters work best when positioned to face the sun for the longest period during the day. In colder months, ensure the heater captures sunlight from a low angle.

By mastering these techniques—wood stoves, rocket stoves, and solar heating—you'll be equipped with versatile, sustainable heating solutions that cater to the diverse needs of off-grid living. Each method has its unique advantages, and incorporating all three ensures you're prepared for any situation, whether it's a cold winter night or a sunny day where fuel conservation is key.

Biomass Heating: Utilizing Natural Waste for Heat

As we transition from the abundant solar and wind energy solutions discussed in previous sections, biomass heating stands as an invaluable alternative for off-grid living. While solar and wind systems are effective for generating electricity, biomass heating leverages natural waste materials to provide consistent warmth, even in the coldest climates. Whether you're in a heavily wooded area or relying on agricultural waste, biomass heating is a sustainable and efficient method to maintain comfort without relying on external fuel supplies.

Understanding Biomass Heating

Biomass heating taps into the energy stored in organic materials like wood scraps, leaves, and agricultural byproducts. These materials are readily available and can be sustainably harvested, making biomass a reliable off-grid fuel source.

Why Biomass Is Valuable:

- **Renewable and Sustainable**: Biomass is a renewable energy source that can be continuously replenished with proper management. Deadwood, fallen leaves, and agricultural waste provide an endless supply of fuel that can be sourced locally.
- **Low-Cost Fuel**: By using materials that would otherwise be discarded, biomass heating keeps costs low while reducing environmental impact.
- **Reliable Heat Source**: Biomass provides steady, long-lasting heat, ideal for maintaining comfortable temperatures in off-grid homes, particularly during cold weather when solar power may be limited.

Examples of Biomass Materials:

- Wood scraps and dead branches from trees
- Fallen leaves, straw, and grass
- Agricultural waste like cornhusks and plant stalks

Creating and Using a Biomass Heater

Building a simple biomass heater allows you to utilize these materials efficiently and provide heat without excessive smoke or waste. Below is a step-by-step guide to constructing your own biomass heater:

1. **Materials**: You'll need heat-resistant materials such as bricks or metal tubing to create the heating chamber. A vertical chamber is ideal for efficient airflow and concentrated combustion.
2. **Structure**: Assemble a cylindrical or box-like structure where biomass materials can be fed through a lower opening, and air is drawn in to fuel combustion.
3. **Combustion Chamber**: The key to an efficient biomass heater is a well-designed combustion chamber that maximizes airflow while concentrating heat. Add a chimney or exhaust system to vent smoke and prevent buildup inside the space.
4. **Ignition**: Load the heater with dry biomass, such as wood scraps or dried leaves, and light from the base. The airflow should ensure a steady burn.

Pro Tip: Always keep your biomass dry before use. Wet biomass can cause incomplete combustion, producing smoke and reducing the efficiency of the heater. Store materials in a sheltered area to maintain optimal fuel conditions.

Efficiently Burning Biomass for Cold Weather Heating

Once your biomass heater is built, maximizing its efficiency is crucial for staying warm with minimal fuel. Here are a few tips for optimal biomass burning:

- **Fuel Selection**: Use dry, lightweight materials like dead branches and dried grass. Larger logs can be added once the fire is well-established to sustain heat for longer periods.
- **Airflow Control**: Ensure proper ventilation for the fire to burn at high temperatures. Adjust the intake of air as needed to control the intensity of the heat.

Pro Tip: Regularly clean the combustion chamber and remove ash to maintain good airflow and prevent blockages that can hinder performance.

Sustainability and Biomass Heating

Biomass heating offers long-term sustainability if managed properly. By integrating a sustainable biomass supply into your off-grid lifestyle, you ensure a consistent fuel source that doesn't deplete local resources.

- **Harvesting Practices**: Only collect deadwood or waste materials to preserve forests and agricultural areas. Avoid cutting down living trees or plants, which can disrupt the local ecosystem.

- **Regeneration**: Replace the biomass materials you use by planting new trees or allowing the natural regeneration of local flora. This practice ensures a continuous supply of biomass without causing environmental damage.

Pro Tip: Establish a biomass stockpile before winter to ensure you have enough fuel stored for the colder months when foraging becomes difficult.

Managing Fire and Heat Indoors and Outdoors

Fire management, both indoors and outdoors, is essential for maintaining efficient and safe heating in an off-grid environment. Whether you're using a biomass heater, wood stove, or open fire pit, controlling airflow, heat output, and safety measures is critical for success.

Indoor Fire Management

Heating indoor spaces with biomass or wood requires careful attention to safety and ventilation. Here's how to safely and efficiently manage indoor fires:

- **Airflow and Burn Rate**: Controlling the airflow in your wood stove or biomass heater is essential for consistent heat. Adjust the intake vents to regulate oxygen supply and control how quickly the fuel burns.
- **Ventilation**: Proper ventilation is crucial for preventing carbon monoxide buildup indoors. Always ensure your stove or heater is vented with a chimney or flue to direct smoke outside.
- **Heat Retention**: Use insulated materials like thermal curtains or blankets to trap heat inside your living space, reducing the need for constant fuel replenishment.

Pro Tip: To prevent carbon monoxide poisoning, make sure to install carbon monoxide detectors and regularly check that your ventilation systems are clear and functioning properly.

Backup Heating Solutions: Propane, Kerosene, and Emergency Systems

Having a backup heating plan is crucial for ensuring warmth and safety in an off-grid environment, particularly when biomass or wood supplies run low. Here are alternative fuel options to keep in mind:

Alternative Fuels for Off-Grid Heating

- **Propane**: Propane heaters are a reliable option for emergency heat when traditional fuel sources are unavailable. These heaters are portable, easy to use, and provide immediate warmth. However, propane must be stored safely in tanks and requires proper ventilation.
- **Kerosene**: Kerosene heaters offer a powerful, portable heating option, ideal for off-grid homes. Kerosene burns hot and can heat large spaces quickly, but like propane, it requires careful storage and ventilation to avoid indoor air quality issues.

Pro Tip: Always use carbon monoxide detectors when operating propane or kerosene heaters indoors. Ventilate the space well to prevent the buildup of toxic gases.

Creating a Redundant Heating System

Building a redundant heating system ensures that if one fuel source fails, you have other options to fall back on. A combination of biomass, propane, and solar heating allows for flexibility in unpredictable weather conditions or during fuel shortages.

- **Fuel Storage**: Keep a reserve of alternative fuels, such as propane tanks or kerosene, as part of your emergency preparedness plan.

- **Multiple Heat Sources**: Incorporate various heating solutions, such as solar heaters or rocket stoves, to diversify your energy sources.

Pro Tip: Regularly check your fuel reserves and ensure your backup systems are in working order before winter hits, giving you peace of mind during colder months.

Energy-Efficient Heating: Maximizing Heat Retention

As you transition from harnessing solar and wind power to creating a truly energy-efficient off-grid home, the next essential step is heat retention. While generating heat is crucial, ensuring that you keep as much of it inside your shelter is equally important. Proper insulation and heat retention strategies can drastically reduce your fuel consumption, allowing you to stay warm with minimal resources. By optimizing how your home retains heat, you can stretch your fuel supplies—whether wood, biomass, or solar—through the coldest months.

Insulating Your Off-Grid Shelter

Insulating your shelter is the foundation of energy-efficient heating. Without proper insulation, even the most powerful heating systems will struggle to maintain comfortable temperatures. Insulation is about trapping the heat you generate, preventing it from escaping, and keeping cold air from entering. Here's how to do it effectively:

1. **Wall and Roof Insulation**: Use materials like straw bales, wool blankets, or foam panels to insulate the walls and roof of your shelter. These materials are effective at trapping heat while also being sustainable and easy to source.
2. **Floor Insulation**: Don't overlook the floor! Cold air can seep through the ground, making your living space chilly. Lay down thick rugs, wool mats, or even insulated flooring to create a barrier between your feet and the cold ground.
3. **Windows and Doors**: The biggest heat loss often occurs through windows and doors. Seal gaps around frames with weatherstripping or caulking. Use heavy curtains or thermal blinds to add an extra layer of insulation during the night.

Pro Tip: Straw bales make excellent, eco-friendly insulation. They are easy to build with, provide excellent thermal resistance, and can be sourced sustainably. For smaller windows or gaps, thermal curtains and blankets work wonders to keep heat in.

Heat Retention Techniques

Designing your shelter for maximum heat efficiency goes beyond insulation. By using passive heating strategies, you can make the most of natural resources like sunlight and the heat generated by daily activities. Here's how:

1. **Maximizing Sunlight**: Position your shelter with southern-facing windows (in the Northern Hemisphere) to capture as much sunlight as possible. Sunlight can naturally warm your living space during the day, reducing the need for active heating systems.
2. **Thermal Mass**: Incorporate materials like brick, stone, or concrete inside your shelter. These materials absorb heat during the day and slowly release it at night, helping to regulate indoor temperatures.
3. **Windbreaks**: Build windbreaks around your shelter using natural barriers like trees or man-made walls. This prevents cold winds from blowing against your home, reducing heat loss and making your living environment more comfortable.

Pro Tip: Use a combination of thermal curtains during the night and sunlight during the day to keep your shelter warm naturally. Heavy curtains at night will trap heat inside, while opening them in the morning will allow sunlight to warm the space.

Draft-Proofing Your Home

Even the best insulation won't help if cold drafts are entering your home. Sealing your home against drafts is one of the easiest and most efficient methods to retain heat.

1. **Sealing Windows and Doors**: Use weatherstripping or caulking to seal any gaps around your windows and doors. These tiny gaps can allow warm air to escape and cold air to creep in, significantly reducing your home's heat efficiency.
2. **Chimney and Vent Sealing**: When not in use, make sure your chimney and vents are closed tightly. Drafts can often enter through these areas, so it's essential to seal them when they're not actively venting.
3. **Rugs and Draft Stoppers**: Place rugs along doorways and draft stoppers at the base of exterior doors to block cold air from seeping inside.

Pro Tip: Draft-proof your home by checking for gaps where cold air could enter. Even small leaks around doors and windows can cause significant heat loss, making your heating efforts less efficient. Use a candle or incense stick to detect airflow near windows and doors.

Maintaining and Protecting Your Heating Tools

Your heating tools—whether they're wood stoves, fire pits, or solar heaters—are critical to keeping your home warm. Proper maintenance ensures these tools function efficiently for years, minimizing breakdowns and maximizing their performance. Let's break down how to care for each heating method:

Caring for Wood Stoves, Fire Pits, and Solar Heaters

1. **Wood Stove Maintenance:**
   o Regularly clean the chimney to prevent dangerous creosote buildup, which can lead to chimney fires.
   o Clean the firebox of ashes regularly to maintain good airflow and efficient burning.
   o Inspect the stove pipes for any blockages or damage and replace worn gaskets to ensure a tight seal.
2. **Fire Pit Maintenance:**
   o After each use, clear out the ashes and unburned wood to allow for better airflow during the next fire.
   o Ensure the surrounding area is clear of debris or vegetation to prevent accidental fire spread.
3. **Solar Heater Maintenance:**
   o Clean the glass or reflective surfaces regularly to ensure maximum sunlight absorption.
   o Inspect the heater for any cracks or damage that might affect performance.
   o Check the insulation of your solar air heater to ensure it's functioning effectively.

Pro Tip: To avoid the buildup of creosote in your wood stove, always burn seasoned wood. Seasoned wood burns more efficiently and produces less creosote than green wood, which can be dangerous.

Protecting Your Fire-Making Tools

Your fire-making tools are indispensable when living off-grid, so it's essential to protect them from the elements and ensure they're always ready for use.

1. **Keep Tools Dry**: Store lighters, matches, and ferro rods in waterproof containers. Wet fire-starting tools are unreliable, and in cold or wet environments, failure is not an option.
2. **Sharpen and Maintain Tools**: Keep your ferro rod and flint properly sharpened to ensure they produce strong sparks. Clean your tools after each use to prevent corrosion and rust.
3. **Carry a Fire Kit**: Always have a backup fire kit that includes matches, lighters, dry tinder, and a ferro rod. Having a reliable way to start a fire is essential, especially in emergencies.

Pro Tip: Attach a small piece of petroleum jelly-soaked cotton to your fire kit. This makes an excellent emergency tinder, igniting easily even in damp conditions.

By insulating your shelter, maximizing heat retention, and maintaining your heating tools, you can ensure efficient energy use in an off-grid lifestyle. Protecting the heat you generate—whether through a wood stove, biomass, or solar heater—minimizes resource consumption and maximizes comfort. Keeping your fire-making tools in peak condition guarantees you're never without the warmth and safety they provide, allowing you to stay prepared no matter the conditions.

Mastering Off-Grid Heating for Sustainable Living

In your journey to live off the grid, mastering efficient heating methods is crucial to ensure your comfort, safety, and overall survival. Throughout this guide, you've explored a wide range of heating solutions that can sustain you in even the harshest environments, from traditional fire-starting methods to modern, energy-efficient systems like solar and biomass. Each method brings unique advantages, and understanding how to use them effectively will allow you to create a sustainable, comfortable, and resilient off-grid lifestyle.

Recap of the Various Heating Solutions

You've learned how to make the most of fundamental heating methods like **fire**, understanding its importance not only for warmth but also for safety and cooking. With **wood stoves**, you've seen how an efficient, long-term heating system can be maintained and optimized for years of reliable use. **Rocket stoves** showed how you can minimize fuel use while maximizing heat output, offering an ideal solution for both heating and cooking. Moving to renewable energy, **solar heating** highlighted the advantages of harnessing the sun's energy to reduce reliance on traditional fuels, while **biomass** systems demonstrated how you can convert waste materials into a valuable heating resource.

Backup heating methods, such as **propane and kerosene**, provided additional security for those times when wood or solar is insufficient. Finally, energy-efficient strategies focused on maximizing heat retention through proper insulation and passive heating techniques, ensuring that you can retain warmth even when the temperature outside drops.

Practice and Mastery

As with any off-grid skill, consistent practice and mastery of these techniques will make you more self-reliant and confident in your ability to thrive. Fire-starting, for instance, is a vital skill that should be regularly honed in different conditions. Understanding the intricacies of maintaining a wood stove or managing the airflow of a rocket stove is essential for optimizing fuel consumption and staying warm efficiently.

By practicing these heating methods in real-world scenarios, you ensure that when an emergency arises or extreme weather strikes, you're prepared. Redundancy in your systems—such as having multiple fire-starting tools, spare propane, or additional wood supplies—will guarantee that you're never caught unprepared.

Final Thoughts on Preparedness and Self-Reliance

Living off the grid requires not only technical knowledge but also the mindset of preparedness and self-reliance. Heating your shelter efficiently, whether through traditional methods or modern solutions, is a core part of this philosophy. The ability to generate, manage, and retain heat is essential to your off-grid survival and well-being.

Through careful planning and consistent effort, you can master the heating techniques discussed in this guide. Whether it's building a wood stove, insulating your shelter, or setting up a solar heating system, the knowledge you've gained will empower you to create a sustainable and comfortable off-grid environment. You are now equipped with the tools, tips, and expert advice necessary to thrive in any situation, no matter how challenging.

With determination, practice, and the right preparation, you're ready to face the demands of off-grid living and maintain a warm, safe, and sustainable lifestyle for the long term. Keep building, keep learning, and keep perfecting your systems—your future off the grid depends on it.

12. Off-Grid Cooking Systems

This guide will walk you through essential systems to cook in the most practical, efficient, and enjoyable way possible, no matter the situation. Building on the knowledge from the previous book on heating, where we explored how to generate and manage heat off the grid, we now shift focus to harnessing that heat for cooking. With no access to electricity or gas, you'll rely on natural heat sources like fire, sun, and alternative fuel methods to cook your meals.

You'll use cookware durable enough to withstand direct flame, and you'll learn to control heat manually, rather than simply turning a dial. Understanding the basics of off-grid cooking is essential, and once mastered, you'll have the confidence to prepare satisfying meals no matter where you are.

Cooking off-grid requires a shift in mindset. Without the conveniences of modern kitchens, you'll discover a world of creativity and resourcefulness. The simplicity and connection to nature that off-grid cooking offers is one of its most rewarding aspects. Before diving into any cooking project, it's important to have the right tools, ingredients, and techniques to ensure your meals are not only successful but also nourishing and sustainable. Let's break down the essentials so you're well-prepared to start cooking without electricity.

What You Need to Start

1. Basic Cookware

The backbone of off-grid cooking is durable cookware that can withstand high, direct heat. **Cast iron** is your best friend here—whether you're cooking over a campfire, rocket stove, or in an oven, cast iron distributes heat evenly and holds up against flames and coals. Invest in a good-quality **cast iron skillet, Dutch oven, and a few sturdy pots and pans**. These will become your go-to for everything from stews and breads to searing and frying.

2. Fuel Sources

Without electricity or gas, your cooking heat will come from **natural fuels** like wood, biomass, or even the sun. The most accessible and reliable fuel source for most off-grid situations is **dry wood**. Focus on gathering small twigs, branches, and dried leaves, which ignite quickly and burn efficiently. It's always a good idea to keep your wood stash **dry** and readily accessible, especially in unpredictable weather.

If you have access to a **solar oven** or plan to build one, then sunshine becomes your fuel. We'll dive deeper into that later, but remember that mastering multiple fuel sources will give you flexibility, no matter the conditions.

3. Ingredients

Your pantry will be the heart of your kitchen, and off-grid cooking requires careful planning around non-perishable ingredients, foraged foods, and items you've grown or stored. Start with a selection of dried beans, grains (rice, quinoa, barley), flours, canned goods, and root vegetables like potatoes or carrots. These ingredients store well for extended periods and provide a solid foundation for meal planning.

Foraged items—like wild herbs, mushrooms, or fruits—will add diversity and nutrition to your meals, while preserved foods from your own garden (canned tomatoes, dried herbs, or pickled vegetables) can be used throughout the year.

Tips for Starting Out

Start simple, especially if you're new to off-grid cooking. One-pot meals are a great way to ease into it. Think stews, soups, and casseroles, which are easy to manage and only require periodic attention once they're on the heat.

Pro Tip: Prepping your ingredients in advance saves time and reduces fuel consumption, especially when you're working with limited resources.

Building and Using a Rocket Stove for Efficient Cooking

One of the most efficient and sustainable cooking methods off-grid is the **rocket stove**. It uses minimal fuel—just small sticks and twigs—and generates intense heat for cooking. Whether you're boiling water, frying vegetables, or simmering a stew, a rocket stove is a versatile and essential tool.

Cooking with a Rocket Stove

Building a rocket stove is a simple process, using just a few basic materials that you likely already have, as we discussed in the previous book on heating systems. There, we explored how to build a rocket stove for efficient heating. But beyond heating, rocket stoves are perfect for boiling water, simmering stews, or whipping up quick-fry meals. They heat up quickly and maintain steady warmth without consuming much fuel. The compact fire chamber encourages efficient cooking, which is especially useful when resources are limited.

- **Cast iron cookware** is the best match for rocket stoves because it distributes heat evenly and can handle high temperatures.
- Adjust the size of the flame by controlling the amount of wood you feed into the stove. You'll get a feel for how much fuel you need based on what you're cooking.

Pro Tip: Keep your wood dry to avoid smoky fires, which can reduce heat efficiency and make cooking more difficult.

Solar Cooking: Harnessing the Sun

Solar cooking is a remarkable technique that uses zero fuel, relying solely on the power of the sun to prepare your meals. It's not just sustainable, but also efficient and cost-free once you have the right setup. In an off-grid scenario, mastering solar cooking ensures you can prepare food without using firewood, propane, or other traditional fuels. Let's break down how to set up a solar oven and cook effectively using the sun's energy.

Building or Setting Up a Solar Oven

You have two main options for solar ovens: buying a pre-made one or building your own from basic materials. Both work on the same principle of capturing sunlight and converting it into heat, but making your own is a simple, cost-effective project.

Pre-Made Solar Ovens:

- These are commercially available and designed for efficiency. If you prefer convenience, buying a pre-made solar oven is a quick solution. Most come with features like adjustable reflectors and insulated chambers for optimal cooking performance.

DIY Solar Oven: Building your own solar oven is an easy project that only requires a few common materials:

- **Materials:** Cardboard box, aluminum foil, glass (or plastic wrap), and black paint or construction paper.

Steps:

1. **Prepare the Box:** Line the inside of the cardboard box with aluminum foil, making sure it's smooth to reflect sunlight efficiently. Paint the bottom of the box black or cover it with black construction paper—this helps absorb the heat.

2. **Make the Reflectors:** Use another piece of cardboard or aluminum foil to create a reflective panel that angles toward the inside of the box. This will direct sunlight into the oven, concentrating the heat.
3. **Cover the Top:** Place a sheet of glass or plastic wrap over the top of the box to trap the heat inside. This creates an insulated space where temperatures can rise high enough for cooking.
4. **Position in Sunlight:** Set the box in direct sunlight, adjusting the reflective surfaces to maximize the sun's rays.

Cooking with Solar Power

Once your solar oven is set up, it's time to start cooking. Solar ovens work best for slow-cooking and baking. While they take longer than traditional methods, the results are tender, well-cooked meals.

Steps for Effective Solar Cooking:

1. **Preheat the Oven:** Like any other oven, it's important to preheat your solar oven. Let it sit in the sun for about 20 minutes before placing any food inside. This will ensure the interior reaches the desired cooking temperature.
2. **Choose the Right Foods:** Solar ovens excel at cooking soups, rice, stews, and baked goods. Because the cooking process is slower, it's a good idea to cut your food into smaller pieces to reduce the overall cooking time.
3. **Adjust for the Sun:** Throughout the cooking process, adjust the angle of your solar oven to track the sun's movement across the sky. This keeps your oven consistently hot. Stir your food occasionally to distribute the heat evenly, especially in dishes like soups or stews.
4. **Cooking Time:** Solar ovens take longer than conventional cooking methods. Meals may take several hours to cook, depending on the sunlight and the type of food. Make sure to plan ahead and have your meal cooking by midday to take full advantage of the sun.

Pro Tip: For optimal results, cook during the brightest part of the day and avoid cloudy conditions, as even slight variations in sunlight can affect your cooking time.

Cooking Over an Open Fire: Mastering the Basics

Cooking over an open flame is a fundamental off-grid skill that has been practiced for centuries. Whether you're roasting a chicken or simmering a stew, fire brings out unique flavors in food and is often the fastest way to cook outdoors. To make the most of this method, you need to know how to set up a cooking fire and manage heat.

Setting Up a Cooking Fire

Building the right type of fire for cooking is key to controlling the heat and ensuring your food cooks evenly. Follow these simple steps to get started:

Steps:

1. **Build a Fire Pit:** Find a safe spot away from any overhanging branches or dry materials. Dig a small pit in the ground and surround it with stones. The stones help contain the fire and reflect heat toward your cooking area.
2. **Start the Fire:** Arrange kindling in a teepee shape using dry twigs or wood shavings in the center, with progressively larger sticks on the outside. Light the kindling, and once it catches, add larger logs to maintain the fire.
3. **Create Different Heat Zones:** For more control over cooking, rake coals to one side of the pit to create different heat zones. This way, you can cook directly over high heat or use the cooler side for simmering and slow-cooking.

Cooking Over the Fire

You have several methods to choose from when cooking over an open flame, depending on the type of meal you're preparing:

1. **Skewer Cooking:**
   - **Method:** Thread pieces of meat or vegetables onto skewers, then hold them over the fire. Rotate frequently to cook evenly. This is great for quick meals like kebabs.
   - **Pro Tip:** Use sturdy, non-flammable skewers (metal or green branches) to avoid them burning in the fire.
2. **Dutch Oven Cooking:**
   - **Method:** Dutch ovens are perfect for soups, stews, and baking. Place the Dutch oven directly on top of coals or hang it over the fire using a tripod. Cover the lid with hot coals for **even heat distribution**.
   - **Pro Tip:** For baking bread or pies, turn the oven halfway through cooking to prevent burning on one side.

Pro Tip: Use a cast iron skillet or grill grate over the fire to expand your cooking options. Cast iron retains heat well and ensures your food cooks evenly.

Preparing Meals from Foraged and Grown Ingredients

In an off-grid setting, you'll often rely on what you can forage or grow to create nutritious meals. These ingredients are not only sustainable but offer essential nutrients. Here's how to make the most of nature's pantry:

Foraged Plants

The key to using foraged ingredients is knowing what's safe to eat and how to prepare it. Some common, easy-to-find wild plants include:

- **Dandelions, nettles, and wild garlic**: These plants can be added to soups, stews, or salads for flavor and nutrition. Foraging takes practice, so always ensure you're confident in identifying safe plants.

Pro Tip: Bring a foraging guide with you to help identify local edible plants. Stick to easily recognizable ones at first to avoid confusion.

Home-Grown Produce

Growing your own food provides a steady source of ingredients, even in challenging environments. Root vegetables, leafy greens, and hardy herbs are ideal for off-grid gardening because they're resilient and easy to store.

Cooking Techniques:

- Roast **root vegetables** like potatoes and carrots directly in the embers of your fire, or use a cast iron skillet for frying.
- Add fresh **herbs** to soups and stews to elevate the flavor of your meal.

Pro Tip: Always wash foraged items thoroughly and avoid plants you're not 100% certain of to prevent poisoning or contamination.

By mastering solar cooking, open fire techniques, and foraging skills, you'll be able to create nutritious, flavorful meals in any off-grid scenario. These methods are practical, sustainable, and offer the flexibility needed to thrive in nature. Remember, practice makes perfect—so use these techniques regularly to hone your skills and ensure you're fully prepared for any situation.

Off-Grid Baking: Bread Without an Oven

Bread is one of the most basic and essential foods, and even without an electric oven, you can easily bake your own off the grid. With a few simple tools and ingredients, you can still enjoy freshly baked bread, whether you're deep in the wilderness or living in an off-grid homestead. The Dutch oven, which can be used directly over a fire or in hot coals, is a perfect tool for this.

How to Bake Bread Using a Dutch Oven

Baking bread off-grid may seem like a challenge, but using a **Dutch oven** simplifies the process and gives you consistent results. Here's how to bake bread without electricity.

Step 1: Mix Your Dough

- **Ingredients**: Start with basic ingredients—flour, water, salt, and yeast (or baking soda if you're making soda bread).
- **Method**: In a large bowl, mix:
  - 3 cups of flour
  - 1 teaspoon of salt
  - 1 packet of yeast (or 1 teaspoon baking soda if you're not using yeast)
  - About 1 ¼ cups of warm water (enough to make a sticky dough)

Stir until the dough comes together. If using yeast, let it sit and rise for an hour in a warm spot, covered with a clean cloth.

Step 2: Heat Your Dutch Oven

- **Fire Preparation**: While the dough is rising, prepare your fire. Create a bed of hot coals using either wood or charcoal. You want enough heat to bake the bread, but not too much to burn the bottom.
- **Preheat**: Place the Dutch oven over the coals or next to the fire to preheat for 10–15 minutes. This ensures even cooking.

Step 3: Place the Dough Inside

- Once the dough has risen (or immediately for quick bread), shape it into a round loaf and place it in the **preheated Dutch oven**. If you like, dust the bottom of the Dutch oven with a little flour or cornmeal to prevent sticking.
- **Cover the Dutch Oven** with its lid to trap the heat, just like you would with a conventional oven.

Step 4: Bake Over Hot Coals

- **Cooking Method**: Position the Dutch oven on top of hot coals and place additional coals on the lid. This ensures even heat distribution, mimicking an oven-like environment.
- **Timing**: Bake for about 30–40 minutes, turning the Dutch oven every 10–15 minutes to prevent hot spots and ensure even baking. The bread is done when it's golden brown and makes a hollow sound when tapped on the bottom.

Step 5: Cool and Enjoy

- Once your bread is fully baked, carefully remove the Dutch oven from the fire using heat-resistant gloves.

- Let the bread cool for 10–15 minutes before slicing to allow the crust to set and the inside to finish cooking. Enjoy fresh, homemade bread with minimal equipment.

Pro Tip: You can also experiment with quick breads like flatbreads or tortillas if you want something faster. These can be cooked directly on a hot cast iron pan or even on flat stones over a fire.

Practical Tips for Off-Grid Cooking Success

Cooking off the grid comes with its own set of challenges, especially when managing your resources. Here are some expert tips to ensure you make the most of your fuel, time, and ingredients while cooking outdoors or in an off-grid setting.

1. Fuel Efficiency

One of the biggest considerations when cooking off the grid is **fuel conservation**. Here's how to make your fuel last longer:

- **Always have extra dry wood, kindling, or biomass** ready before you start cooking. Running out of fuel mid-cook can cause delays and uneven cooking.
- For longer cooking processes, use **smaller sticks or twigs** for steady heat, especially when using a rocket stove or Dutch oven.

2. Organize Your Cooking

Being organized is crucial for efficiency. It's not just about preparing food—it's about maximizing the energy you spend on cooking:

- **Prep ingredients ahead of time**. This not only helps save time but also ensures that everything is ready when your fire or solar oven is at its optimal temperature.
- **Cook in bulk** when possible. If you're making bread, soups, or stews, double the recipe. Leftovers can be stored for later meals, conserving your cooking fuel and effort.

3. Maximize Heat

Efficient heat management is key to successful off-grid cooking:

- **Use lids on your pots and pans** to retain heat. This not only speeds up cooking time but also ensures that your meals are evenly cooked with minimal fuel consumption.
- In solar ovens or while cooking over a fire, positioning is important. **Adjust your pots and pans closer or further from the heat source** to control cooking speed. You can create multiple heat zones in a fire by separating coals—one for high heat, one for low simmering.

Self-Sufficient Cooking for Survival

Mastering off-grid cooking is more than just a skill—it's a cornerstone of true self-reliance. By learning to cook without electricity and gas, you're not only ensuring your family's nourishment but also preparing for long-term sustainability, regardless of the circumstances.

When living off the grid, you have to rely on natural resources, ingenuity, and the techniques you've honed through practice. From rocket stoves and solar ovens to cooking over open flames, each method teaches you how to adapt to your environment and make the most of what nature provides. The key is to practice these methods regularly, so when modern conveniences are unavailable, you can confidently prepare nutritious meals using only the resources at hand.

Practical Mastery of Off-Grid Cooking

The transition to off-grid living means shifting from reliance on appliances to more hands-on, efficient cooking methods. Here are key steps to ensure you are well-prepared:

1. **Practice Cooking in Different Conditions**: Whether it's clear skies for solar cooking or windy weather that makes fire management tricky, practice cooking in all kinds of situations. This ensures you can adapt and be ready for anything nature throws your way.
2. **Master Efficient Fuel Use**: Understanding how to conserve fuel, whether it's wood for a rocket stove or positioning pots correctly over a fire, helps you make your resources last longer. Efficiency means fewer trips to gather wood and a smaller environmental impact.
3. **Prep and Plan Meals Ahead**: Cooking off-grid requires forethought. Prepping ingredients and knowing what dishes cook best under different conditions will save you time and energy. Bulk cooking is especially useful when resources are limited, allowing you to cook once and eat multiple meals.
4. **Grow and Forage**: Incorporating fresh, foraged plants and homegrown produce into your meals brings variety and nutrition. Whether it's using wild herbs or roasting root vegetables, this connection to your land strengthens your self-sufficiency.
5. **Maintain Your Tools**: Cast iron pans, Dutch ovens, and essential utensils require care. Regularly season your cast iron to prevent rust and keep them in prime condition. Proper tool care ensures your cooking methods remain effective and reliable.

Your Path to Food Independence

The ability to prepare nourishing meals with minimal resources is at the core of self-sufficient living. Off-grid cooking is not about surviving on the bare minimum; it's about thriving by using the tools and techniques that connect you back to nature.

By practicing these methods, you're creating a food system that doesn't rely on power grids or external sources. You're taking control of your food security and ensuring that, no matter the challenges, you and your family can enjoy warm, healthy meals. Whether you're slow-cooking a stew over an open fire, baking bread in a Dutch oven, or harnessing the sun's energy for a solar-cooked meal, each step brings you closer to true independence.

This journey toward off-grid living is deeply rewarding, allowing you to live in harmony with the land while learning valuable, timeless skills. Keep refining your techniques, experimenting with new recipes, and adapting to the ever-changing conditions that off-grid life presents. This mastery over your food and resources is not just a survival skill—it's a lifestyle of resilience and self-reliance.

With dedication, you'll not only become an expert at cooking off the grid but also a living example of how to thrive without relying on modern conveniences.

13. DIY Lighting Systems for Off-Grid Homes

Introduction to Off-Grid Lighting Systems

As we move from the essential topic of heating and cooking systems discussed in the last books, it's time to focus on another crucial aspect of off-grid living: lighting. Whether you're cooking after sunset, working on projects, or simply navigating your home at night, having a reliable, sustainable lighting system is non-negotiable.

Lighting in an off-grid setting comes with its own set of challenges. Since you're not connected to the grid, you need to utilize renewable energy sources such as solar or wind, as well as efficient technologies that minimize power consumption. The key to an effective off-grid lighting system is balance—between energy efficiency, cost, and maintenance. These factors will determine how well your system works for you in the long run, and how easily you can maintain it with limited resources.

By embracing low-power, sustainable lighting solutions, you're not just saving energy—you're creating a system that supports your off-grid lifestyle in a way that's environmentally conscious, cost-effective, and adaptable to any situation.

Solar Lighting Systems: Harnessing the Sun's Energy

Solar power, as covered in previous sections on off-grid energy solutions, remains one of the most reliable and accessible sources of power for lighting. Utilizing the sun's energy means you can have a **constant, renewable** source of power, even in remote areas. Now, let's explore how to set up your off-grid solar lighting system.

Choosing the Right Solar Setup

The foundation of any solar lighting system lies in selecting the right **solar panels**. These panels will capture sunlight during the day and convert it into usable energy for lighting during the night.

- **Solar Panels**: The size and wattage of the panels are crucial for providing enough energy. Here's a step-by-step guide to calculate your energy needs:
    1. **Assess your lighting requirements** by calculating the wattage of the bulbs you'll be using and the number of hours you expect to need them each day.
    2. Multiply these figures to find your **total daily energy consumption**.
    3. Choose panels that can generate enough energy based on your geographical location and available sunlight.

Pro tip: Ensure your panels are positioned at the right angle for **maximum sunlight exposure** throughout the day. Track the sun's movement over the seasons to make adjustments as needed.

- **Solar Batteries**: Storing energy is essential for night lighting or cloudy days. The most common choices are **lead-acid** and **lithium-ion** batteries. Here's what you need to know:
    1. **Lead-acid batteries** are are cost-effective but demand frequent maintenance and have shorter lifespans.
    2. **Lithium-ion batteries** come with a higher price tag but offer greater efficiency and longevity.

Sizing your battery bank is crucial. It needs to hold enough charge to power your lights through the night and during overcast days. Regular maintenance is essential to ensure long-term performance, particularly for lead-acid batteries, which need to be checked for water levels and charge cycles.

DIY Solar Lighting Projects

Setting up a solar-powered lighting system can be a rewarding DIY project that ensures you're in full control of your lighting needs.

- **Installing Solar-Powered Lights**: To set up a basic solar system for indoor and outdoor use, follow these steps:
  1. **Wire your solar panels** to a charge controller, which manages the flow of energy going into the battery.
  2. Connect the controller to your battery bank to store energy.
  3. **Link your lights** to the battery, ensuring the voltage matches the system.

Pro tip: Solar-powered lights can be set up for both indoor use and garden or pathway lighting, providing safe, energy-efficient lighting throughout your property.

- **DIY Solar Garden and Pathway Lights**: For outdoor areas, building a simple solar lighting system is both cost-effective and practical. Use inexpensive materials like small solar panels, rechargeable batteries, and LED lights to create lighting for pathways, gardens, or even outdoor seating areas.

Low-Power LED Lighting: Maximizing Efficiency

When you're living off the grid, every watt counts. That's why LED lights are the best choice for off-grid lighting. They're not only energy-efficient but also have a long lifespan, which means less frequent replacements and reduced maintenance.

Why LEDs Are the Best Choice for Off-Grid Homes

- **Energy Efficiency**: LEDs use far less energy compared to incandescent or CFL bulbs. For off-grid living, where power resources are limited, this energy efficiency is invaluable. On average, LEDs use 75% less energy than traditional incandescent bulbs and have a lifespan up to 25 times longer.

Pro tip: LEDs also generate very little heat, which helps in reducing cooling costs during warmer months.

- **Selecting the Right LED Bulbs**: When choosing LED bulbs for your off-grid home, it's important to consider lumens (brightness) and color temperature. Warm lights (2700K-3000K) are suitable for living spaces, while cooler lights (4000K-5000K) are better for task-oriented areas like kitchens or workshops.
  - **Minimize power draw** by selecting bulbs that offer the appropriate wattage for the area they will light. This prevents energy waste while providing adequate illumination.

Wiring LEDs to Solar Power

Once you've chosen your LEDs, the next step is to wire them into your solar power system.

- **DIY Installation**: For a basic 12V or 24V LED lighting setup, follow these steps:
  1. **Wire the LED lights** directly to your solar battery system, ensuring the voltage matches the output of your battery.
  2. If your lights require a different voltage, you can use a **step-down transformer** to match the power requirements.

Pro tip: Always use appropriate fuses and switches to prevent electrical issues or overloading.

- **Battery Backup Options**: Even with a reliable solar system, it's wise to have an emergency backup plan. Installing a small battery backup system ensures that your lighting will continue to function even if your primary battery runs low. This system can be wired to automatically kick in when energy levels drop.

Building a DIY Wind-Solar Hybrid Lighting System

In the previous chapters, we covered essential off-grid energy solutions such as solar power, which plays a key role in off-grid living. Now, it's time to enhance that system by integrating wind energy, a complementary and renewable energy source. A **wind-solar hybrid lighting system** is an excellent way to ensure that your off-grid home is consistently powered, regardless of weather conditions. By combining these two energy sources, you can create a robust system that maximizes efficiency and reliability.

Adding Wind Power to Your Lighting Setup

Wind energy can significantly bolster your off-grid energy system, especially during times when solar output may be lower, like during nighttime or on overcast days. By incorporating a **small wind turbine** into your system, you can continuously generate energy, making your lighting system more sustainable.

- **Choosing a Small Wind Turbine**: When selecting a wind turbine for your off-grid lighting, the most important factors are size, wattage, and compatibility with your existing solar setup. To make an informed choice:
    1. **Calculate your energy needs**: Start by determining how much additional energy your lighting system requires. This will help you select a wind turbine that meets your needs without overburdening your system.
    2. **Consider local wind conditions**: Turbines work best in areas with consistent wind speeds. Research your location's wind profile to ensure your turbine will produce enough energy.
    3. **Select the right turbine**: For most off-grid homes, a small wind turbine with a capacity of around 400 to 1,500 watts is sufficient for lighting and other basic needs.

Pro tip: Position your turbine at a height where wind exposure is optimal—typically at least 30 feet above the nearest obstruction (trees, buildings) to ensure efficient energy capture.

Combining Solar and Wind Energy: Maximizing Off-Grid Lighting Efficiency

Now that you've chosen the right turbine, it's time to integrate it with your existing solar setup. A **hybrid system** allows you to switch between energy sources, ensuring a seamless power supply to your lighting system.

- Step-by-Step Guide to Integration:
    1. **Connect both systems to a charge controller**: This device regulates the energy coming from both your solar panels and wind turbine, ensuring your battery bank receives the correct charge.
    2. **Monitor energy flow**: The charge controller will prioritize energy from solar panels when the sun is shining and switch to wind energy when the sun isn't available. This prevents overcharging and ensures efficient energy use.
    3. **Balance your system**: Make sure your charge controller and inverter are designed to handle dual inputs, ensuring smooth operation without energy surges or overloads.

Pro tip: Test your hybrid system regularly to ensure it transitions between solar and wind energy smoothly. Regular checks will help prevent energy loss and keep your lighting system reliable.

DIY Wind-Solar Lighting Projects

Building a **wind-solar lighting circuit** can sound complex, but with the right tools and guidance, it's an achievable and rewarding project. Here's how to wire a simple hybrid system:

- Building a Wind-Solar Lighting Circuit:
    1. **Gather your components**: You'll need solar panels, a small wind turbine, a charge controller, batteries, an inverter, and LED lights.

2. **Wiring the components**: Start by wiring both the solar panels and wind turbine to the charge controller. The controller regulates the power before sending it to the battery storage.
3. **Connecting the lights**: Once the energy is stored in your batteries, connect your LED lighting system to the inverter, which transforms DC power stored in the batteries into AC power to run your lights and other household appliances.

Pro tip: Use a system that can switch automatically between wind and solar energy, allowing you to fully leverage both sources without manual intervention.

Off-Grid Lighting for Emergencies

One of the key challenges of off-grid living is preparing for unexpected system failures. Having **backup lighting solutions** ensures that you're never left in the dark, no matter what happens.

- **Portable Solar Lighting Solutions**: Having **solar lanterns** and flashlights at your disposal ensures you have a reliable backup in case your main system goes down.
  1. **Build your own solar-powered lantern**: Using recycled materials, you can create a simple lantern powered by small solar panels.
  2. **Portable solar lights**: These can be charged during the day and used anywhere at night, offering a versatile solution for emergencies.
- **Hand-Crank and Pedal-Powered Lights**: In the event of long-term system failure, hand-crank and pedal-powered lights provide an additional layer of security.
  1. **DIY Hand-Crank Generator**: A hand-crank generator allows you to generate light with minimal effort. Simply crank the handle to power small LED lights.
  2. **Pedal-Powered Lighting**: For larger lighting needs, a pedal-powered generator can provide more substantial energy by converting mechanical energy into electricity.

Pro tip: Both hand-crank and pedal-powered systems are excellent backup options, especially in remote locations where solar or wind energy may not always be reliable.

Reducing Energy Consumption and Maximizing Lighting Efficiency

In an off-grid setting, every watt matters. To extend the life of your battery and minimize energy waste, it's crucial to optimize your lighting system for maximum efficiency.

- **Using Motion Sensors**: Motion sensors ensure that lights are only used when needed, reducing unnecessary energy consumption. Install sensors in high-traffic areas like hallways or outdoor entry points to activate lights when movement is detected.

Pro tip: Motion sensors are especially useful for outdoor lighting, where lights might only be needed for short periods, like when you're coming home at night.

- **Light Reflectors and Placement**: Strategically placing mirrors or reflective surfaces can help maximize the effectiveness of your lighting system by bouncing light into darker areas, reducing the need for additional lighting.

Pro tip: Use natural light during the day by incorporating large windows or skylights into your home design, further reducing the need for artificial lighting.

- **Smart Lighting Tips for Off-Grid Living**: Smart lighting solutions like dimmers and timers allow you to control when and how much energy is used for lighting. Installing dimmer switches lets you adjust the brightness of your lights based on current needs, while timers ensure that lights turn off automatically after a set period.

Pro tip: Create lighting zones in your home, where lights are only used in areas of high activity, helping to conserve energy in less-used spaces.

By incorporating wind power into your solar system, building reliable backup options, and optimizing energy use, your off-grid lighting system will be efficient, reliable, and resilient. Taking a practical, step-by-step approach to setting up your wind-solar hybrid lighting ensures a system that provides light when you need it most, all while maintaining the independence and sustainability that off-grid living offers.

Mastering Off-Grid Lighting for Long-Term Sustainability

As we wrap up our exploration of off-grid lighting, it's clear that lighting plays a vital role in ensuring a safe, functional, and comfortable off-grid lifestyle. Throughout this book, we've covered the most efficient ways to harness renewable energy sources like solar and wind, how to implement energy-efficient lighting systems using LED technology, and how to build hybrid setups that provide reliable lighting regardless of the weather.

Recap of Efficient Off-Grid Lighting Systems

Your lighting system is at the core of your off-grid living experience, and getting it right is essential. From setting up solar-powered lights to building wind-solar hybrid systems, the key is maximizing energy efficiency while minimizing waste. Here's a quick recap of what we've covered:

- **Solar Power**: We explored how to harness solar energy with the right solar panels, batteries, and installation techniques to create a sustainable lighting solution.
- **Wind Power**: We looked at complementing your solar system with wind energy, adding resilience to your setup by utilizing both renewable resources.
- **LED Lighting**: We dove into the benefits of using low-power LED bulbs that consume less energy and last longer, making them ideal for off-grid homes.
- **Backup Solutions**: From hand-crank generators to solar lanterns, we discussed various emergency lighting solutions to ensure you're never without light, even during system failures.

Adapting and Improving Your System

Off-grid living is about flexibility and constant improvement. As your energy needs evolve, so should your lighting system. Perhaps you'll expand your lighting setup by adding more panels, upgrading your battery bank, or incorporating advanced controls like dimmers and timers to reduce consumption further.

Remember, off-grid living isn't static—it's about continuously optimizing your setup to ensure your home remains comfortable, efficient, and resilient. Always be on the lookout for ways to improve your system, whether by upgrading components, integrating new technologies, or simply adjusting your light placement to maximize natural light.

Pro tip: Regularly assess your energy usage and make adjustments based on seasonal changes or shifts in your off-grid lifestyle. Adapting your system ensures it remains efficient and sustainable in the long run.

Final Thoughts on Long-Term Off-Grid Lighting Sustainability

Your off-grid lighting journey doesn't end with the final installation. It's an evolving project that will grow with your home and your energy needs. By continually refining and adapting your setup, you'll ensure that your home remains illuminated in a way that is both efficient and sustainable for years to come.

With the right approach, your lighting system will be a shining example of how renewable energy can power a brighter, more sustainable future for your off-grid home.

14. Foundations of Sustainable Gardening: Soil, Water, and Garden Structures

After mastering the essentials of off-grid living—such as heating, cooking, and energy systems—the next vital step on your journey toward complete self-sufficiency is building a sustainable food source. A thriving, self-sustaining garden serves as the cornerstone of off-grid living, providing a consistent supply of fresh, organic food year-round. Beyond reducing your reliance on external food systems and cutting costs, a well-maintained garden fosters a deep connection with the land you live on, contributing to environmental stewardship and sustainable practices that benefit both you and the ecosystem.

In Foundations of Sustainable Gardening: Soil, Water, and Garden Structures, we will lay the groundwork for a thriving garden by focusing on the core elements needed for long-term success. This book is designed as an introduction to the fundamental concepts of soil management, water conservation, and garden structures like raised beds and vertical gardening. These are the building blocks of a resilient and productive garden that will serve you well, no matter your growing conditions.

The topics explored in this guide will prepare you for a more in-depth exploration of advanced gardening techniques in the next book. Here, we will start with the basics—understanding soil composition, efficient water use, and maximizing space with garden structures. From the importance of nutrient-rich soil to efficient irrigation systems and space-saving growing methods, these foundational principles ensure that your garden not only survives but thrives with minimal external inputs.

In this first step toward mastering self-sufficient gardening, you will learn how to build and maintain healthy soil, make the most of available water, and design a garden layout that maximizes productivity. These key concepts will form the backbone of your gardening practice, setting the stage for the more advanced techniques we will explore in the subsequent volume.

By the time you finish, you'll have a solid grasp of the essential elements that will sustain your garden and support your off-grid lifestyle for years to come.

Starting Small: A Simple Garden to Get You Going

Building a self-sustaining garden doesn't have to be daunting. Starting small allows you to ease into the process, learn key gardening skills, and make mistakes without feeling overwhelmed. Once you master the basics, you can expand your garden as your confidence and experience grow.

Example Garden Setup:

- **Crops:** Tomatoes, lettuce, carrots, beans, spinach.
- **Why these crops?** These plants are hardy, quick to grow, and provide essential nutrients, making them perfect for beginners. They offer a solid foundation for building your self-sustaining garden.

Step-by-Step Guide:

1. Prepare the Soil:
   o Till the soil to a depth of at least 12 inches to loosen it and create space for roots to grow.
   o Mix in organic compost or well-rotted manure to enrich the soil with nutrients. This will give your plants a strong start and promote healthy growth.
2. Planting:

o Follow the spacing recommendations on seed packets to prevent overcrowding, which can lead to disease and stunted growth.
o For leafy greens like spinach and lettuce, stagger your plantings by sowing seeds every two weeks. This will ensure a continuous harvest throughout the season.

3. Watering:
   o Water deeply once a week to encourage the roots to grow deeper into the soil. Adjust your watering schedule depending on weather conditions, increasing it during hot spells and reducing it during rainy periods.
   o Early morning watering is ideal, as it reduces evaporation and helps prevent fungal diseases from developing overnight.

4. Maintenance:
   o Regularly weed the garden to eliminate competition for nutrients and space.
   o Keep an eye out for pests and diseases, addressing them early with natural solutions like neem oil or hand-picking larger pests.
   o Prune plants like tomatoes to encourage better air circulation and fruit production.

5. Harvesting:
   o Start harvesting leafy greens like lettuce and spinach within 30 to 40 days of planting. These crops can be harvested multiple times by cutting the outer leaves and allowing the inner ones to keep growing.
   o Root crops like carrots and tomatoes will be ready in 60 to 70 days, depending on your growing conditions.

Pro Tip: Keep a garden journal. Document your planting dates, harvests, and any observations you make along the way. Tracking what works best in your specific climate and soil will help you refine your gardening approach each year, making your garden more productive and sustainable over time.

By starting small and building on your successes, you can confidently develop a thriving, self-sustaining garden that will feed you year-round. With careful planning and ongoing maintenance, you'll gain the skills and knowledge needed to manage a larger, more complex garden over time.

Soil Management: The Foundation of Your Garden

When it comes to cultivating a thriving off-grid garden, nothing is more important than your soil. Just as a solid foundation supports a home, nutrient-rich soil is the key to growing strong, healthy plants. Without the right soil composition, even the best seeds and most diligent care won't yield the results you're aiming for. Proper soil management ensures that your garden will flourish, reducing the need for synthetic fertilizers and keeping your ecosystem in balance.

Key Components of Soil:

• **Soil Composition**: The ideal soil is a balanced mix of sand, silt, and clay. This balance improves drainage, allows air circulation around roots, and retains enough moisture to keep your plants hydrated without drowning them. • **Composting**: One of the easiest and most sustainable ways to enrich your soil is through composting. Using kitchen scraps, leaves, and grass clippings creates a nutrient-rich amendment that enhances the texture and fertility of your garden's soil over time.

Step-by-Step Guide to Building and Maintaining Healthy Soil

Step 1: Testing Your Soil

Before planting, it's crucial to assess your soil's composition and nutrient content. Testing helps you identify what needs to be improved for optimal growth.

- **Purchase a soil test kit**: These are available at most garden centers or online. They measure pH, nitrogen, phosphorus, and potassium levels—key nutrients for plant growth.
- **Ideal pH range**: Most plants thrive in soil with a pH between 6.0 and 7.0. Too acidic or too alkaline, and your plants won't be able to absorb nutrients properly.
- **Amending soil**: If your pH is too low (acidic), add lime. If it's too high (alkaline), incorporate sulfur to bring it into balance.

Step 2: Building a Compost Pile

Composting transforms organic waste into rich, nutrient-dense soil conditioner.

- **Layering**: Start your pile with alternating layers of green materials (kitchen scraps, grass) and brown materials (dry leaves, straw).
- **Watering**: Maintain the compost at a moisture level similar to that of a wrung-out sponge. Be careful not to over-saturate it, as this can slow the decomposition process.
- **Turning**: Every few weeks, turn the pile with a pitchfork to aerate it. This speeds up decomposition by ensuring oxygen reaches all parts of the compost.

Step 3: Soil Enrichment

Each season, rejuvenate your garden by adding compost and organic materials to the soil.

- **Spread compost**: After your compost has broken down (typically 6-12 months), spread it across your garden, focusing on the root zones of your plants.
- **Integrate cover crops**: In the off-season, consider growing cover crops such as clover or rye to prevent erosion, naturally enrich the soil, and add nitrogen back into the soil.

Expert Tip: Using Cover Crops

Sowing cover crops during the off-season can significantly improve soil health. These crops help prevent erosion, control weeds, and enrich the soil's structure. Once they've grown, simply till them back into the soil to create a green manure that boosts organic matter and nutrients.

Irrigation Techniques: Maximizing Water Efficiency

Water is a valuable resource, especially in an off-grid lifestyle where you might not have unlimited access to a water supply. Efficient irrigation is vital for keeping your garden healthy without wasting water. The key to maximizing water efficiency is ensuring that your plants receive just enough to thrive—no more, no less.

Techniques to Consider:

• **Drip Irrigation**: This approach channels water directly to the root zone, effectively minimizing both evaporation and runoff. It's a highly efficient way to keep your garden hydrated.

• **Rainwater Harvesting**: Collecting rainwater in barrels connected to your roof gutters can provide a free and sustainable water source.

• **Mulching**: By covering the soil around your plants with organic materials like straw or wood chips, you can retain moisture, suppress weeds, and keep the soil temperature stable.

Step-by-Step Drip Irrigation Installation

Step 1: Laying the Hoses
- **Position hoses**: Lay drip irrigation hoses along plant rows, ensuring that the perforations or emitters are positioned near the root zones of each plant. This ensures that water is delivered right where it's needed.

Step 2: Connecting to a Water Source
- **Rain barrel or tap**: Attach the hoses to a rain barrel if you're collecting rainwater, or connect them to a garden tap. A rain barrel is especially useful for sustainable water use in off-grid environments.

Step 3: Automating the Process (Optional)
- **Timers**: If you want to make your irrigation system fully automatic, install a timer. This way, your garden will be watered at consistent intervals, even when you're not around to manually manage it.

Step 4: Maintenance
- **Check regularly**: Periodically inspect the system to ensure there are no leaks or blockages. Clean any clogged emitters to maintain consistent water flow.

Pro Tip: Morning Watering

Water your plants early in the morning to minimize evaporation and prevent the growth of fungal diseases, which tend to develop in damp conditions.

By mastering soil management and irrigation techniques, you'll lay the foundation for a healthy, productive garden that requires minimal external inputs. Strong soil leads to strong plants, and efficient water use ensures sustainability in even the most challenging off-grid environments. With these skills, your garden will thrive year after year, no matter the conditions.

Raised Bed Gardening: Maximizing Space and Soil Quality

Raised bed gardening is an excellent solution for anyone seeking more control over soil quality and drainage, especially in off-grid settings. These beds not only prevent waterlogging but also allow for a more concentrated area of nutrient-rich soil. Raised beds are easier to maintain, reduce strain on your back, and extend your growing season by warming the soil earlier in the spring.

Benefits of Raised Beds:
- **Improved Drainage**: Raised beds help prevent water from pooling around your plants, which can lead to root rot.
- **Rich Soil Amendments**: They offer the opportunity to enrich the soil more efficiently by adding organic material directly to the concentrated space.
- **Extended Growing Season**: Raised beds warm up more quickly in the spring, enabling you to start planting earlier and enjoy a longer growing season.

Step-by-Step Guide to Building and Managing a Raised Bed

Step 1: Building the Bed

Choose a location with plenty of sunlight and begin constructing the bed.

- **Materials**: Use untreated wood, bricks, stones, or even old metal panels. Make sure the bed is 12–18 inches tall to provide enough depth for root growth.
- **Dimensions**: Build your raised bed about 3 to 4 feet wide so you can easily reach the center from both sides. The length can be adjusted to fit your space.
- **Site Prep**: Clear the area of grass or weeds, and loosen the soil where the bed will sit to improve drainage.

Step 2: Layering the Soil

The foundation of a good raised bed is healthy, nutrient-dense soil. A balanced mixture will ensure your plants get the nutrients and drainage they need.

- **Layer 1 (Base)**: Start with larger organic materials like branches or wood chips. This provides good drainage and long-term nutrients as they break down.
- **Layer 2 (Compost)**: Add a layer of compost, which will provide nutrients to your plants.
- **Layer 3 (Topsoil)**: The final layer should be high-quality garden soil mixed with organic matter like leaves or straw to enhance moisture retention and soil structure.

Step 3: Planting in Raised Beds

Once the bed is ready, it's time to plant your crops. One of the great advantages of raised beds is that you can plant more intensively, maximizing space and yield.

- **Companion Planting**: Use companion planting techniques to grow crops that benefit each other. For example, plant basil next to tomatoes to improve flavor and repel pests.
- **Efficient Spacing**: Follow the recommended spacing for each plant type to avoid overcrowding. Raised beds can handle closer planting because of the rich soil.

Step 4: Watering and Maintenance

Raised beds require more frequent watering as they dry out faster than in-ground beds.

- **Deep Watering**: Water the beds deeply, ensuring that water reaches the roots. Depending on your climate, you may need to water daily during hot periods.
- **Mulch**: Use mulch to help retain moisture and suppress weeds. Organic mulches like straw or grass clippings are perfect for raised beds.

Expert Tip:

In colder climates, you can extend the growing season by covering your raised beds with plastic or fabric row covers. These create a greenhouse effect, trapping heat and protecting your plants from frost.

Vertical Gardening: Grow More in Less Space

Vertical gardening is a game-changer for small gardens or when space is limited. By growing upward instead of outward, you can increase productivity, improve air circulation, reduce the risk of pests, and make harvesting easier. Vertical gardens are perfect for urban spaces, backyards, or even alongside your raised beds.

Benefits of Vertical Gardening:

- **Maximizes Space**: Vertical gardens use the height of your space, allowing you to grow more plants without expanding your garden horizontally.
- **Pest Control**: Growing vertically lifts plants off the ground, which reduces the risk of certain pests and diseases.
- **Easier Harvesting**: Harvesting is more accessible because fruits and vegetables are within reach.

Step-by-Step Vertical Garden Setup

Step 1: Build Trellises or Frames

For a successful vertical garden, you'll need to provide support for your climbing plants.

- **Materials**: Use sturdy materials like wood, wire, or metal frames to create a trellis or structure. Choose materials that can withstand the weight of growing plants.
- **Placement**: Place trellises or vertical frames on the north side of your garden beds to avoid shading smaller plants.

Step 2: Choose Your Plants

Not all plants are suitable for vertical gardening, so selecting the right crops is essential.

- **Vining Plants**: Cucumbers, peas, pole beans, and squash are ideal for vertical gardening as they naturally climb.
- **Stacked Planters**: Use tiered or stacked planters for smaller plants like herbs (basil, parsley) or leafy greens (spinach, kale).

Step 3: Train the Plants

As your plants grow, they'll need a little help to climb.

- **Tie Gently**: Use soft ties or twine to gently secure vines to the trellis. Regularly tie the plants as they grow to guide them upward.
- **Pruning**: Prune any damaged or unruly vines to encourage healthy growth and make sure the plant stays productive.

Step 4: Watering and Fertilization

Vertical gardens, like raised beds, tend to dry out faster. Consistent watering is crucial to ensure proper growth.

- **Drip Irrigation**: A drip irrigation system works well for vertical gardens, delivering water directly to the roots without wasting water through evaporation.
- **Fertilize Regularly**: Since plants in vertical gardens are often in smaller containers or limited soil, they benefit from regular fertilization. Use organic compost or liquid fertilizers every few weeks during the growing season.

Expert Tip:

Install a drip irrigation system to keep your vertical garden well-watered, even in the hottest weather. This ensures even water distribution and minimizes manual labor.

By implementing raised bed and vertical gardening techniques, you can maximize the productivity of your off-grid garden, even in limited space. These methods not only improve soil quality and drainage but also provide an efficient way to grow a variety of crops in a sustainable, manageable way.

Hugelkultur: A Sustainable Soil-Building Technique

Hugelkultur is a gardening method designed for sustainability, making it ideal for off-grid living. This technique relies on decaying wood and organic matter to create raised beds that not only retain moisture but also provide nutrient-dense soil for long-term plant growth. By building a Hugelkultur bed, you're essentially creating a slow-decomposing compost heap, which supplies your plants with continuous nutrients while reducing the need for constant watering.

Benefits of Hugelkultur:

- **Moisture Retention**: Hugelkultur beds retain water exceptionally well, meaning you won't need to water as often. This is particularly valuable in dry climates.
- **Sustainable Soil**: As the wood and organic matter decompose, they enrich the soil with vital nutrients, creating a self-fertilizing system.
- **Natural Heat Generation**: The decomposition process generates heat, helping to extend the growing season, especially in cooler climates.

Step-by-Step Guide to Building a Hugelkultur Bed

Step 1: Base Layer – Large Logs or Branches

The foundation of your Hugelkultur bed is the base layer of large logs or tree branches.

- **Material Selection**: Use untreated, natural wood. Ideally, choose hardwood like oak or beech for long-lasting beds, though softer woods like pine will work as well. Avoid using chemically treated wood or wood that contains toxins like walnut, which can harm plants.
- **Placement**: Lay the large logs or branches directly on the ground in the area where your bed will be. You can create a mound or dig a shallow trench to secure the logs. The larger the bed, the more water it can hold.

Step 2: Organic Material Layer

After placing your logs, add a thick layer of organic material to enhance moisture retention and nutrient content.

- **What to Use**: Include leaves, grass clippings, straw, or even cardboard. This layer adds to the decomposition process, creating a nutrient-dense environment for plant roots.
- **Layering**: Pile the organic material on top of the logs until you've filled the gaps and created a mound. This helps improve airflow while maintaining moisture within the bed.

Step 3: Top Layer – Garden Soil

The top layer of your Hugelkultur bed will be your growing medium.

- **Soil**: Use a good-quality garden soil mixed with compost or well-rotted manure. The top layer should be thick enough (8–12 inches) to support the roots of your plants.
- **Smoothing**: Spread the soil evenly over the mound, making sure it's compact enough for planting but not so tightly packed that water can't penetrate.

Step 4: Planting

Now that your Hugelkultur bed is ready, it's time to start planting.

- **Deep-Rooted Plants**: Begin by planting deep-rooted varieties like tomatoes or beans at the top of the mound where they can reach the richer layers as the bed decomposes.

- **Shallow-Rooted Plants**: Plant shallow-rooted crops like lettuce or strawberries along the sides of the mound, where they will benefit from the top layer of nutrient-rich soil.

Expert Tip:

Hugelkultur beds require less frequent watering, making them perfect for dry climates. The decomposing wood acts as a sponge, retaining moisture and releasing it slowly to your plants over time.

Composting: Turning Waste into Nutrient-Rich Soil

Composting is an essential process for anyone living off-grid, providing a sustainable way to recycle kitchen scraps and yard waste into rich, organic material that will nourish your garden. It's easy to set up, and the payoff is immense, offering a constant supply of nutrient-rich compost that will improve your soil's texture, drainage, and fertility.

What to Compost:

- **Green Materials:** Nitrogen-rich materials such as vegetable scraps, coffee grounds, and fresh grass clippings.
- **Brown Materials:** Carbon-rich materials like dried leaves, straw, and cardboard. Aim for a balance between green and brown materials to create a compost that breaks down efficiently.

Step-by-Step Composting Process

Step 1: Start a Pile or Bin

The first step to successful composting is deciding where to place your pile or bin.

- **Location:** Choose a shaded spot that's easily accessible. If you're using a bin, ensure it's well-ventilated. A simple compost pile works well too, but bins can help contain and speed up the process.
- **Base Layer:** Start with a layer of brown materials like straw or cardboard at the base of the pile. This allows air to circulate from the bottom and helps prevent compaction.

Step 2: Layer Green and Brown Materials

Create alternating layers of green and brown materials to maintain the right balance of nitrogen and carbon, essential for effective decomposition.

- **Green Layer:** Add your vegetable scraps, grass clippings and coffee grounds.
- **Brown Layer:** Follow up with dry leaves, shredded paper, or straw. These layers help absorb moisture and prevent the pile from becoming too wet.

Step 3: Keep it Moist

The compost pile should be kept moist but not soggy. Think of it like a wrung-out sponge.

- **Watering:** If the pile is too dry, sprinkle some water over it to maintain moisture. If it's too wet, add more carbon-rich materials, such as dried leaves or straw to absorb excess water.

Step 4: Turn the Pile

Turning the compost pile introduces oxygen, which accelerates the breakdown of organic materials.

- **When to Turn**: Every two to three weeks, use a pitchfork or shovel to mix the pile. This adds oxygen, which helps the microorganisms break down the organic material more quickly.
- **Check for Heat**: A properly functioning compost pile will heat up, reaching temperatures of 130–160°F, which helps kill off weed seeds and pathogens.

Step 5: Harvest Compost

After about six to twelve months, your compost will be ready to use.

- **Finished Compost**: The compost will be dark, crumbly, and have an earthy smell. You can now mix it into your garden beds, enriching the soil with vital nutrients.

Expert Tip:

Chop larger materials like sticks or vegetable scraps into smaller pieces before adding them to the pile. This speeds up the decomposition process and helps your compost break down more evenly.

With the foundational principles of soil management, water conservation, and garden structures now in place, you've taken the first crucial steps toward building a thriving, self-sustaining garden. These core techniques will not only help you cultivate healthy plants but also ensure long-term resilience in your off-grid lifestyle. As you continue on your gardening journey, these basics will serve as the backbone for more advanced methods, which we will explore in the next volume. By mastering these essentials, you're well on your way to creating a productive and sustainable food source for years to come.

15. Advanced Gardening Techniques: Self-Sustaining Systems and Production

After laying the groundwork with foundational gardening skills, the next step in your journey toward true off-grid self-sufficiency is mastering advanced techniques. While creating a sustainable garden begins with the basics of soil, water, and structure, the real key to long-term productivity lies in refining these systems and expanding your capabilities. This volume delves into the more complex aspects of gardening that allow you to produce more food, conserve resources, and foster a garden that can support you year-round.

In Foundations of Sustainable Gardening, you established the essential elements needed to cultivate a resilient garden. Now, it's time to build on that foundation, enhancing your methods through innovative techniques like aquaponics, vertical gardening, and advanced pest control strategies. These approaches will not only help you maximize your harvests but also create a more integrated, self-sustaining ecosystem within your garden.

Whether you're looking to increase efficiency, diversify your crops, or extend your growing season, this book is designed to guide you through the next phase of your off-grid gardening experience. From setting up aquaponic systems that produce both fish and vegetables to learning how to protect your garden from pests naturally, you'll be equipped with the knowledge needed to ensure your garden thrives in any environment.

This introduction to advanced gardening techniques serves as your gateway to the next level of self-sufficiency, building on the strong foundation you've already created. Together, these methods will deepen your connection to the land and solidify your ability to produce your own food, no matter the challenges ahead.

Aquaponics: A Self-Sustaining Food and Water System

Aquaponics is a brilliant combination of aquaculture (fish farming) and hydroponics (soilless plant cultivation), where the two systems work together: fish waste acts as a nutrient-rich fertilizer for the plants, and the plants, in turn, purify the water for the fish. It's an incredibly efficient, self-sustaining method for producing food, making it ideal for off-grid living. With the right setup, you can grow fresh vegetables and raise fish for food simultaneously while conserving water and minimizing the need for external resources.

Benefits of Aquaponics:

- **Water Efficiency**: Aquaponics conserves up to 90% more water compared to traditional soil-based gardening, making it perfect for regions where water is scarce.
- **Dual Yield**: You can produce both fish and vegetables in the same system.
- **No Soil Needed**: Ideal for those with poor soil quality or no land space for a traditional garden.

Step-by-Step Guide to Setting Up an Aquaponics System

Step 1: Set Up a Fish Tank

The fish tank is the heart of your aquaponics system. Start with hardy fish species that are easy to maintain, such as tilapia or catfish.

- **Size**: The size of the tank depends on how many plants you want to grow and the space available. For a beginner, a 100-gallon tank is sufficient.
- **Location**: Place the tank in an area with partial sunlight, ideally outdoors or in a greenhouse.
- **Stocking**: Start with fewer fish (1 fish per 5 gallons of water) to prevent overloading the system initially. You can always add more later as the system stabilizes.

Step 2: Build or Install Grow Beds

The grow beds sit above or beside the fish tank and are where your plants will thrive, supported by nutrient-rich water from the fish tank.

- **Media**: Fill the grow beds with inert media like gravel, expanded clay pellets, or lava rock. These provide a stable environment for plant roots and allow beneficial bacteria to break down fish waste into nutrients.
- **Size and Setup**: Ensure the grow beds are proportional to the fish tank—about half the tank's volume in grow bed space. Position them to allow water from the fish tank to flow freely through the media and back into the tank.

Step 3: Install a Water Circulation System

Water must be continually circulated between the fish tank and the grow beds for your aquaponics system to function. This is where pumps and gravity come into play.

- **Pump**: Install a submersible water pump in the fish tank to move water up into the grow beds. The pump should be able to circulate the entire tank's volume at least once per hour.
- **Plumbing**: Use PVC pipes to direct the water flow from the fish tank to the grow beds. Ensure proper drainage back to the tank, allowing gravity to return the filtered water.

Step 4: Monitor Water Quality and Balance

Maintaining a healthy balance in your aquaponics system is essential to ensuring that both the fish and plants flourish.

- **pH Levels**: The ideal pH range for an aquaponics system is between 6.8 and 7.2. Test your water regularly with a pH testing kit and adjust as necessary with natural pH adjusters.
- **Ammonia, Nitrites, and Nitrates**: Test for ammonia, nitrite, and nitrate levels using a water test kit. Ammonia and nitrites should remain at 0 ppm, while nitrates (which feed plants) should be kept below 50 ppm. This balance ensures healthy fish and plant growth.

Step 5: Introduce Plants

Once the water circulation system is up and running, it's time to plant your crops.

- **Best Plants for Aquaponics**: Leafy greens like lettuce, spinach, and herbs like basil are excellent for beginners. You can also grow tomatoes, cucumbers, and peppers once your system matures.
- **Planting Method**: Insert seeds or seedlings directly into the media. The nutrient-rich water will provide everything the plants need to grow. Ensure adequate spacing between plants to allow for proper growth.

Pro Tip:

Add an aerator or air pump to the fish tank to keep oxygen levels high. This is critical for the health of your fish and the efficiency of the system.

Pest Control: Natural Solutions to Common Problems

Even in a well-maintained off-grid garden, pests can become a challenge. Instead of relying on chemical pesticides, which aren't sustainable for off-grid living, you can turn to natural methods that protect your plants and keep your environment healthy. By combining companion planting, natural sprays, and other eco-friendly approaches like diatomaceous earth, you can maintain a balanced, pest-resistant garden.

Natural Pest Control Solutions

1. Companion Planting

Companion planting is a highly effective method for deterring pests naturally. By planting specific plants together, you create natural barriers that protect your crops without needing synthetic chemicals.

- Best Companion Plants:
  - *Marigolds*: Repel nematodes and aphids.
  - *Basil*: Keeps flies, mosquitoes, and beetles away.
  - *Garlic and Onions*: Naturally repel aphids, mites, and other pests.

Implementation: Plant marigolds, basil, or garlic around crops like tomatoes, peppers, and leafy greens. These plants act as a natural shield, preventing pests from harming your garden.

Pro Tip: Add aromatic herbs like rosemary or lavender to further deter pests. Their strong scents confuse and repel harmful insects.

2. Neem Oil Spray

Neem oil is a versatile and natural pesticide, perfect for dealing with soft-bodied pests like aphids, mites, and whiteflies. It disrupts their life cycle without harming beneficial insects.

- How to Use:
  - Mix 2 tablespoons of neem oil with 1 gallon of water.
  - Add a few drops of dish soap to help the solution adhere better to the plants.
  - Spray the solution on the leaves, covering both sides. Apply weekly or after rain for maximum protection.

Neem oil is a safe and eco-friendly option, especially for an off-grid garden where chemical-free solutions are preferred.

3. Diatomaceous Earth

Diatomaceous earth is a non-toxic, natural powder derived from fossilized diatoms. It's highly effective against crawling pests such as ants, beetles, and slugs by damaging their exoskeletons, causing dehydration.

- How to Use:
  - Dust a thin layer of food-grade diatomaceous earth around the base of plants and along pathways where pests are known to travel.
  - Reapply after rain, as moisture can reduce its effectiveness.

Diatomaceous earth is safe for humans, pets, and beneficial insects like bees, making it a great addition to your natural pest control toolkit.

Pro Tip: Use diatomaceous earth in dry conditions for optimal results. Apply it early in the morning when the ground is still damp with dew to ensure it sticks to pests as they move.

4. Handpicking Pests

For larger pests, such as caterpillars and beetles, handpicking can be an effective and chemical-free method. While it requires regular monitoring, it's a straightforward way to protect your plants.

- **Method**: Inspect your plants every few days, particularly the undersides of leaves where pests like to hide. Pick off any visible pests and drop them into soapy water to kill them.

Step-by-Step Pest Management

Step 1: Plant Companion Crops

- Interplant companion plants like marigolds, basil, or garlic near crops vulnerable to pests. This method works best if implemented early in the growing season.

Step 2: Monitor for Damage

- Conduct weekly checks for indications of pest damage, including leaf holes or wilting. Early detection prevents infestations from spreading.

Step 3: Apply Natural Remedies

- For plants showing signs of pests, apply neem oil or dust with diatomaceous earth to protect them. Reapply these solutions after rain or as needed.

Pro Tip: Encourage beneficial insects like ladybugs and praying mantises by planting dill, fennel, or sunflowers. These natural predators help keep harmful pest populations in check, creating a balanced ecosystem in your garden.

Extending Your Growing Season: Greenhouses and Cold Frames

Growing your own food year-round is one of the key benefits of off-grid living, and extending your growing season helps maximize your harvests, even in colder months. By using greenhouses and cold frames, you can protect your crops from frost and create a controlled environment that supports plant growth, no matter the season. Whether you live in a region with severe winters or just want to boost your food production, these structures will provide the necessary shelter to keep your garden productive.

Cold Frames

Cold frames are simple, low-cost structures designed to shield plants from frost and extend their growing season. They act as mini-greenhouses, capturing solar heat and maintaining a more stable temperature inside, perfect for cool-weather crops like leafy greens, carrots, and herbs.

Materials You'll Need:

- Wooden planks or reclaimed materials for the frame
- An old window, glass door, or clear plastic for the top
- Hinges for easy opening and closing
- Soil and mulch for insulation

Step-by-Step Cold Frame Setup:

1. **Choose the Right Spot**: Place your cold frame in a south-facing location with plenty of sunlight throughout the day. The more sun it gets, the warmer it will be inside.
2. **Build the Frame**: Use untreated wood or other natural materials to build a frame that's roughly 12–24 inches tall. The back should be slightly higher than the front to allow for slanted glass, which maximizes sunlight exposure.
3. **Add the Lid**: Attach the window or clear plastic sheet to the top of the frame with hinges. This makes it easy to open during warmer parts of the day to avoid overheating and promote airflow.
4. **Insulate for Extra Warmth**: If you're expecting harsh cold, add a layer of mulch or straw around the outside of the frame to help keep it insulated.
5. **Monitor Temperature**: Open the cold frame on warm, sunny days to prevent the plants from overheating. Close it during cold nights to trap heat.

Pro Tip: If you're in a region with heavy snowfall, make sure the lid is sturdy enough to withstand the weight, or plan to regularly brush snow off to keep sunlight coming in.

Greenhouses

Greenhouses offer even more protection, providing a warm, controlled environment where you can grow crops all year long. They allow for a more diverse range of plants, including those that typically wouldn't survive in colder climates.

Materials You'll Need:

- PVC pipes or wood for framing
- Clear plastic sheeting or glass for covering
- Raised beds or planters for growing crops
- Ventilation system (vents or fans)

Step-by-Step Greenhouse Setup:

1. **Choose a Location**: Like cold frames, your greenhouse should be in a spot that receives full sun exposure, preferably facing south. This will ensure the plants inside get plenty of light.
2. **Build the Frame**: Use PVC pipes or wood to construct the framework. The size can vary depending on how much space you have, but a simple tunnel or A-frame structure works well for beginners.
3. **Cover the Frame**: Stretch clear plastic sheeting tightly over the frame, securing it with clips or nails. Make sure it's taut to avoid flapping in the wind and to provide a stable environment inside. If you're using glass, ensure all panes are securely fastened.
4. **Install Shelving or Raised Beds**: Organize your plants with shelving to make the most of vertical space or use raised beds to keep the plants warm and well-drained. Raised beds also provide additional protection from frost creeping in from the ground.
5. **Add Ventilation**: To prevent your greenhouse from overheating, install windows or vents that can be opened during the warmer part of the day. A small fan can help circulate air and maintain even temperatures inside.

Pro Tip: Use thermal mass—such as water barrels painted black—to absorb warmth throughout the day and slowly emit it during the night, keeping your greenhouse at a more stable temperature.

Tips for Extending Your Growing Season

1. **Grow Cool-Weather Crops**: Focus on plants that naturally thrive in cooler conditions, such as spinach, kale, lettuce, carrots, and broccoli. These crops don't require intense heat and will continue to produce well into the winter with a little protection.
2. **Use Row Covers Inside**: Even within a greenhouse or cold frame, using lightweight row covers can provide additional insulation for your plants, especially on extremely cold nights.
3. **Monitor Temperature and Humidity**: Keep a close eye on temperature and humidity levels inside the greenhouse or cold frame. Opening the lids or vents during warm spells will prevent overheating, while closing them at the right time ensures the plants stay protected during cold spells.

Final Thoughts: A Balanced Approach to Year-Round Production

Creating a self-sustaining garden is not an overnight achievement, but with patience, persistence, and a clear plan, you can gradually transform your outdoor space into a reliable food source that serves you year-round. Whether you're starting with a small raised bed or aiming for a complex aquaponics system, the key is to take it one step at a time and adapt your approach as you learn in this guide and in the previous one.

Begin with manageable projects like raised bed gardening, where you can control soil quality and make the most of your space. As you grow more confident, experiment with other techniques like vertical gardening, which maximizes limited space, or hügelkultur, which creates nutrient-rich soil that requires less maintenance. If you're aiming to elevate your sustainability to the next level, consider incorporating aquaponics, a highly efficient system that produces both fish and vegetables while conserving water.

Pro Tip: Adaptability is Key

As an off-grid gardener, you'll quickly learn that nature doesn't always cooperate with your plans. Be ready to adapt based on what your climate and soil are telling you. Observe the growth patterns of your plants, note what techniques work best for your environment, and don't hesitate to make adjustments. Keep a journal to document your progress—this will help you refine your strategy year after year.

Step-by-Step Guidance for Long-Term Success:

1. **Start Small**: Focus on building confidence and learning the basics of gardening with small projects like raised beds or simple cold frames.
2. **Expand Gradually**: Once you've mastered the essentials, introduce new techniques like vertical gardening or hugelkultur to diversify your growing methods and increase your yield.
3. **Incorporate Water Efficiency**: As your garden grows, invest in water-saving methods like drip irrigation or rainwater harvesting. This ensures that even during dry spells, your plants are getting the water they need without unnecessary waste.
4. **Plan for All Seasons**: Utilize greenhouses and cold frames to protect your crops and extend your growing season. With a little effort, you can harvest fresh produce even in the middle of winter.
5. **Stay Flexible**: Gardening is an ongoing learning process. Be open to experimenting, and if something doesn't work, tweak it. There's always another season to improve upon your efforts.

A Sustainable Lifestyle

By dedicating time and energy to creating a year-round garden, you not only secure a fresh food source but also cultivate a deeper connection with the land. This garden becomes a representation of your off-grid lifestyle—a practical tool for survival and a symbol of your self-reliance.

Pro Tip: The Joy of Self-Sufficiency

The satisfaction that comes from growing your own food is unmatched. It's more than just sustenance—it's knowing that your efforts directly contribute to your independence. Celebrate every small victory, from the first ripe tomato to your flourishing garden at the peak of summer. These moments will remind you why you embarked on this journey in the first place.

The Journey Ahead

With each new season, you'll fine-tune your approach, build on your successes, and adapt to the challenges that come your way. The key to a thriving, self-sustaining garden is continuous learning and a willingness to grow alongside your plants. Keep nurturing, keep experimenting, and enjoy the fruits of your labor. Before long, your garden will be a thriving ecosystem that sustains you in every season, providing nourishment and peace of mind.

With thoughtful planning and steady effort, your garden will not only meet your needs but exceed your expectations, helping you truly live off the land in harmony with nature.

16. Raising Small Livestock: Chickens, Rabbits

Raising livestock is one of the most fulfilling ways to guarantee a sustainable and reliable food source when living off the grid. Whether you're new to this lifestyle or experienced, raising animals such as chickens and rabbits can provide a steady supply of eggs, meat, and natural resources. These smaller livestock options are ideal for beginners due to their low maintenance and adaptability. As you gain confidence and experience, you can explore expanding into larger animals like pigs and cattle, which will be discussed in the following book. In this guide, we'll walk you through the step-by-step process of raising chickens and rabbits, two of the easiest and most rewarding animals to start with. By the end, you'll have the knowledge and practical know-how to manage a small flock and harvest meat when necessary.

Starting with Chickens: Your First Step

Chickens are the perfect starting point for anyone new to raising livestock off the grid. They are low-maintenance, adaptable, and provide two essential resources: eggs and meat. Additionally, they require minimal space and are relatively inexpensive to feed, making them ideal for beginners. Here's how you can get started with your flock.

Step-by-Step: Raising Chickens

Set Up a Coop:

The coop is your chickens' home, and it needs to be secure and predator-proof to keep your flock safe. Here's how to set up a coop that ensures your chickens stay healthy and productive:

- **Space**: A helpful guideline is to allow 2 to 3 square feet of space per bird within the coop. This gives them enough room to roost, lay eggs, and move around comfortably.
- **Nesting Boxes**: You'll need nesting boxes where your hens can lay their eggs. Plan for one nesting box for every 3-4 hens. Keep the boxes filled with clean bedding like straw or hay.
- **Ventilation**: Proper airflow is critical to prevent moisture buildup, which can lead to respiratory problems or mold in the coop. Ensure there are windows or vents that allow fresh air to circulate.
- **Perches**: Chickens like to roost on perches at night. Add perches inside the coop that are about 1-2 feet off the ground.

Pro Tip: To keep predators like foxes or raccoons from digging under the coop, bury hardware cloth (a strong wire mesh) about 12 inches deep around the perimeter.

Feeding and Watering:

Chickens require a balanced diet to stay healthy and productive. Here's how to keep their nutrition and hydration on track:

- **Feed**: Provide high-quality chicken feed, which you can supplement with kitchen scraps, garden waste, and grains. Let them forage for insects and greens if you allow them to free-range, which will reduce feed costs and improve egg quality.
- **Water**: Always have a constant supply of clean, fresh water. Make sure the water container is elevated or placed in a way that keeps dirt and debris from contaminating it.

Pro Tip: Adding apple cider vinegar to your chickens' water can boost their immune system and keep their digestive tract healthy.

Egg Collection:

Daily egg collection is essential to maintain hygiene and avoid attracting predators. Here's what to keep in mind:

- Collect eggs at least once a day, preferably in the morning.
- If you leave eggs too long in the nesting boxes, they can become dirty or get broken. Additionally, hens may start eating them, which can become a habit.
- Gently clean any dirty eggs by wiping them with a dry cloth. Avoid washing them unless absolutely necessary, as washing can remove the protective bloom that keeps the egg fresh longer.

Pro Tip: Rotate your hens into different areas to graze. This not only keeps their diet diverse but also allows your land to recover, reducing wear on the soil.

Basic Health Care:

While chickens are generally hardy, they are susceptible to common issues like mites, respiratory infections, and egg-laying problems. Here's how to keep them healthy:

- **Coop Maintenance**: Keep the coop dry and clean. Replace bedding regularly, and remove waste to prevent the spread of diseases.
- **Mite Control**: Dust baths are a natural way for chickens to control mites. Provide a dry area filled with dirt, sand, and wood ash where chickens can bathe.
- **Disease Prevention**: If you notice any chickens with signs of illness (such as coughing, sneezing, or lethargy), isolate them from the flock immediately. Consult a local vet or use herbal remedies to treat common issues like respiratory infections.

Pro Tip: Adding garlic and apple cider vinegar to their feed or water occasionally can boost their immune systems and keep internal parasites at bay.

Slaughtering Chickens for Meat

Harvesting your chickens for meat is a necessary part of raising livestock, and doing it humanely and efficiently is key. Here's a detailed step-by-step guide to walk you through the process.

Step 1: Catching the Chicken

Gently catch the chicken, ensuring you don't stress or injure the bird. It's easiest to catch chickens at night when they're calm or early in the morning while still in the coop. Once caught, place the chicken into a restraining cone or tie its legs securely.

Step 2: Slaughter

The most humane way to slaughter a chicken is by cutting the artery in the neck. Here's how to do it:

- Position the chicken in the cone with its head pointing downward. This keeps the bird calm and minimizes movement.
- Using a sharp knife, swiftly cut the artery on the side of the neck. This allows the blood to drain quickly, ensuring a humane death.

Pro Tip: Make sure your knife is very sharp to avoid prolonging the process and causing unnecessary pain to the animal.

Step 3: Plucking and Butchering

After slaughter, the next step is plucking and butchering the chicken. This is essential to prepare the bird for cooking or storage:

- **Scalding**: To loosen the feathers, submerge the bird in hot water (about 140°F) for 30-60 seconds. This will make plucking the feathers much easier.

- **Plucking**: After scalding, manually pluck the feathers from the chicken. You can use a mechanical plucker if available, but hand-plucking works just as well for small-scale operations.
- **Butchering**: Once the bird is plucked, make an incision at the base of the breastbone. Carefully remove the internal organs, being sure not to puncture the intestines. Rinse the bird thoroughly inside and out to remove any remaining blood or debris.

Pro Tip: Save the internal organs (liver, heart, gizzard) for use in soups, stocks, or pâtés. They are nutritious and flavorful.

Raising chickens is an incredibly rewarding and practical way to secure a steady supply of food in an off-grid setting. Not only will you gain fresh eggs and meat, but you'll also develop valuable skills in animal care and sustainability. By following these simple, actionable steps, you'll have a healthy, productive flock that provides for you and your family.

Rabbits: A Great Source of Lean Meat

Rabbits are an ideal livestock option for those starting their off-grid journey. They are highly efficient in terms of space and resources, reproduce quickly, and provide lean, high-protein meat. Whether you're aiming to diversify your food supply or looking for a sustainable source of meat, rabbits are a great choice. In this section, I'll guide you through the essential steps of raising and caring for rabbits, followed by a clear, humane process for harvesting their meat.

Step-by-Step: Raising Rabbits

Housing Your Rabbits

Building a proper hutch or cage is the first step to raising healthy rabbits. Here's what you need to keep in mind:
- **Space Requirements**: Each rabbit needs about 3-4 square feet of space. Make sure their housing allows enough room for movement but is also secure from predators. A simple wooden hutch or a wire cage with a solid base works well.
- **Ventilation**: Rabbits are sensitive to heat and poor air circulation, so ensure their hutch has proper ventilation. Open sides with a roof will allow for airflow while protecting them from rain and harsh weather.
- **Bedding**: Use straw or hay as bedding material. It provides comfort, absorbs moisture, and can be easily replaced.
- **Predator Protection**: Ensure the enclosure is sturdy and elevated to prevent predators like foxes or raccoons from accessing your rabbits.

Pro Tip: Place the hutch in a shaded area during summer months to keep the rabbits cool. Extreme heat can stress them, so try to avoid direct sunlight.

Feeding Your Rabbits

Rabbits are low-maintenance when it comes to feeding. Here's how to keep them healthy and nourished:
- **Primary Diet**: Hay should make up the bulk of their diet, as it aids digestion and maintains dental health. Fresh, green hay is ideal.
- **Supplementary Feed**: Offer fresh greens like dandelion leaves, clover, and vegetable scraps from your garden. Commercial rabbit pellets can also be included to ensure a balanced diet.
- **Water Supply**: Always provide fresh, clean water. Use a hanging water bottle or a bowl, and make sure it is always filled.

Pro Tip: Rotate the types of greens and vegetables you feed your rabbits to avoid any nutrient imbalances. Introduce new foods gradually to prevent digestive issues.

Breeding and Growth

One of the major benefits of raising rabbits is their rapid reproduction. Here's how to manage breeding effectively:

- **Breeding Cycle**: A female rabbit (doe) can start breeding at 6 months old. Rabbits have a short gestation period of about 30 days, and a single pair can produce multiple litters per year.
- **Litter Size**: Each litter can consist of 6-12 kits (baby rabbits), making it easy to scale up your meat production quickly.
- **Weaning**: Kits can be weaned from their mother at about 4-6 weeks old. At this point, they can begin eating solid food.

Pro Tip: To avoid overbreeding, separate the male rabbits (bucks) from the females when not intending to breed. This also helps maintain the health of the breeding does.

Slaughtering Rabbits for Meat

Harvesting rabbits is straightforward but requires care and skill. Here's how to do it humanely and efficiently:

Stunning the Rabbit

The first step is to stun the rabbit to ensure a quick and humane process:

- **How to Stun**: Hold the rabbit securely and deliver a swift, firm hit to the back of its head. This will render the rabbit unconscious, reducing any stress or pain during the slaughter process.

Pro Tip: Practice this technique carefully beforehand to ensure you can perform it swiftly and effectively when the time comes.

Bleeding the Rabbit

Once the rabbit is stunned, the next step is to bleed it:

- **How to Bleed**: After stunning, hang the rabbit by its back legs. Using a sharp knife, make a clean cut at the throat to allow the blood to drain fully.

Pro Tip: Always use a sharp knife to minimize pain and ensure a clean cut. Dull blades can make the process more difficult and stressful for both you and the rabbit.

Skinning and Gutting the Rabbit

Now that the rabbit has been bled, you can move on to skinning and gutting:

- **Skinning**: Make a small incision at the hind legs, near the feet, and start peeling the skin downward like a glove. Rabbit skins come off easily, so this step should be smooth once you get the hang of it.
- **Gutting**: Once the skin is removed, open the belly with a careful incision and remove the internal organs. Take care not to puncture the intestines, as this could contaminate the meat.

Pro Tip: Save the organs like the liver, heart, and kidneys—they are highly nutritious and can be used in soups or stews.

Starting your off-grid journey with chickens and rabbits is an excellent way to build a sustainable, reliable food system. These animals are manageable, productive, and offer valuable resources like eggs, meat, and manure to support your self-sufficient lifestyle. By mastering the basics outlined in this guide, you'll be well-prepared to expand your livestock operation and take the next steps toward larger-scale farming with pigs and cattle, which will be covered in the following book. Keep refining your skills, and enjoy the rewards of a thriving, sustainable homestead.

17. Advanced Livestock and Integrated Systems: Pigs Goats, and Cattle

Pigs: A Larger Meat Source

After mastering chickens and rabbits, raising pigs is the logical next step for increasing your meat production. Pigs are versatile, grow quickly, and can thrive on a varied diet of kitchen scraps, grains, and garden waste. As you progress, this book will also guide you through raising goats and cattle, which offer valuable sources of milk and meat, as well as the essentials of beekeeping, providing honey and natural pollination for your crops. These steps will further enhance the sustainability of your off-grid lifestyle.

Step-by-Step: Raising Pigs

Housing Your Pigs

Pigs are strong animals, so their housing must be robust:

- **Sturdy Pen**: Pigs need a sturdy enclosure that can withstand their rooting behavior. Use strong fencing and make sure there's a covered area to protect them from extreme weather.
- **Space**: Each pig should have at least 50-100 square feet of space. Pigs enjoy rooting and need enough room to roam and stay healthy.

Pro Tip: Pigs are excellent at turning over soil and clearing land. If you have overgrown areas, let them work the land while they forage.

Feeding and Growth

Pigs are omnivores, and their diet can include a wide variety of foods:

- **Feed Variety**: You can feed pigs food scraps, grains, garden waste, and even forage. Make sure their diet is balanced to support fast growth.
- **Water Supply**: Fresh water is essential. Use automatic waterers or large troughs to ensure they stay hydrated.

Pro Tip: Incorporating a variety of foods into your pigs' diet not only saves on feed costs but also results in better-tasting pork.

Breeding Pigs

Pigs are prolific breeders, and you can easily grow your herd:

- **Breeding Age**: Pigs can start breeding at about 6-8 months old. Sows typically have litters of 8-12 piglets, which are ready for weaning after about 6 weeks.

Pro Tip: Separate pregnant sows from the rest of the herd in the later stages of pregnancy to prevent stress and ensure a safe birth.

Harvesting Pork

Slaughtering pigs is a more complex process than harvesting smaller animals like rabbits or chickens, often requiring extra help:

Slaughtering Pigs

It's best to work with an experienced butcher or have someone assist you:

- **Stunning**: Pigs are typically stunned using a captive bolt or gunshot to the head. This ensures a humane and quick process.
- **Bleeding and Scalding**: After stunning, the pig is bled out by cutting the main artery in the neck. The carcass is then scalded in hot water to loosen the hair, making it easier to remove.

Pro Tip: Scalding and scraping can be labor-intensive, but it is crucial for removing the tough hair on the pig's skin. Use a large tub or trough for this step.

Butchering the Pig

Once the pig has been cleaned, it's time to butcher the meat:

- **Breaking Down the Carcass**: Divide the pig into primal cuts such as the shoulder, loin, ham, and ribs. These cuts can be further processed into pork chops, bacon, sausage, and roasts.

Pro Tip: Save every part of the pig—fat can be rendered into lard, bones can be used for broth, and scraps can be turned into sausages. Nothing should go to waste.

Goats and Cattle: Milk and Meat for Sustainable Off-Grid Living

Expanding your livestock to include goats and cattle is a powerful way to ensure a steady supply of both milk and meat. These animals not only provide essential nutrition, but they also help create a sustainable off-grid farm. Goats are a more manageable option for smaller properties, while cattle are ideal if you have ample space and resources. Let's break down how to raise both goats and cattle effectively, focusing on practical, step-by-step guidance to ensure success.

Step-by-Step: Raising Goats

Goats are an excellent addition to any off-grid homestead due to their versatility. They can be raised for both milk and meat, are relatively low-maintenance, and adapt well to different climates and environments. Here's how to get started:

Housing for Goats

Goats need secure, comfortable housing that allows them to roam but also protects them from predators and harsh weather:

- **Space Requirements**: Each goat should have access to at least 15 square feet of indoor shelter, with an additional 25-50 square feet of outdoor roaming space. Ensure there's plenty of room for grazing if possible.
- **Enclosure Setup**: Goats are excellent climbers and can jump over low fences. A sturdy fence that is at least 4 feet high is essential to prevent escapes. Ensure the shelter is windproof, waterproof, and well-ventilated.
- **Bedding**: Use straw or wood shavings as bedding, which should be replaced regularly to keep the shelter clean and dry.

Pro Tip: Goats love to climb and explore, so adding logs or raised platforms inside their enclosure can keep them entertained and prevent boredom.

Feeding Your Goats

Goats are browsers, meaning they prefer to eat shrubs, leaves, and a variety of plants rather than just grass:

- **Primary Diet**: The majority of a goat's diet should consist of grass, hay, and browse (shrubs, bushes). Ensure you provide high-quality hay, especially during winter or dry seasons when fresh forage is limited.
- **Supplemental Feed**: Provide goats with a mineral supplement, especially one rich in calcium and phosphorus, to support healthy milk production and overall health.

- **Water**: Always provide fresh water. Goats are notorious for tipping over water containers, so use a secure, non-tippable water trough.

Pro Tip: To avoid overeating or malnutrition, offer feed in measured amounts and monitor their intake. Goats are curious and will try to eat anything, so make sure their diet is balanced and safe.

Milk Production

Female goats, or does, are excellent milk producers. Here's how to ensure steady, high-quality milk production:

- **Milking Setup**: You'll need a clean, quiet space to milk your goats, ideally with a milking stand to keep them still. Milking should be done twice a day to maintain a steady supply.
- **Lactation**: Does typically produce milk for 8-10 months after giving birth. To keep milk production going, plan to breed your goats annually.
- **Milking Procedure**: Wash the udder with warm water and dry it before milking to ensure cleanliness. Gently squeeze the teats, starting from the top and working downward, to collect the milk.

Pro Tip: Freeze any excess milk to preserve it for later use, or use it to make cheese, yogurt, or soap. Goat milk is easier to digest than cow's milk and has a variety of uses in an off-grid home.

Step-by-Step: Raising Cattle

Cattle are a significant commitment but offer tremendous benefits in terms of both meat and milk. If you have the space and resources, they can be a cornerstone of your off-grid farm. Here's how to raise cattle efficiently:

Housing and Space for Cattle

Cattle require much more space than goats, so make sure you have ample land for grazing and shelter:

- **Pasture Space**: A small herd of cattle will need at least 1-2 acres per cow for grazing. The more land you have, the better, as it allows for natural grazing and minimizes the need for supplemental feed.
- **Shelter Requirements**: Cattle need basic shelter to protect them from extreme weather. A three-sided barn or lean-to structure is sufficient, providing shade in summer and protection from wind and rain in winter.
- **Fencing**: Use sturdy, high-tensile fencing to contain cattle. Electric fencing is also a good option to prevent cattle from wandering.

Pro Tip: Rotational grazing, where you divide the pasture into smaller sections and move cattle between them, ensures the grass has time to regrow and helps prevent overgrazing.

Feeding Your Cattle

Cattle primarily rely on grass for their diet, but they will need supplemental feed during the winter or in dry conditions:

- **Grazing**: Grass should be the main component of your cattle's diet. Ensure the pasture has a mix of grasses and legumes to provide balanced nutrition.
- **Hay and Grain**: During winter or when grass is scarce, provide hay. You can also supplement their diet with grains like corn or barley for extra calories, especially for cattle raised for meat production.
- **Water**: Cattle need access to clean water at all times. Each cow can drink up to 30 gallons of water a day, so ensure your water supply is consistent and reliable.

Pro Tip: In cold weather, cattle will need extra energy to stay warm, so adjust their feed accordingly. A high-fiber diet helps them generate heat during digestion.

Managing Cattle for Meat and Milk

Cattle can be raised for either milk or meat, depending on your needs:

- **Milk Production**: If raising dairy cows, expect a consistent supply of milk once the cow calves. Cows generally produce milk for 10 months a year and should be milked twice daily.
- **Breeding**: Plan to breed your cows annually to maintain milk production. A gestation period for cows is about 9 months, and calves are weaned after 6-8 months.
- **Meat Production**: If raising cattle for meat, focus on breeds like Angus or Hereford, known for their quality beef. Cattle are typically ready for slaughter at 18-24 months of age.

Pro Tip: Always maintain good health practices for your cattle, such as regular deworming, vaccinations, and hoof care. Healthy animals produce better meat and milk.

Expert Tips for Raising Goats and Cattle

- **Keep Records**: Track feeding schedules, health issues, and breeding cycles to ensure the well-being of your herd.
- **Get a Veterinarian**: Build a relationship with a local vet who can help with any health issues or emergencies, especially with larger animals like cattle.
- **Use Every Resource**: Goat and cattle manure can be used to enrich your soil for gardening. Composting manure creates a sustainable cycle on your homestead.

By raising goats and cattle, you significantly enhance your off-grid self-sufficiency. Goats are easier to manage, provide a consistent supply of milk, and are a great entry point for livestock farming. Cattle, while requiring more space and resources, offer larger quantities of meat and milk, making them ideal for expanding your operation. By following these step-by-step guidelines, you can create a thriving system that produces high-quality food while ensuring the long-term sustainability of your farm. Keep refining your approach, and soon you'll master the art of raising livestock for off-grid living.

As you continue your journey toward a sustainable off-grid lifestyle, the skills and knowledge gained from raising smaller livestock like chickens and rabbits (discussed in the previous book) lay the foundation for scaling up. With those initial steps mastered, this book has guided you through the more advanced and rewarding practices of raising pigs, goats, and cattle, expanding your ability to produce both meat and dairy on a larger scale. These animals not only diversify your food supply but also enhance the sustainability of your farm through integrated systems.

Pigs, as we've explored, are incredibly efficient animals that quickly contribute to your meat production. As you grow comfortable with them, introducing goats and cattle will further expand your farm's potential. Goats offer an excellent balance of manageable size, milk production, and meat, while cattle provide larger quantities of both, making them a valuable addition for those with ample space and resources. Each step toward raising these larger animals adds another layer to your self-sufficiency, increasing the variety of your food sources and ensuring long-term resilience.

As you move forward, continue to pace your growth according to your resources and experience. Start with smaller projects and animals, like those outlined in the previous book, and expand at a rate that feels manageable. Whether it's raising pigs or integrating cattle for dairy and meat, each addition to your homestead brings you closer to achieving true off-grid self-sufficiency.

The road to a fully sustainable off-grid farm is one of continuous learning and adaptation. By building on the foundational practices from the previous book and mastering the advanced techniques shared here, you'll find yourself well-equipped to create a thriving, resilient farm that supports your independence and nourishes your household for years to come. Keep expanding, keep refining, and watch your off-grid farm flourish as you continue this rewarding journey.

18. Beekeeping: Nature's Pollinators and Honey Producers

As you continue expanding your off-grid homestead, adding beekeeping to your repertoire brings an entirely new dimension to sustainable living. In previous books, we focused on the foundational aspects of raising livestock, from chickens and rabbits to pigs, goats, and cattle—ensuring a steady supply of meat, dairy, and other essential resources. Beekeeping complements these efforts by offering something equally vital but often overlooked: pollination and honey production.

While livestock provides your household with protein and nutrients, bees contribute to the broader ecosystem. Their role in pollinating plants supports your garden, fruit trees, and crops, increasing overall farm productivity. Additionally, beekeeping introduces the benefit of honey—an energy-rich, natural sweetener that can be harvested sustainably year after year. With a few hives on your property, you'll not only enrich your food supply but also ensure that your plants thrive with the help of nature's best pollinators.

In this guide, we'll walk through the simple yet fascinating process of setting up a beekeeping operation on your off-grid farm. From choosing the right type of hive to harvesting honey, this book will provide the practical know-how to get started with bees—an essential step in rounding out your sustainable, self-sufficient lifestyle.

Step-by-Step: Starting Beekeeping

Beekeeping might seem complex at first, but with the right guidance, you'll find it to be a rewarding and relatively low-maintenance activity. Follow this practical guide to get started:

Set Up a Hive

The first step to beekeeping is setting up a proper hive. You can either purchase a pre-built hive or build your own. Here's what you need to know:

- **Choosing a Hive Type**: The most common hives for beginners are **Langstroth hives**, which are made up of stacked boxes with removable frames. These are easy to manage and ideal for honey harvesting.
- **Location**: Place the hive in a sunny, sheltered spot that's protected from strong winds. Bees prefer warmth, so make sure the hive faces southeast to catch the morning sun.
- **Hive Stand**: Elevate the hive slightly off the ground to prevent moisture from accumulating and to protect it from small predators.

Expert Tip: Bees are most active during the day, so ensure your hive is located in a quiet part of your homestead where they won't be disturbed by constant activity.

Feeding and Care for Bees

Bees are efficient foragers, but in colder months, you may need to supplement their diet with sugar water to keep them strong and healthy. Here's how to care for them year-round:

- **Foraging Season**: During the warmer months, bees will forage on their own, collecting nectar and pollen from flowers within a 2-3 mile radius of the hive. Ensure your homestead has plenty of flowering plants to support their activity.
- **Winter Feeding**: As winter approaches, supplement their food supply with a mixture of sugar and water (2:1 ratio of sugar to water). Place the sugar water in a feeder inside the hive to prevent freezing.
- **Water Supply**: Bees need a consistent water source. Place a shallow water dish near the hive, and add stones or sticks so bees can land safely while drinking.

Pro Tip: Keep an eye on the hive during winter. Check for signs of condensation inside the hive, as moisture can be more dangerous to bees than cold temperatures. Proper ventilation is key to keeping the hive dry.

Harvesting Honey

After a few months, once the bees have built up their honey stores, you can start harvesting. This usually occurs in late summer or early fall, depending on your local climate and the bees' productivity.

- **Honey Super**: Place a **honey super** (a smaller box placed on top of the hive) to encourage the bees to store honey there. This makes harvesting easier and ensures you don't disturb their brood chambers.
- **Timing**: Harvest honey when the frames in the honey super are fully capped (covered with beeswax). This indicates the honey has the right moisture content and is ready for extraction.
- **Harvest Process**: Use a **honey extractor** or manually crush and strain the honey from the combs. Ensure you leave enough honey behind—about 60-80 pounds for an average-sized colony—to sustain the bees through winter.

Pro Tip: Always wear protective clothing (beekeeping suit, gloves, veil) when working with the hive. Bees are generally docile, but they can become defensive during harvesting. Move calmly to avoid agitating them.

Making a Solar Dehydrator for Preserving Meat

Once you've established a steady source of meat from your livestock, preserving it for long-term storage becomes essential. A **solar dehydrator** is a simple, off-grid solution to drying meat and making jerky. This method uses the sun's energy to remove moisture from the meat, ensuring it can be stored for months without refrigeration.

Step-by-Step: Building a Solar Dehydrator

Building your own solar dehydrator is a straightforward project that requires basic materials. Here's how to construct one and start preserving your meat:

Gather Materials

You'll need the following materials to build your solar dehydrator:

- **Wood for the Frame**: Choose untreated wood for the frame to avoid harmful chemicals leaching into your food. Pine or cedar works well.
- **Fine Mesh or Screen**: This is where you'll lay out the meat. Use a non-toxic, food-safe mesh that allows airflow while keeping insects out.
- **Glass or Clear Plastic**: This acts as the top cover, allowing sunlight to pass through while creating a greenhouse effect to dry the meat.
- **Additional Items**: Screws, nails, and hinges for assembly, and some dark paint (optional) to improve heat absorption.

Build the Dehydrator Frame

Construct a rectangular or square frame for the dehydrator. This will hold the mesh racks and the clear cover.

- **Base and Sides**: Cut the wood into the desired size for your frame. Build a slanted base so the dehydrator can catch maximum sunlight. The frame should be at least 2 feet tall and wide, depending on how much meat you want to dry at once.
- **Mesh Racks**: Inside the frame, install mesh racks to hold the meat. You'll want at least 2-3 racks spaced evenly, allowing airflow between layers. Attach the mesh securely to the frame.

Pro Tip: Paint the inside of the frame black to absorb more heat from the sun, speeding up the drying process.

Install the Clear Cover

The top cover of the dehydrator is crucial for trapping heat and creating the right environment for drying.

- **Glass or Plastic**: Attach a sheet of glass or clear plastic to the top of the frame, angled toward the sun. Make sure it fits securely to prevent moisture from getting in. You can install this cover on hinges for easy access.

Pro Tip: Place the solar dehydrator in a sunny, breezy spot where it will get at least 6 hours of sunlight a day. The airflow will help wick away moisture from the meat.

Using the Dehydrator

Once your solar dehydrator is built, it's time to put it to use.

- **Prepare the Meat**: Slice the meat into thin strips, about 1/8 to 1/4 inch thick. Season with salt, spices, or marinades as desired. Thinner slices dry faster and more evenly.
- **Lay Out the Meat**: Spread the strips of meat in a single layer on the mesh racks. Make sure they're not overlapping so air can circulate around each piece.
- **Drying Process**: Leave the meat in the dehydrator for 2-4 days, depending on the weather and how thick the slices are. Turn the meat occasionally to ensure even drying. The meat is ready when it is dry and leathery, but not brittle.

Pro Tip: To test if the meat is fully dehydrated, bend a strip. It should be flexible but firm, with no moisture visible inside. Properly dried meat will last for months when stored in an airtight container.

As you've now discovered, beekeeping is a vital aspect of fostering a thriving off-grid ecosystem. Bees play an essential role in pollinating your crops, fruit trees, and wild plants, amplifying the productivity of your entire homestead. Beyond the invaluable role of pollination, they also provide a renewable source of honey, which is both a delicious sweetener and a nutritious addition to your off-grid pantry.

Like the livestock and agricultural skills discussed in previous books, beekeeping helps ensure a balanced, self-sustaining environment. Bees may be small, but their impact on your farm's resilience and productivity is enormous. By understanding their habits, nurturing their colonies, and practicing sustainable harvesting techniques, you're adding another layer of security and sustainability to your off-grid lifestyle.

As you continue on this journey, remember that each element—whether it's raising animals, growing food, or keeping bees—works together in harmony. This holistic approach will strengthen your homestead, ensuring that it flourishes for years to come. Keep honing your skills, expanding your knowledge, and enjoying the rich rewards that come with true self-reliance. Your bees will not only provide you with honey, but they will also be an enduring symbol of the natural balance and sustainability you've worked so hard to create.

19. Off-Grid Food Preservation: Tools and Techniques for Long-Term Survival

Preserving food off-grid is a natural next step after raising livestock and cultivating a garden, both of which were covered in earlier sections. While you've learned how to raise animals for meat, eggs, and dairy, and how to grow a productive garden, this guide now focuses on ensuring those resources are available long after the harvest, covering the essential tools and methods needed to ensure your harvested produce and prepared foods remain safe and usable for the long term. From canning to dehydrating and root cellar storage, you'll learn the key techniques that will help you store food effectively, without relying on electricity or modern conveniences.

Equipping Yourself for Off-Grid Preservation Success

Before you dive into any preservation project, having the proper tools is crucial. When you're living off the grid, you need to rely on durable, non-electric equipment that will stand the test of time and function reliably without modern conveniences. Here's what you need to get started.

Gathering the Right Tools for Preservation

Start by choosing high-quality, long-lasting equipment. This isn't the place to cut corners—your tools need to last. Here's a basic checklist to follow:

- **Hand-Operated Jar Lifters**: These are essential for safely removing hot jars from boiling water.
- **Non-Electric Canning Funnels**: A funnel will help you avoid spills and keep jar rims clean, which is critical for creating a proper seal.
- **Mason Jars**: Invest in heavy-duty jars like Ball or Kerr, which are designed to withstand repeated use and temperature fluctuations.
- **Manual Grinders & Choppers**: These will save you time when prepping fruits and vegetables without electricity.

By having reliable tools, you set yourself up for success in off-grid food preservation. Make sure you also stock up on replacement parts, such as extra rubber seals and lids for your jars, so you're not caught unprepared.

Ensuring Proper Sterilization with Off-Grid Solutions

Sterilization is non-negotiable. Contaminated jars or tools can lead to spoiled food and serious health risks. But how do you sterilize without electricity? Follow these steps:

1. **Boiling Water Sterilization**: Boil your jars and tools in a large pot over an open flame or a solar-powered heat source. Ensure they are submerged in boiling water for at least 10 minutes to kill bacteria and mold.
2. **Solar Sterilization**: If firewood or fuel is scarce, a solar cooker can do the job. Set up your solar cooker, place your tools inside, and let the sun work its magic. This may take longer than boiling, so plan accordingly.
3. **Alcohol Wipes for Utensils**: For smaller tools like canning funnels or jar lifters, wipe them down with alcohol-soaked cloths for added sterilization before use.

Proper sterilization will prevent the growth of harmful bacteria like botulism, so never skip this step.

Building a Root Cellar for Year-Round Storage

A root cellar is an off-grid game changer. It naturally keeps food cool, extending the life of fruits, vegetables, and even canned goods without electricity. Building one may seem intimidating, but with the right approach, you can create a reliable storage space that lasts for years.

Selecting and Preparing the Perfect Location

To ensure your root cellar functions efficiently year-round, choosing the right location is key:

- **Natural Shade and Drainage**: Select a spot that naturally stays cool, such as on the north side of a hill or under tree cover. Avoid areas prone to flooding—proper drainage is critical.

- **Slope for Insulation**: If possible, build on a slope to take advantage of natural insulation and airflow. A sloped site will help regulate temperature inside the cellar.

- **Distance from Your Shelter**: Keep your root cellar close enough to your home for convenience, but far enough to avoid heat from your living space.

Constructing Your Root Cellar for Optimal Storage

Once you've chosen your location, it's time to build:

1. **Excavation**: Dig deep—aim for at least 8 to 10 feet underground. This depth helps maintain a stable temperature of around 32-40°F, perfect for preserving food.
2. **Insulation**: Line the walls with natural materials like stone or wood to create insulation. You can also use straw bales or earth bags for added thermal mass.
3. **Ventilation**: Install two pipes—one near the floor and one near the ceiling—to ensure proper airflow. This prevents condensation and mold, keeping your food dry and safe.
4. **Shelving**: Build sturdy shelves to keep your food off the floor, which helps prevent moisture buildup. Use untreated wood or metal racks to avoid contamination.

Pro Tips for Root Cellar Success

- **Monitor the Temperature**: A thermometer will help you track the internal temperature. Too hot, and your food will spoil; too cold, and it may freeze.
- **Pest Control**: Seal all entry points to keep rodents and insects out. Consider adding a wire mesh barrier around the entrance.
- **Seasonal Adjustments**: In extreme heat or cold, add or remove insulation as needed to maintain the optimal temperature.

With your root cellar in place, you'll have a reliable, year-round storage solution that keeps your food fresh and safe, no matter the season.

Supplementing Your Off-Grid Pantry: Long-Lasting Supermarket Foods for Emergencies

While your off-grid food sources—such as homegrown vegetables, fruits, and livestock—are the foundation of your self-sufficient lifestyle, it's always wise to keep additional food reserves. Certain supermarket products have long shelf lives and can serve as an emergency buffer when your off-grid reserves are low, or you face unforeseen circumstances.

In this section, we'll go over a list of supermarket foods that store well and can easily be integrated into your stockpile. These hybrid resources are affordable, durable, and ensure you're always prepared, no matter what.

1. Dried Grains and Legumes

Dried grains and legumes are nutritional staples that can last for years when stored properly. They provide essential carbohydrates and proteins, making them valuable for long-term storage.

- **Rice (White Rice)**: Can last **30+ years** when stored in an airtight container or Mylar bags with oxygen absorbers. Brown rice, though nutritious, has a shorter shelf life due to its higher fat content (around **6 months to 1 year**).
- **Pasta**: Stores well for **2-3 years**, and is a versatile base for many meals.
- **Lentils and Dried Beans**: Last **10+ years** when stored properly. These can be used in soups, stews, or as side dishes, and provide a solid source of plant-based protein.
- **Quinoa**: Has a shelf life of **2-3 years** and is a great gluten-free alternative to rice.

2. Canned Goods

Canned foods are among the most reliable store-bought items for long-term storage. They can last years, require no refrigeration, and provide a quick, ready-to-eat solution during emergencies.

- **Canned Vegetables**: These can last **2-5 years** depending on the type. Green beans, corn, carrots, and peas are great additions to any off-grid meal when fresh produce is low.
- **Canned Fruits**: Typically last **1-2 years**, providing a good source of vitamins when fresh fruit isn't available.
- **Canned Meat (Chicken, Tuna, Beef)**: High in protein, canned meats can last **2-5 years**. They are an excellent backup when your livestock reserves are low.
- **Canned Soup and Stews**: These can last **2-5 years** and provide complete, ready-to-eat meals in a pinch. Look for nutrient-rich options like chili or vegetable-based soups.
- **Canned Fish (Sardines, Salmon, Mackerel)**: Typically lasts **2-5 years**, and these fish are packed with omega-3 fatty acids and protein.

3. Dehydrated and Freeze-Dried Foods

Dehydrated and freeze-dried foods are designed for long shelf life and can be easily rehydrated with water, making them perfect for off-grid living.

- **Freeze-Dried Vegetables**: Last up to **25 years**. These are excellent for adding to soups, stews, or casseroles.
- **Dehydrated Fruits**: Such as bananas, apples, or berries, last **up to 25 years** when sealed properly. They make for great snacks or additions to cereals and desserts.
- **Powdered Milk**: Lasts **10-20 years**, and is essential for baking, drinking, or adding to recipes that call for milk.
- **Freeze-Dried Meals**: Prepackaged meals designed for camping or emergency use can last up to **25 years**. These can be a lifesaver when time and resources are limited.

4. Dry Baking Ingredients

Dry ingredients used in baking can be stored long-term and provide the essentials for making bread, pastries, or pancakes.

- **Flour (White)**: Can last **1-2 years** if stored in a cool, dry place. Whole wheat flour has a shorter lifespan of about **3-6 months**.
- **Baking Powder and Baking Soda**: Typically last **1-2 years**. These are crucial for making baked goods when yeast isn't available.
- **Yeast (Dry)**: Can last **1-2 years** if unopened and stored in a cool, dry place. Ideal for making homemade bread.
- **Sugar**: Can last indefinitely when stored properly. White sugar, brown sugar, and powdered sugar are all essentials in baking and preserving.

5. Cooking Oils and Fats

Cooking oils are a necessary component of any off-grid kitchen, though they don't last as long as some other products.

- **Olive Oil**: Can last **1-2 years** if stored in a cool, dark place.
- **Coconut Oil**: Has a slightly longer shelf life, typically **up to 2 years**, and can be used for cooking and baking.
- **Ghee (Clarified Butter)**: Ghee is butter that has been treated to remove its water content, allowing it to last up to **1 year** without refrigeration.

6. Nuts, Seeds, and Nut Butters

Rich in fats and protein, nuts and seeds make excellent emergency foods. They can be eaten on their own, added to meals, or used to make homemade nut butter.

- **Peanut Butter**: Lasts **1-2 years**, providing a shelf-stable source of protein and healthy fats.
- **Almonds, Cashews, and Walnuts**: Can last **6-12 months** when stored in airtight containers in a cool, dark place.
- **Chia Seeds**: These tiny seeds have a shelf life of **2-4 years** and are a great source of omega-3 fatty acids.

7. Honey and Syrups

Honey is a near-perfect survival food—it never spoils, provided it's stored correctly.

- **Honey**: Lasts indefinitely. As long as it's stored in a tightly sealed container, honey is an excellent natural sweetener.
- **Maple Syrup**: Has a shelf life of **2 years** unopened and can be used for sweetening, cooking, or baking.

8. Salt and Seasonings

Salt is essential for preserving food, seasoning meals, and making food more palatable.

- **Table Salt and Sea Salt**: Last indefinitely and are crucial for food preservation and flavoring.
- **Dried Herbs and Spices**: Typically last **1-4 years**, though their potency diminishes over time. Stocking up on essential spices like garlic powder, chili powder, and dried oregano will keep your meals flavorful.

9. Powdered and Canned Beverages

Certain beverages can last for years, providing both comfort and nutrition.

- **Coffee (Instant)**: Lasts **up to 20 years**. Instant coffee is lightweight and easy to store.
- **Tea (Dried)**: Lasts **2-3 years** and can be a comforting addition to your off-grid stockpile.
- **Hot Cocoa Mix**: Lasts **6-12 months** and is a comforting beverage for cold nights.

These supermarket staples, combined with your off-grid resources, create a hybrid strategy for food security. Stocking up on these long-lasting items ensures that even in the toughest circumstances, you can supplement your off-grid diet with reliable, nutrient-dense foods. Rotate these items regularly, monitor their shelf life, and integrate them into your everyday meals to keep your emergency stockpile fresh and ready.

Conclusion: Securing Your Off-Grid Food Supply

By now, you've gained a deep understanding of the vital off-grid food preservation techniques necessary for long-term survival. Mastering these skills isn't just about learning how to can, dehydrate, or ferment; it's about building a reliable, sustainable food supply that can support you and your family, no matter the circumstances. The beauty of these methods is that they allow you to preserve your harvest, manage your resources efficiently, and maintain your independence from modern conveniences like electricity.

Here's how you can ensure that your food supply stays secure:

Maintain Vigilance and Practice Rotating Your Stock

Preserving food is only half the battle. To truly secure your food supply, you must stay vigilant and actively manage your stock. Regularly inspect your stored jars for signs of spoilage, such as bulging lids, rust, or leaks. Be proactive with your inventory—use the oldest jars first by following a "first in, first out" system to prevent any food from spoiling unnecessarily.

Tip: Make it a routine to check your stockpile every month. This way, you'll catch any potential issues early, keeping your supply safe and fresh.

Adapt and Improve Your Preservation Skills

The techniques you've learned—whether canning, dehydration, or fermentation—are time-tested, but there's always room for refinement. Keep experimenting with different foods, adjusting techniques, and learning from any challenges you face. Your ability to adapt and improve ensures that your preservation methods will continue to evolve, making your food supply more secure with each season.

Diversify Your Food Supply

Reliance on a single preservation method or type of food is risky. The key to true off-grid resilience lies in diversifying both your methods and your food sources. Rotate between canning, drying, and fermenting a variety of fruits, vegetables, and meats to ensure you have a well-rounded stockpile.

Tip: Keep a balance between fast-consumed and long-lasting food. For example, fermented vegetables might be ready to eat within a month, while pressure-canned meats can last over a year. Having this mix ensures flexibility in your food supply.

20. Mastering Food Preservation: From Canning to Fermentation and Dehydration

After gaining a strong foundation in essential off-grid preservation tools, this booklet takes your skills to the next level. You'll now explore a wider range of techniques for long-term food storage, from water bath canning to fermentation and dehydration. These methods not only help preserve your harvest but also ensure that you have access to a diverse and nutritious food supply, no matter the season. By mastering these techniques, you'll enhance your ability to store food efficiently, supporting your self-sufficient, off-grid lifestyle year-round.

Water Bath Canning: Preserving Fruits, Jams, and Pickles

Step 1: Gather Your Equipment

First, you'll need to assemble the right tools:

- **A Large, Deep Pot or Water Bath Canner**: This needs to be deep enough to fully submerge your jars in water, with at least an inch or two of water above the jar lids.
- **Mason Jars**: Use heat-resistant, high-quality jars with two-piece lids (flat lids with rubber seals and metal bands).
- **Jar Lifter**: To safely lift hot jars out of the boiling water
- **Canning Funnel**: To make sure you fill the jars cleanly without spilling on the rims.

Make sure everything is clean and sterilized. You can sterilize your jars and tools by boiling them in water for a minimum of 10 minutes or using a solar cooker if you're off-grid and low on fuel.

Step 2: Prepare Your Food

High-acid foods like fruits and pickles are ideal for water bath canning. Whether you're preserving tomatoes, making jam, or pickling cucumbers, the preparation is key.

- **Fruits**: Wash, peel, and cut them as needed. If you're making jam or jelly, follow your recipe to cook the fruit and sugar to the right consistency.
- **Pickles**: Prepare your brine with vinegar, water, and salt. Ensure the acidity is high enough to prevent spoilage. You can add spices like dill, garlic, or mustard seeds for extra flavor.

Always follow a trusted recipe, especially when working with acidity levels, to ensure food safety.

Step 3: Fill and Seal Your Jars

Now, it's time to pack your jars.

- **Use a Funnel**: Place your funnel in the jar and fill it with your hot food or brine, leaving the correct amount of **headspace**—typically about 1/2 inch for most fruits and pickles. This space allows the contents to expand during processing without breaking the jar.
- **Eliminate Air Bubbles**: Use a non-metallic spatula or tool to carefully run along the inner edge of the jar, freeing any trapped air pockets. This step is critical because trapped air can interfere with the sealing process.
- **Wipe the Rims**: Before sealing, make sure to wipe the jar rims with a damp, clean cloth. Any residue left on the rim could prevent a proper seal, leading to spoilage.
- **Apply the Lids**: Place the flat lids on the jars, ensuring the rubber seal is clean, and screw the metal bands on **fingertip tight**—secure, but not too tight. The bands will allow air to escape during the canning process, creating a vacuum seal.

Step 4: Process the Jars in Boiling Water

Once your jars are filled and sealed, it's time for processing.

- **Submerge the Jars**: Use your jar lifter to carefully lower the jars into your large pot or water bath canner. Make sure the jars are completely submerged with at least 1-2 inches of water covering the tops.
- **Boil and Process**: Bring the water to a full, rolling boil. Once boiling, set your timer. The processing time will depend on what you're canning and your altitude. For most jams and fruits, you'll need to process the jars for about 10 to 15 minutes. Pickles may take 10 to 20 minutes. **Tip**: If you're at a higher altitude, you'll need to increase your processing time. Check a trusted altitude chart to get this right.
- **Maintain a Steady Boil**: Make sure the water keeps boiling throughout the entire process. If it drops below a boil, you'll need to restart your timing from scratch.

Step 5: Cool and Check the Seal

Once the processing time is complete, turn off the heat and let the jars sit in the hot water for about 5 minutes to stabilize. This helps avoid thermal shock, which could crack the jars.

- **Carefully Lift the Jars**: Using a jar lifter, gently remove the jars from the pot and place them on a towel or cooling rack in a draft-free location. Allow the jars to sit undisturbed for 12-24 hours.
- **Inspect the Seals**: Once the jars have completely cooled, press the center of the lids to ensure a proper seal. A properly sealed jar will have a concave lid that doesn't move or pop. If a jar hasn't sealed correctly, you'll need to refrigerate it and use it within a few days.

Step 6: Store Your Jars

Label the jars: Mark each jar with the contents and the date of preservation. Store them in a cool, dark, and dry location like a root cellar or pantry. Properly processed and sealed jars can last for up to a year or more, giving you a reliable source of food.

Expert Tips for Water Bath Canning Success

- **Altitudes Matter**: If you're canning at high altitudes, increase your processing time to compensate for the lower boiling point of water.
- **Batch Size**: Don't overload your canner. Too many jars can cause uneven heat distribution. Process in manageable batches for best results.
- **Flavor Boost**: When making jams, try adding a squeeze of lemon juice or a dash of vanilla extract to enhance flavor. For pickles, experiment with garlic, dill, or red pepper flakes.
- **Inspect Jars**: Before each canning session, check your jars for cracks or chips, especially on the rims. Any imperfections can prevent a proper seal.

Water bath canning is an invaluable skill for off-grid living, allowing you to preserve the best of your harvest. With these clear, practical steps, you're ready to start preserving high-acid foods like fruits, jams, and pickles safely and efficiently. Just remember, attention to detail at every stage ensures that your food stays safe, delicious, and ready to enjoy long after the harvest season ends.

Pressure Canning: The Key to Preserving Low-Acid Foods

When it comes to preserving low-acid foods like meats, vegetables, and legumes, pressure canning is your go-to method. Unlike high-acid foods that can be preserved with water bath canning, low-acid foods require much higher temperatures to eliminate bacteria like **Clostridium botulinum**, which causes botulism. Pressure canning ensures that your food reaches the necessary heat levels for long-term, safe storage. With the right approach and tools, you can store a variety of nutrient-rich foods for months or even years—keeping your off-grid pantry well-stocked and reliable.

Mastering Pressure Canning for Vegetables and Meats

Step 1: Prepare Your Equipment

Before you begin pressure canning, ensure that you have the necessary tools:

- **Pressure Canner**: This is different from a pressure cooker. A pressure canner is specifically designed for safely canning foods at high pressure. Choose a model that suits your setup—whether it runs on wood, propane, or solar-powered heat.
- **Mason Jars**: Just like with water bath canning, you'll need durable, heat-resistant jars. Ensure they're in good condition with no cracks or chips.
- **Lids and Bands**: Use new flat lids with rubber seals for each batch, and check that your metal bands are clean and rust-free.

Thoroughly inspect your pressure canner for any issues. Check the seal, gasket, and pressure gauge (if applicable). If your canner has a **weighted gauge**, no calibration is necessary, but make sure it moves freely.

Step 2: Prepare Your Food

Whether you're canning fresh vegetables or meats, preparation is key:

- **Vegetables**: Wash and peel your vegetables. Depending on the type, you may need to blanch them briefly in boiling water to preserve their color and texture.
- **Meats**: Trim any excess fat from your meats and, if desired, brown the pieces lightly in a pan to enhance flavor before canning. Alternatively, you can raw-pack meats directly into jars for a simpler approach.

Once your ingredients are prepped, pack them into jars, leaving about **1 inch of headspace** at the top. This space allows the food to expand during processing. Adding boiling water, broth, or tomato juice (for some meats) helps fill the jars while maintaining moisture during storage.

Step 3: Fill and Seal the Jars

To ensure a successful seal, follow these steps carefully:

1. **Use a Funnel**: Place a funnel over the jar to fill it without spilling food on the rim. Keeping the rim clean is essential for a proper seal.
2. **Remove Air Bubbles**: Slide a non-metallic tool, like a plastic spatula, along the inside of the jar to release trapped air. Any remaining air bubbles can interfere with the pressure canning process.
3. **Wipe the Rim**: Clean the rims of the jars with a damp cloth to remove any food particles or liquid that could affect the seal.
4. **Seal**: Place the flat lids on top and screw on the metal bands until they're fingertip-tight—snug but not too tight. This allows air to escape during processing.

Step 4: Process in the Pressure Canner

Now that your jars are packed and sealed, it's time to process them:

1. **Add Water**: Pour 2-3 inches of water into your pressure canner. Unlike water bath canning, the jars do not need to be fully submerged. The steam generated by the boiling water will provide the heat necessary for canning.
2. **Load the Jars**: Place the jars on the canning rack inside the pressure canner. Be sure they are not touching each other or the sides of the canner to allow for proper steam circulation.

3. **Secure the Lid**: Lock the lid in place according to your canner's manual. If you're using a weighted-gauge canner, ensure the vent is open to allow steam to escape.
4. **Vent Steam**: Let the steam vent for about 10 minutes to purge any air from the canner. This is crucial for maintaining the right pressure inside.
5. **Build Pressure**: Close the vent (or add the weight) and bring the canner to the required pressure—usually **10-15 pounds of pressure**, depending on your altitude and what you're canning. Follow your pressure canner's instructions closely.

Step 5: Monitor the Pressure

Maintaining steady pressure is critical during the canning process. Once the pressure is reached, adjust the heat to keep it steady. The processing time will vary depending on what you're canning and the size of the jars:

- **Vegetables**: Typically require 20-40 minutes, depending on the type.
- **Meats**: Usually take between 75-90 minutes for quarts.

Keep an eye on the pressure gauge or listen to the steady rocking of the weight to ensure everything stays consistent. If the pressure drops too low, you'll need to start the timing over to ensure the food reaches the necessary temperature for safe storage.

Step 6: Cool and Check the Seals

After the processing time is finished, turn off the heat and allow the pressure to decrease naturally. This cooling phase is crucial—don't rush it by forcing the lid open or running cold water over the canner, as this can lead to jar breakage or improper sealing.

1. **Open the Lid**: Once the pressure is fully released and the gauge reads zero, carefully remove the lid, opening it **away from your face** to avoid a rush of steam.
2. **Remove the Jars**: Use a jar lifter to transfer the hot jars to a towel-covered surface. Allow them to cool undisturbed for 12-24 hours.

Once the jars have fully cooled, verify the seals by pressing the center of each lid. If it **pops** up and down, the jar hasn't sealed properly and should be refrigerated and used within a few days.

Step 7: Store Your Canned Goods

Once you've confirmed that the jars are sealed, label them with the date and contents, and store them in a cool, dark, and dry place. Properly processed and sealed low-acid foods can last for **12 to 18 months**, giving you a reliable source of vegetables and meats in your off-grid pantry.

Expert Tips for Pressure Canning Success

- **Adjust for Altitude**: If you're canning at higher altitudes, you'll need to increase the pressure to account for the lower boiling point of water.
- **Inspect Your Canner**: Before every use, check the gasket, vent, and gauge to ensure everything is in good working order. A faulty canner can lead to dangerous results.
- **Batch Size**: Don't overcrowd your canner. Keep batches manageable to ensure proper steam and pressure circulation.
- **Avoid Siphoning**: Siphoning occurs when liquid is drawn out of your jars during processing. To prevent this, avoid overfilling and make sure the temperature doesn't fluctuate too rapidly.

By mastering pressure canning, you'll have the ability to safely preserve a wide variety of low-acid foods for long-term storage, ensuring that your off-grid pantry is well-stocked and ready for any situation. With careful attention to detail and patience, pressure canning can provide you with nutritious, shelf-stable food for months or even years.

Solar Dehydration: Harnessing the Sun to Preserve Food

Solar dehydration is a simple, sustainable, and efficient method to preserve fruits, vegetables, and even meats without using electricity. It's especially suited for off-grid living, where resources may be limited, but the sun is abundant. By drying your food naturally, you reduce its water content, which prevents spoilage and extends its shelf life for months. With the right setup and approach, solar dehydration can become one of your most reliable food preservation techniques.

Building a Solar Dehydrator for Sustainable Food Drying

You don't need complicated tools or a lot of materials to create a solar dehydrator. A basic setup can be built using wooden frames and mesh trays, and it can be placed anywhere you have good sunlight. Here's how to do it:

1. **Gather Materials:**
   o **Wooden Frames**: Use untreated wood to build a sturdy frame. The size depends on how much food you plan to dry, but a simple 3x2-foot frame works well for most purposes.
   o **Mesh Trays**: These should be fine enough to hold fruits, vegetables, or meat but allow airflow. You can use food-grade nylon mesh or metal screen trays.
   o **Clear Plastic Cover**: This will act as a heat trap, allowing sunlight in but keeping moisture out. You can use clear plastic sheeting or an old glass windowpane for this.
2. **Build the Frame**: Construct a frame with the wooden pieces, ensuring it has enough depth to hold at least 2-3 trays. Attach the mesh trays at even intervals so air can circulate around the food. The cover should be slanted, allowing maximum sun exposure while encouraging airflow.
3. **Position in Direct Sunlight**: Place the solar dehydrator in a sunny location, ideally facing south if you're in the Northern Hemisphere. The more direct sunlight it receives, the more efficiently it will dry your food. Ensure that it is slightly elevated from the ground to avoid moisture buildup.
4. **Loading and Drying Food:**
   o **Cut Uniformly**: Slice fruits, vegetables, or meat into thin, even pieces. The thinner and more uniform your slices, the faster and more evenly they will dry.
   o **Arrange on Trays**: Spread the food in a single layer across the mesh trays. Avoid overlapping pieces, as this will slow the drying process.
5. **Drying Time**: Depending on the weather and the thickness of your slices, drying times can vary between **6–12 hours** for most fruits and vegetables. Meat may take longer, so always check that it has dried thoroughly before storing it.

Monitoring and Storing Dried Goods for Maximum Longevity

Once your food is dried, proper storage is critical to maintaining its longevity. Follow these steps for effective storage:

1. **Check for Complete Drying**: Before removing your food from the dehydrator, check that it's fully dried. Fruits should be leathery but not sticky. Vegetables should be brittle, and meat should be tough but pliable. If any part feels damp, leave it in the dehydrator longer.
2. **Cool Before Storing**: Allow your dried food to cool completely before placing it in containers. If stored while still warm, condensation can occur, leading to mold.

3. **Store in Airtight Containers**: Place your dried goods in airtight containers like glass jars or vacuum-sealed bags. Keep them in a cool, dark place to maximize their shelf life. Label each container with the type of food and the date it was dried to make inventory management easier.

Fermentation: Preserving Vegetables the Natural Way

Fermentation is one of the oldest and simplest ways to preserve vegetables without electricity. It uses naturally occurring bacteria to convert sugars into lactic acid, which acts as a preservative. Not only does fermentation increase the shelf life of your vegetables, but it also enhances their flavor and nutritional value. With minimal tools and ingredients, fermentation is perfect for off-grid living.

The Basics of Fermenting Vegetables for Long-Term Storage

Fermenting vegetables is incredibly straightforward. You can ferment almost any vegetable, but cabbage (for sauerkraut) and cucumbers (for pickles) are some of the most common choices. Here's how to get started:

1. **Gather Ingredients and Tools:**
   o **Fresh Vegetables**: Cabbage, cucumbers, carrots, and radishes are ideal for fermentation.
   o **Salt**: Use non-iodized salt, such as sea salt or kosher salt, to create the brine.
   o **Clean Jars or Crocks**: Use wide-mouth Mason jars or fermentation crocks that are clean and sterilized.
2. **Prepare the Vegetables:**
   o Wash and chop the vegetables into your desired size. For cabbage, remove the outer leaves, core the cabbage, and shred it finely.
   o Sprinkle salt over the vegetables (about 1-2 tablespoons per pound of vegetables) and massage it in. This draws out the moisture and begins the fermentation process.
3. **Pack into Jars or Crocks:**
   o Pack the salted vegetables tightly into the jars or crock, pressing them down so the natural brine covers the vegetables. If there isn't enough liquid, you can add a brine made from 1 tablespoon of salt dissolved in 1 cup of water.
   o Weigh down the vegetables to ensure they remain submerged under the brine. You can use a fermentation weight or a clean, heavy object.
4. **Ferment in a Cool, Dark Place**: Store the jars in a cool, dark area. The temperature should be around **60-75°F (15-24°C)** for optimal fermentation. In about 3-10 days, depending on the temperature and the vegetable, the fermentation process will be complete.

Storing and Monitoring Fermented Foods for Safety

Once the fermentation process is complete, follow these steps to ensure your fermented foods stay safe and delicious:

1. **Taste Test**: After a few days, taste your fermented vegetables to see if they've reached the desired flavor and tang. If they taste too mild, let them ferment longer.
2. **Transfer to Airtight Containers**: Once you're satisfied with the fermentation, transfer the vegetables to airtight containers, like Mason jars with tight lids. This helps preserve them for longer.
3. **Store in a Cool, Dark Place**: Fermented vegetables are best stored in a root cellar or a similar cool, dark location. You can also refrigerate them if space allows. Properly stored, fermented vegetables can last for months.
4. **Monitor Regularly**: Check your fermented vegetables periodically for signs of spoilage, such as mold or off-smells. Fermented foods should smell tangy and fresh—never foul or rotten.

Expert Tips for Off-Grid Success:

- **Solar Dehydrator Positioning**: If you notice your food isn't drying as quickly as expected, try adjusting the angle of your solar dehydrator to catch more sunlight. Moving it a few degrees can make a big difference.
- **Fermentation Time**: The longer you ferment vegetables, the tangier they will become. You can stop the process early if you prefer a milder flavor or let them ferment longer for a more intense taste.
- **Label and Rotate**: Always label your dried and fermented goods with the date they were processed, and use the oldest items first. Rotating your stock helps prevent spoilage and waste.

By incorporating solar dehydration and fermentation into your off-grid food preservation strategies, you'll have a well-rounded approach that ensures you can store your harvest long-term. Both methods require minimal resources and are easy to adapt to different environments, making them perfect for an off-grid lifestyle.

Storing Your Preserved Food for the Long Haul

Once you've successfully preserved your food through canning, dehydration, or fermentation, the next crucial step is ensuring that it remains safe and ready for consumption over the long term. Proper storage practices can make the difference between a secure food supply and one compromised by spoilage or contamination. Let's walk through how to store your preserved food effectively, so it's always ready when you need it.

Organizing and Labeling Your Stockpile for Easy Rotation

The first step in maintaining an efficient off-grid food supply is organization. Keeping your stockpile orderly and rotating it regularly will ensure you're always consuming the oldest preserved items first, minimizing waste and spoilage. Here's how to manage this step-by-step:

1. **Labeling Your Jars or Containers:**
   o **Date**: Always label your jars with the date they were preserved. Use a waterproof marker or adhesive label to write the exact day, month, and year of preservation.
   o **Contents**: Clearly label what's inside the jar—whether it's pickled vegetables, dried fruits, or fermented cabbage. This helps avoid confusion and keeps your inventory management simple.
   o **Storage Method**: If you're using different preservation methods (canning, dehydration, fermentation), note the method on the label for easy reference.
2. **Plan a Rotation System:**
   o Arrange your jars and preserved food items so the oldest jars are placed at the front and the newest at the back. This makes it easy to rotate your stockpile and ensures you always use the older items first.
   o Implement the **FIFO method** (First In, First Out): This is the simplest way to maintain a fresh stockpile. Each time you add a new batch of preserved food, push the older jars forward and place the new ones behind.
3. **Inventory Management:**
   o Keeping a small logbook or digital record of your preserved food can help you track what you've stored and when it should be used. This is especially helpful if you have a large stockpile and don't want to rely on memory.
   o Include the type of food, preservation date, quantity, and method used. This level of organization will keep you on top of your supplies, making it easier to manage during an emergency.

Maintaining the Right Conditions to Prevent Spoilage

Your storage environment is just as important as your preservation methods. To ensure that your preserved food lasts for the long term, you need to create the right conditions. Here are the key factors:

1. **Temperature:**
   - **Cool Temperatures**: A stable, cool environment is ideal for long-term food storage. Aim for a temperature range of **50–70°F** (10–21°C). Higher temperatures can degrade the quality of the food, while fluctuating temperatures may cause condensation, leading to spoilage.
   - If you have a root cellar, this is an excellent storage option. If not, find a cool area of your home or property that maintains a consistent temperature year-round. Avoid attics or other spaces that experience extreme temperature swings.
2. **Darkness:**
   - **Protect from Light**: Light, especially sunlight, can break down the nutrients in preserved food and degrade the quality of your jars. A dark environment, like a root cellar, basement, or pantry, is ideal. If your storage area has windows, cover your jars or install curtains to block out the light.
3. **Humidity:**
   - **Keep it Dry**: Excess moisture in the air can cause rust on your jar lids and bands, which may compromise the seal and lead to spoilage. Ensure your storage area has good airflow to prevent dampness. In high-humidity environments, consider using **desiccants** (like silica gel packs) to absorb moisture and protect your stockpile.
4. **Jar Inspection:**
   - **Regular Checks**: At least once a month, inspect your jars for signs of spoilage or compromised seals. Look for **bulging lids**, **rust**, or **leaks**. These are clear indicators that the jar is no longer sealed properly and the contents are unsafe to eat.
   - **Smell Check**: If you open a jar and notice an off-smell, discard the contents immediately. Fermented foods should have a tangy smell, while canned goods should have no unpleasant odors.
5. **Preventing Rodents and Pests:**
   - Rodents and insects can quickly ruin your stockpile if they gain access. Ensure your storage area is **sealed tightly** to prevent pests from entering. Keep food jars on **sturdy, elevated shelves**—never directly on the ground. Consider using metal or hard plastic storage bins for added protection.

Expert Tips for Long-Term Storage Success

- **Inspect Seals**: Each time you retrieve a jar from storage, check the lid for any signs of failure. A properly sealed lid should still be **concave** and shouldn't flex or pop when pressed. If the seal has broken, discard the food inside.
- **Clean Lids**: After processing, remove the bands and wipe the lids clean. Leaving the bands on during storage can trap moisture and lead to rust, which may weaken the seal. Store the jars **without the bands** to prevent this issue.
- **Separate Canning Methods**: Keep jars preserved by different methods (e.g., pressure-canned meats, water bath fruits, fermented vegetables) organized in separate areas or shelves. This helps you quickly access what you need without confusion.
- **Rotate Seasonally**: Adjust your storage system seasonally, ensuring that preserved goods from previous harvests are used before the latest batches. This prevents older items from sitting too long and ensures you're eating your freshest food.

By following these practical storage tips, you'll maintain the integrity of your preserved food for the long haul. With a well-organized system and proper environmental conditions, your food stockpile will stay safe, delicious, and ready to support you through any challenge. Whether you're storing canned goods, dried fruits, or fermented vegetables, diligent storage practices are the key to off-grid food security. Keep your food well-labeled, well-protected, and regularly inspected, and you'll always have access to nutritious, shelf-stable provisions.

Create a Safe and Organized Storage Environment

A proper storage environment is essential to long-term food security. Ensure that your storage area is cool, dark, and dry to prevent spoilage. Whether it's a root cellar or a pantry, keep your food organized by type and date to make rotation seamless. Label each jar with clear, detailed information about when it was preserved and what's inside.

Tip: If you don't have a dedicated root cellar, consider using an insulated basement or even a closet away from heat sources. A consistent, stable environment is key to keeping your food in top condition.

Final Words: Stay Ready, Stay Resilient

The key to success lies in continuous learning and adapting to your environment. As seasons change and conditions evolve, so should your approach to food preservation.

Keep honing your skills, maintain your stockpile, and be ready for whatever challenges come your way. Your resilience is your greatest asset—combined with the knowledge you've gained here, you're fully prepared to secure your off-grid food supply for the long haul.

21. Hunting, Fishing, and Foraging

Introduction to Off-Grid Hunting, Fishing, and Foraging

As you expand your off-grid food supply beyond gardening and livestock raising, hunting, fishing, and foraging become essential skills. While cultivating your own food provides a stable base, nature's resources can offer much-needed variety and sustenance. In an off-grid lifestyle, sustainable food sourcing ensures that you make the most of your surroundings without depleting them. Hunting, fishing, and foraging allow you to work in harmony with the environment, providing vital protein and nutrients while promoting self-reliance.

Sustainable food sourcing in an off-grid context is about more than just survival—it's about respecting the ecosystems that support your livelihood. The key lies in adopting low-tech, efficient methods that minimize your impact on the environment. Whether you're setting snares, fishing in local streams, or gathering edible plants, your approach should be mindful and rooted in long-term balance with nature. By learning these methods, you ensure that your off-grid lifestyle not only thrives but also sustains itself for years to come.

Practical Off-Grid Hunting Methods

Hunting off the grid doesn't have to rely on modern equipment or high-tech tools. Instead, you can use natural materials and simple techniques to hunt small game efficiently. Building traps, in particular, allows you to set up passive hunting systems that require minimal intervention and energy on your part—ideal for those balancing multiple tasks in an off-grid environment.

Crafting Simple and Effective Traps

One of the most efficient ways to hunt small game like squirrels, rabbits, and other wildlife is through traps. These traps work while you attend to other tasks, making them an essential part of your off-grid toolkit. With the right knowledge, you can create effective snares and traps using only the natural materials you find around you—vines, branches, stones, and even small pieces of cordage. The following guide covers two simple yet highly effective traps you can build and set with ease.

Natural Snares and Traps

1. Figure-4 Deadfall Trap

The figure-4 deadfall trap is a classic and highly effective trap that uses a simple mechanism to catch small game. This trap works by using the weight of a rock or log to crush the animal when it triggers the trap. It's particularly useful for catching ground-dwelling creatures like rabbits or squirrels.

Materials:

- A heavy flat stone or log
- Three sticks (about the thickness of a pencil) or carved wood
- A knife to carve notches
- Bait (such as nuts, fruit, or anything that attracts your target game)

Step-by-Step Guide:

Prepare the Sticks:
- o Carve one stick into an upright post (Stick A), which will be vertical and act as the main support. Cut a notch at the top.
- o Carve the second stick into a horizontal piece (Stick B) with notches on both ends to interact with the other two sticks.
- o The third stick (Stick C) will serve as the trigger and should be cut at an angle to fit snugly into the notches of Sticks A and B.

2. **Set the Deadfall:**
- o Position the heavy stone or log above your trap. This weight will fall when the trap is triggered.
- o Insert Stick A vertically into the ground and place Stick B horizontally, balanced between the upright stick and the trigger (Stick C).
- o When the animal nudges Stick C while trying to get the bait, it dislodges the entire mechanism, causing the heavy object to fall and trap the animal.

3. **Bait and Placement:**
- o Place bait on the end of Stick C. Position your trap near known animal paths or feeding spots, where you've seen signs of activity like tracks or droppings.
- o Check the trap frequently to retrieve your catch or reset it if needed.

Pro Tip: Practice carving the notches and assembling the figure-4 mechanism before you rely on it for hunting. It takes time to perfect, but once mastered, it's an incredibly reliable trap.

2. Spring Snare Trap

The spring snare trap relies on the tension of a bent sapling or flexible branch to snap upwards when triggered. It's an excellent trap for small game, such as rabbits or squirrels, and can be crafted using simple natural materials found in your environment.

Materials:

- A flexible sapling or small tree for tension
- Cordage (vines or natural cord)
- Two small sticks to create the trigger mechanism
- A knife to sharpen sticks and cut notches

Step-by-Step Guide:

1. **Find a Sapling:**
- o Choose a small, flexible sapling that can be bent down without breaking. This will act as the spring mechanism that provides the trap's power.

2. **Prepare the Trigger:**
- o Sharpen two sticks (around 6 inches long) and carve notches in one of them to act as the trigger arm. The second stick will be driven into the ground and serve as the anchor.
- o Tie one end of your cordage to the sapling and the other end to form a noose. This noose will be placed in the animal's path.

3. **Set the Snare:**
- o Bend the sapling down and attach the trigger mechanism. One stick will hold the sapling in place, and the other will be connected to the noose. When an animal steps into the noose or disturbs the trigger, the sapling snaps upward, tightening the noose around the animal.

4. **Placement:**
   o   Set your snare in a well-trafficked game trail or near a food source. Look for signs of animal activity, such as tracks or droppings, to improve your chances of success.

Pro Tip: Always make sure your cordage or snare is strong enough to hold the weight of the animal you're targeting. Check your snare frequently to ensure it's functioning correctly and hasn't been disturbed by non-target animals.

Best Locations for Setting Traps

The placement of your traps is just as important as their design. To improve your chances of success, observe the habits of the animals in your area. Look for signs such as well-worn paths, feeding spots, and areas with fresh tracks or droppings. Some of the best locations to set your traps include:

- **Game Trails:** Look for narrow, beaten-down paths in the forest where animals frequently move. These trails are often used by multiple species and are prime spots for trap placement.
- **Water Sources:** Small animals tend to frequent areas near water sources, such as streams, ponds, or rivers. Position your traps near these areas, where animals come to drink.
- **Sheltered Areas:** Animals seek out shelter in thick brush or wooded areas. Setting traps near these shelters increases your chances of catching game.

Using Practical Hunting Tools

In off-grid living, efficient and practical hunting tools are key to sustaining yourself while keeping your impact on the environment to a minimum. Traditional firearms might not always be the best option for off-grid hunting, as they can be loud, require ammunition that can be hard to replace, and cause significant disruption to the local wildlife. Instead, tools like air rifles, pellet guns, and crossbows offer quieter, more sustainable alternatives that are just as effective for small and medium game.

Here, we'll explore the best hunting tools to use in an off-grid environment, how to select the right equipment, and the safety and maintenance tips to ensure your tools remain in optimal condition for years.

Air Rifles and Pellet Guns: Environmentally Safer Hunting Tools

Air rifles and pellet guns are fantastic choices for hunting small to medium game in an off-grid setting. These tools are much quieter than traditional firearms, allowing you to hunt without alerting other animals or disturbing the ecosystem. They also cause less damage to the environment, making them a sustainable option for long-term use.

Choosing the Right Air Rifle or Pellet Gun for Small to Medium Game

When selecting an air rifle or pellet gun, consider the type of game you're targeting. For small animals like rabbits, squirrels, and birds, a .177 or .22 caliber air rifle is generally sufficient. The .22 caliber offers a little more stopping power, which can be useful for slightly larger game like raccoons or groundhogs.

Look for an air rifle that offers both accuracy and power. Break-barrel air rifles are common and easy to use, but pump-action or CO2-powered rifles may provide better consistency, especially for beginners. Consider the velocity of the rifle, as speeds of at least 700 feet per second (FPS) are typically needed for effective small game hunting.

Safety and Maintenance: How to Care for Your Air Rifle

To ensure your air rifle remains in good condition for the long haul, regular maintenance is essential. Here's a simple guide:

1. **Clean the Barrel Regularly**: After each hunt, clean the barrel of your air rifle using a cleaning rod or pull-through with a patch to remove any buildup or residue.
2. **Lubricate the Mechanism**: Utilize premium gun oil to properly lubricate the moving parts of your rifle. However, be sure to avoid over-lubricating the seals, as this can cause malfunctions.
3. **Check for Loose Parts**: Periodically check for any loose screws or bolts, especially around the stock and scope mounts. Tighten these as necessary.
4. **Store Safely**: Store your air rifle in a dry, secure location to prevent rust and keep it ready for use when you need it.

Pro Tip: Practice regularly with your air rifle to improve accuracy, and always be mindful of where you're aiming. Air rifles may be quiet, but safety is still paramount.

Crossbows for Larger Game

For larger game like deer, wild boar, or elk, a crossbow offers the accuracy and power needed while maintaining a quiet profile. Crossbows provide greater precision and distance than air rifles and are particularly useful in environments where you want to minimize noise.

How to Safely Use and Maintain a Crossbow for Hunting Larger Game

Using a crossbow for hunting requires more skill and practice than a rifle, but it's a rewarding and effective tool when used correctly. Here's a basic guide to get you started:

1. **Choosing the Right Crossbow**: Look for a crossbow that suits your strength and hunting style. A draw weight of 150 to 175 pounds is typically sufficient for hunting large game, but make sure you can comfortably cock the bow. Recurve crossbows are simpler and easier to maintain, while compound crossbows offer more power but require more upkeep.
2. **Aiming and Shooting**: Practice is key to becoming proficient with a crossbow. Start by practicing at shorter distances, like 20-30 yards, and gradually increase as you become more accurate. Always aim for vital areas on larger game, such as the heart and lungs, for a humane and effective kill.
3. **Maintaining Your Crossbow**: Keep the string and cables well-lubricated and inspect them regularly for wear. Replace any damaged parts promptly. Clean the rail after each use and wax the string to keep it in top condition.
4. **Safety Considerations**: Always use a proper crossbow cocking device to prevent injury, and never dry fire (fire without an arrow). Ensure your arrows or bolts are of the correct size and weight for your crossbow to avoid damage to the equipment or yourself.

Best Practices: Where and How to Hunt Larger Game

Hunting large game with a crossbow requires patience and strategy. Look for well-traveled game trails and use natural cover like trees or brush to hide your movements. It's also important to understand animal behavior—most large game will be active at dawn and dusk, so plan your hunts accordingly.

Pro Tip: Always aim for the animal's vital organs to ensure a clean, ethical kill. This not only guarantees a humane hunt but also makes it easier to recover the animal.

Tracking and Stalking Animals

Tracking and stalking are crucial skills for any hunter, particularly in off-grid environments where efficiency is key. Knowing how to read the signs of wildlife will improve your chances of success and reduce unnecessary waste of time and energy.

Learning Natural Animal Behaviors

Animals leave a variety of signs that can help you track them, including footprints, scat, feeding patterns, and bedding areas. By learning how to read these signs, you can pinpoint the locations where animals are most likely to be found and anticipate their movements.

1. **Footprints**: Look for tracks in soft soil or muddy areas near water sources. The size and shape of the prints will help you identify the species. Deer, for instance, have distinct two-toed prints, while rabbits leave smaller, rounded prints with a distinct hopping pattern.
2. **Scat**: Animal droppings are a clear indicator of the presence of game. Fresh scat tells you that the animal was recently in the area. Learn to distinguish between different types of scat to determine which animals are nearby.
3. **Feeding Patterns**: Watch for signs of feeding, like chewed leaves, bark stripped from trees, or disturbed soil where animals may have been digging for food. This can lead you to nearby game trails.

Stalking Tips: Moving Silently and Using Natural Cover

When stalking animals, silence is your greatest asset. Move slowly and deliberately, stepping heel-to-toe to minimize noise. Use natural cover, such as trees, bushes, or rocks, to shield yourself from the animal's line of sight. Pay attention to the wind direction, as animals can easily detect human scent.

Pro Tip: Wear soft, muted clothing that blends with your surroundings to reduce your visibility and noise while stalking.

By mastering the use of practical hunting tools like air rifles, pellet guns, and crossbows, and honing your tracking and stalking skills, you'll be well-equipped to source food sustainably in an off-grid lifestyle. With careful preparation and regular practice, you'll become more efficient, confident, and successful in your hunting endeavors.

Off-Grid Fishing Techniques

Fishing off the grid requires simplicity, resourcefulness, and a deep connection to nature. With the right techniques, you can source food sustainably without modern equipment. Off-grid fishing doesn't need to rely on complex gear—you can succeed with basic methods and natural materials. Whether you're using handlines, crafting a spear, or building DIY fish traps, these techniques are efficient and effective for catching fish in rivers, lakes, and oceans. Let's explore some of the best off-grid fishing methods and how to use them.

Traditional Hand Fishing and Trapping Methods

Fishing with minimal tools is a skill that allows you to catch fish even when rods or nets aren't available. Two of the most effective methods are **handlining** and **spearfishing**.

Handlining: How to Fish with a Simple Line, Hook, and Bait

Handlining is an old-school technique that requires nothing more than a line, hook, and bait. It's lightweight, portable, and easy to set up, making it perfect for off-grid living.

1. **Setting Up Your Handline**: To start, you'll need a sturdy fishing line—about 20-50 feet should do, depending on the depth of the water you're fishing in. Attach a hook to the end, and consider adding a sinker to help the bait reach the desired depth.

2. **Bait**: Forage for worms, insects, grubs, or even small fish as bait. Digging in moist soil or flipping over logs are easy ways to find bait. You can also craft lures from reflective materials if bait is scarce.
3. **Knotting and Securing**: Tie your hook using a strong knot, like the Palomar knot, and use a rock or natural weight as a sinker. This will ensure the hook stays submerged. Cast the line by gently throwing it into the water, then let the weight sink the bait.
4. **Catching Fish**: Wait patiently and feel for any tugs on the line. When you feel a bite, pull the line in by hand. Be steady to avoid snapping the line.

Pro Tip: If you're fishing in a strong current, tie the line to a solid object, like a tree root or rock, and let the current move the bait for you.

Spearfishing: Hunting Fish in Shallow Waters

Spearfishing is another effective off-grid method, especially in shallow, clear waters where you can see fish swimming.

Step-by-Step Guide to Crafting a Fishing Spear:
1. **Finding Materials**: Start by finding a sturdy, straight stick about 5-6 feet long. Hardwoods like oak or hickory are ideal because of their durability.
2. **Crafting the Spear**: Sharpen one end of the stick to a fine point using a knife or stone. For better results, split the tip into three or four prongs and sharpen each one. This increases your chance of catching fish with a single thrust.
3. **Using the Spear**: Wade into shallow water and remain as still as possible to avoid scaring the fish. Aim slightly below the fish (because of water refraction) and thrust with a quick, deliberate motion.

Best Locations: Spearfishing works best in shallow streams, lakes, and coastal areas where fish tend to gather near rocks or vegetation.

Pro Tip: Practice your aim on still objects before trying to spear fish. Accurate thrusts are key to success.

Building DIY Fish Traps from Natural Materials

Fish traps are a low-maintenance, passive way to catch fish, allowing you to attend to other tasks while your trap does the work. There are two main types of traps you can build with natural materials: woven fish baskets and rock weirs.

Woven Fish Baskets

A **woven fish basket** is a funnel-shaped trap made from branches, vines, and flexible sticks. It works by allowing fish to swim in but preventing them from swimming out.

Step-by-Step Guide to Crafting a Woven Fish Basket:
1. **Gather Materials**: Collect long, flexible branches or vines. Willow branches or bamboo shoots work well for weaving.
2. **Weaving the Basket**: Start by weaving a circular base, about the size of a dinner plate. Then weave vertical sticks around the base to create the sides, gradually narrowing the opening as you go. The funnel shape should guide the fish into the basket but make it difficult for them to escape.
3. **Setting the Trap**: Place the basket in shallow water where fish are likely to pass, such as near rocks or vegetation. Weigh it down with stones to keep it submerged.
4. **Checking and Maintaining**: Check the trap every few hours and remove any fish. Be sure to regularly inspect the weave for damage and repair as necessary.

Pro Tip: Add bait, like worms or small fish, inside the basket to attract more fish.

Rock Weirs and Dams: Manipulating Water Flows

Rock weirs are simple structures built in rivers or streams to funnel fish into a small area, where they can be easily caught by hand or with a net.

Guide to Building a Rock Weir:

1. **Choosing the Location**: Find a narrow section of a stream or river where fish naturally pass. Look for areas with natural barriers, like rocks or logs, to help funnel the fish.
2. **Building the Weir**: Stack rocks to form two V-shaped walls that converge downstream. Leave a small gap at the point of the V, where fish will be funneled into a pool or shallow area.
3. **Harvesting**: Once the fish are trapped in the pool, you can easily catch them by hand or with a net.

Pro Tip: This method is particularly useful in fast-moving streams where fish are naturally funneled by the current.

Ice Fishing in Cold Environments

In colder climates, **ice fishing** is a great way to source food during winter months. It requires minimal gear and can be done in frozen lakes and rivers.

How to Safely Ice Fish with Minimal Gear:

1. **Cutting Through the Ice**: Use a hand auger, chisel, or even a sharpened stick to create a hole in the ice. The hole should be at least 8 inches in diameter. Be cautious and make sure the ice is at least 4 inches thick to safely support your weight.
2. **Making a Fishing Line**: A simple handline setup works well for ice fishing. Use bait like small fish or grubs, and drop the line into the hole. Attach a small piece of wood or rock to the line to help it sink deeper.
3. **Checking the Line**: Be patient and check your line regularly. Fish often move more slowly in colder temperatures, so bites may be less frequent.

Making Lures and Bait: In winter conditions, natural bait can be scarce. Forage for grubs or insects, or use bits of meat or fish to attract larger fish. Flashy, reflective materials can also be used to make improvised lures.

Pro Tip: Always dress in layers and bring plenty of insulation when ice fishing, as sitting still in the cold can quickly sap your body heat.

By mastering these simple yet effective off-grid fishing techniques, you'll be able to catch fish sustainably without relying on modern equipment. Handlining, spearfishing, and building DIY traps offer reliable ways to source fish in any environment, while ice fishing ensures you have access to fresh protein even in the harshest winter conditions. Practice these methods regularly, and you'll have a steady supply of fish for both immediate consumption and preservation.

Mastering Hunting and Fishing for Off-Grid Living

Mastering the skills of hunting and fishing is a crucial step in building a self-sustaining off-grid lifestyle. These practices provide not only an essential source of protein but also the means to rely less on external resources. By honing your ability to catch wild game and fish, you create a more resilient and balanced food supply, one that can sustain you year-round, even when other sources are limited.

As you continue to develop these skills, remember that sustainability and respect for the environment are key. Ethical hunting and fishing practices ensure that local ecosystems remain healthy and can continue to provide for the long term. The methods you've learned in this guide—whether it's setting snares, using practical fishing tools, or tracking animals— will equip you to thrive in the wild, using simple, effective techniques.

By combining these low-tech, mindful approaches with an understanding of local wildlife patterns, you'll not only improve your off-grid food security but also foster a deeper connection with the natural world around you. Every successful hunt or catch is not just a step toward self-sufficiency but a reminder of the balance required to live sustainably off the land. Keep practicing, refining your techniques, and exploring the abundance that nature offers.

Foraging for Wild Edible Plants

Foraging is one of the most sustainable and rewarding ways to source food in an off-grid lifestyle. The knowledge of identifying, harvesting, and preparing wild edible plants provides a dependable source of nutrition and helps you maintain a closer connection with the natural environment. This section will guide you through identifying common edible plants, understanding seasonal foraging, and gathering nutrient-rich roots and grains.

Identifying Edible Plants in Your Area

Before you start foraging, it's essential to become familiar with the wild plants in your region. While some plants offer abundant nutrition, others can be toxic, so learning how to correctly identify edible plants is critical to your safety.

Common Edible Plants

Here are some easily recognizable, nutrient-rich plants that you can forage for in various environments:

- **Dandelions**: Found in most temperate regions, dandelions are fully edible—from the leaves to the roots. The leaves are great for salads or stir-fries, while the roots can be roasted and used as a coffee substitute.
- **Wild Garlic**: Known for its garlic-like flavor, wild garlic is often found in moist woodlands. It's easy to identify by its broad green leaves and small white flowers. It makes an excellent addition to soups, stews, and pesto.
- **Clover**: White and red clover are widespread and can be foraged from fields and meadows. Clover leaves and flowers can be eaten raw or cooked and are often used in teas or soups.
- **Berries**: Wild berries, such as blackberries, raspberries, and blueberries, are rich in vitamins and make for easy snacks or preserves.

Seasonal Foraging: What to Gather in Each Season

Foraging opportunities change with the seasons, and understanding when certain plants are at their peak will help you optimize your harvest.

- **Spring**: This is the best time to forage for **greens** like dandelion leaves, wild garlic, and chickweed. These plants are tender and nutrient-rich after the winter thaw.
- **Summer**: Look for **berries** and flowering plants. Wild berries are in full bloom during summer, and herbs like mint, wild basil, and yarrow can be collected.
- **Fall**: Focus on **roots and tubers** like burdock and cattails, as well as **nuts** from trees like walnuts and chestnuts. These energy-rich foods can be stored for winter use.
- **Winter**: Foraging in winter is more challenging, but you can still gather **evergreens** like pine needles for teas or medicinal purposes. **Roots** from hardy plants like wild carrots and burdock can also be dug up.

Pro Tip: Keep a journal of the local flora and their seasonal cycles. This will help you remember where to return each season and what's available at different times of the year.

Step-by-Step Guide: How to Harvest and Prepare Plants for Safe Consumption

1. **Identification**: Before harvesting any plant, make sure you positively identify it as edible. Misidentification can lead to dangerous consequences, so use a field guide to confirm the plant's features.

2. **Harvesting**: When harvesting, always use a sharp knife or scissors to avoid damaging the plant. For leaves, snip them carefully at the base, and for roots, use a digging tool to extract them without disturbing the surrounding area.
3. **Cleaning**: Wild plants often carry dirt and bacteria, so always clean them thoroughly. Rinse leaves, berries, and roots in cool, running water.
4. Preparation:
   o **Leaves**: Can be eaten raw in salads or lightly cooked in soups and stir-fries.
   o **Roots**: Slice and roast roots like burdock and cattails, or boil them for soups and stews.
   o **Berries**: Eat them fresh, dry them, or turn them into jams and preserves for longer storage.

Pro Tip: When trying a new wild plant, always sample a small amount first to ensure it agrees with you. Some wild foods can cause mild allergic reactions or digestive discomfort in certain individuals.

Gathering Wild Grains, Nuts, and Roots

In addition to leafy greens and berries, the off-grid lifestyle benefits greatly from foraging grains, nuts, and roots, which are excellent sources of carbohydrates, fats, and proteins.

Collecting Wild Grains and Seeds

Wild grains such as **wild oats, millet,** and **quinoa** can be gathered in the wild and processed to provide long-term sustenance.

1. **Identification**: Look for wild grains growing in open fields or along riverbanks. These grains typically grow in clusters on tall stalks.
2. **Harvesting**: Use a sharp knife or your hands to cut the grain heads. Shake them over a basket or container to collect the seeds.
3. **Processing**: Dry the grains by laying them out in a sunny spot or hanging them in a dry area. Once dried, you can grind the grains into flour or cook them as they are for porridge or bread.
4. **Storage**: Keep the grains in airtight containers to prevent moisture and pests from spoiling your harvest.

Foraging for Roots and Tubers

Roots and tubers are another reliable source of calories, especially in colder months when other plants are scarce. **Cattails, burdock,** and **wild potatoes** are some of the most nutritious and widely available options.

Step-by-Step Guide to Digging and Preparing Roots:

1. **Identification**: Identify the plants by their leaves or stalks, which are often visible above ground. Cattails are easily recognizable by their tall, reed-like stalks, while burdock has large, broad leaves.
2. **Digging**: Use a spade or digging stick to carefully dig around the root, loosening the soil until you can pull the root free. Be careful not to break the root, as damaged roots may spoil more quickly.
3. **Cleaning**: Rinse the roots thoroughly to remove any dirt. For cattail roots, you can peel away the outer layer to access the starchy core.
4. **Cooking**: Slice the roots into thin pieces and roast them in an open fire or boil them in water. Cattails and burdock roots are particularly good when roasted, giving them a rich, nutty flavor.
5. **Storage**: Store any excess roots in a cool, dry place for future use. Many roots can be dried for long-term storage and rehydrated when needed.

Pro Tip: Roots like burdock and wild potatoes are perfect for soups and stews, providing essential carbohydrates that are slow to digest, keeping you fueled for longer.

By following these steps and using the techniques described, you'll be well-prepared to forage effectively for wild edible plants, grains, nuts, and roots. These resources are not only abundant in nature but also provide critical nutrients for an off-grid lifestyle. Practice sustainable foraging, rotate your harvesting spots, and respect the environment to ensure these natural resources remain available for years to come.

Ethical Considerations and Sustainability: Balancing Harvesting with Nature

Living off-grid requires a deep connection with nature, but it also comes with the responsibility to maintain balance and ensure that your harvesting practices are sustainable. The goal is not just to survive, but to live in harmony with the environment, allowing nature to replenish and thrive while meeting your needs. By following sustainable practices, rotating foraging spots, and respecting wildlife and ecosystems, you can protect your local environment for future generations and sustain the delicate balance of your off-grid ecosystem.

Sustainable Practices

When hunting, fishing, or foraging off-grid, sustainability should be at the forefront of your mind. Over-harvesting can deplete natural resources, leaving you and your community with fewer options in the future. To avoid this, it's essential to implement thoughtful harvesting practices.

Harvesting Limits:

- **Take Only What You Need:** Whether you're hunting, fishing, or gathering wild plants, always take only the amount that you and your household need. This ensures that local wildlife and plant populations have time to recover and regenerate.
- **Observe and Monitor:** Pay attention to the population levels of the plants and animals you rely on. If you notice that a particular species is becoming scarce, adjust your harvesting habits accordingly.

Pro Tip: Keep track of your hunting, fishing, and foraging activities in a logbook. This will help you monitor how much you've taken from the environment and whether certain areas or species need time to recover.

Rotating Foraging Spots

One of the easiest yet most effective methods to prevent overharvesting is by rotating your foraging spots. This practice ensures that no single area is overly depleted and allows nature to recover between harvests.

Spread Out Foraging Efforts:

- **Rotate Locations:** Don't rely on the same spot for gathering food every time. Spread your efforts across different areas to give plants and wildlife time to regenerate.
- **Seasonal Adjustments:** Some species thrive in specific seasons. By adjusting your foraging habits throughout the year, you allow different ecosystems to flourish during their peak times.

Pro Tip: Create a foraging map of your surroundings and mark down the areas you've already harvested from. This will remind you to rotate spots and keep track of when you last visited each area.

Respecting Ecosystems

Living off the land means being part of the ecosystem, not just taking from it. It's vital to respect local wildlife and plant life, ensuring that your actions do not disrupt the delicate balance of nature.

Leave Certain Species Untouched:

- **Protect Endangered or Vulnerable Species:** If a plant or animal is rare or struggling in your region, avoid harvesting it. Doing so allows these species to continue to grow and multiply, which ultimately benefits the entire ecosystem.
- **Avoid Disruptive Techniques:** When hunting or foraging, use methods that cause the least amount of disturbance to the land. For example, avoid trampling plant life or cutting down large areas of vegetation for temporary needs.

Pro Tip: Consider planting native species in your garden or homestead to support the local environment. This helps replenish the natural resources you've harvested and ensures a healthy ecosystem in the long run.

Waste Nothing Philosophy

A core tenet of sustainable off-grid living is minimizing waste. Every part of your catch or harvest can be repurposed for something useful, whether it's food, tools, or even clothing.

Repurposing Bones, Hides, and Other Materials:

- **Bones:** After consuming meat, bones can be turned into tools, needles, or fishing hooks. They can also be used to create broth, adding extra nutrition to your meals.
- **Hides and Skins:** The hides of animals you've hunted can be transformed into clothing, blankets, or shelter materials. Tanning the hides ensures they last for years.
- **Foraged Plants:** Even parts of plants you don't eat can be useful. Stems and leaves can be composted to improve soil quality, while fibrous materials can be woven into baskets or used for fire-starting.

Pro Tip: Learning traditional skills like tanning hides, weaving, and bone carving can help you get the most out of your harvests, turning every part of your catch into something valuable.

By incorporating these ethical and sustainable practices into your off-grid lifestyle, you'll not only ensure your own survival but also contribute to the longevity and health of the environment. Living in harmony with nature means understanding the limits of your resources, using every part of what you gather, and allowing ecosystems to flourish alongside you. In the end, this balance between harvesting and sustainability will provide you with long-term security and a deeper connection to the world around you.

22. Preserving Game and Fish: Harnessing Nature's Bounty

Extending Nature's Bounty

Building on the foundations of hunting, fishing, and foraging discussed in the previous guide, this book shifts focus to a crucial aspect of off-grid living: preserving the fruits of your efforts. Once you've successfully sourced meat and fish from nature, the next step is ensuring that your harvest can sustain you for months to come.

This guide dives deep into preservation techniques specifically tailored for game and fish. Methods like sun drying, smoking, and salting have been used for centuries to preserve meat without the need for refrigeration or modern technology. These time-tested approaches allow you to store your hard-earned harvests safely, making sure you have a steady food supply throughout the year.

With a focus on practical and efficient methods, you'll learn how to properly prepare, preserve, and store the meats and fish you gather, ensuring that nothing goes to waste and that your off-grid lifestyle remains sustainable.

Preserving Your Harvest: Natural Preservation Methods

This section will guide you through practical, time-tested methods like sun drying, smoking, and salting, which allow you to store your harvest safely for extended periods. Let's dive into the step-by-step processes of preserving using minimal resources and maximum efficiency.

Sun Drying and Smoking Meat

Sun drying and smoking are two of the oldest, most reliable methods for preserving meat and fish. They require little more than sunlight, wood, and a basic setup, making them perfect for off-grid living.

Sun Drying Meat

Sun drying is an easy and efficient way to preserve smaller cuts of meat and fish by removing moisture to prevent spoilage. This method works best in warm, dry climates with consistent sunlight.

Step-by-Step Guide to Sun Drying Meat:

1. **Preparation:**
   - Choose lean cuts of meat (wild game or fish works well). Fatty pieces are prone to spoilage because fat doesn't dry well.
   - Cut the meat into thin strips, approximately 1/4 inch thick. Thinner strips will dry more quickly and evenly.

2. **Salting:**
   - Lightly salt the meat strips on both sides. Salt draws out moisture and helps prevent bacterial growth.
   - Let the salted meat rest for about 30 minutes.
3. **Drying Setup:**
   - String the meat strips onto a thin rope or skewer. Make sure the strips aren't touching, so air can circulate freely.
   - Hang the strips in direct sunlight, in a well-ventilated area. Avoid places where animals or pests could reach the meat.
   - Turn the strips periodically to ensure even drying.

4. **Timeframe:**
   - o Depending on the climate and thickness of the meat, sun drying can take anywhere from 1 to 3 days. The meat is ready when it feels leathery but still bendable.

Pro Tip: If you live in a humid area, you may need to bring the meat inside at night to avoid moisture buildup from dew.

Smoking Meat and Fish

Smoking is a method that not only preserves meat but also adds a rich, smoky flavor. There are two main types of smoking: hot smoking, which cooks the meat as it smokes, and cold smoking, which dries the meat without fully cooking it.

Step-by-Step Guide to Smoking Meat and Fish:

1. **Building a Basic Smokehouse or Drying Rack:**
   - o **Smokehouse:** If you have the resources, you can build a simple smokehouse from wood or stone. It should be tall enough to hang meat and have an enclosed area to trap smoke.
   - o **Drying Rack:** For smaller operations, use a wooden frame covered with mesh or chicken wire. Position this over a smoldering fire.
2. **Preparing the Meat:**
   - o Similar to sun drying, slice your meat or fish into thin strips.
   - o Lightly salt the strips or marinate them in a brine solution (water, salt, and any preferred spices) for added flavor and preservation.
3. **Setting Up the Fire:**
   - o Use hardwoods like applewood, hickory, or oak for the fire. These woods burn slowly and produce a clean, flavorful smoke.
   - o Start a small fire and allow it to burn down to hot coals. Place wet wood chips on top of the coals to create smoke.
   - o Hang the meat strips in the smokehouse or on the drying rack above the fire.

4. **Smoking Duration:**
   - o For **hot smoking**, maintain a temperature between 150°F and 200°F. Smoke the meat for 4 to 6 hours.
   - o For **cold smoking**, keep the temperature below 90°F. This process can take 12 to 48 hours, depending on the meat and weather conditions.

Pro Tip: Make sure the smoke is consistent and not too thick. Too much smoke can lead to a bitter taste. Ventilate your smokehouse or rack for the best results.

Salting: Preserving Meat and Fish Naturally

Salting is one of the most effective preservation techniques, as salt draws out moisture and creates an environment where bacteria cannot thrive. This method is ideal for preserving meat and fish, especially in regions without consistent sunlight or smoking conditions

Making Salt from Seawater

If you're near the coast, you can harvest your own salt by evaporating seawater. This natural salt can be used in your preservation processes.

Step-by-Step Guide to Making Salt:

1. **Gather Seawater:**
   - Collect clean seawater in a large container. Make sure the water is free from pollution.
2. **Evaporation:**
   - Pour the seawater into a shallow pan and leave it out in the sun. As the water evaporates, salt crystals will begin to form. This can take several days to a week, depending on the climate.
   - Once all the water has evaporated, collect the salt crystals and store them in an airtight container.

Pro Tip: In areas with less sun, you can heat the seawater over a fire to speed up evaporation.

Using Salting as a Preservation Method

Salting is straightforward and doesn't require special equipment. All you need is salt and time.

Step-by-Step Guide to Salt Preservation:

1. **Preparation:**
   - Clean and dry the meat or fish. Remove as much moisture as possible by patting it dry with a cloth or paper towel.
2. **Salt Application:**
   - Coat the meat or fish thoroughly with salt. Ensure every surface is covered, including any crevices. For large cuts, you can make shallow cuts into the meat to allow the salt to penetrate deeper.
   - For long-term preservation, use about 1/4 inch of salt around each piece.
3. **Curing Time:**
   - Place the salted meat or fish in a cool, dry area. Ideally, this should be in a non-humid space where air can circulate.
   - Leave the meat to cure for 1 to 5 days, depending on the thickness. Check the meat daily and drain any excess liquid.
4. **Storing the Cured Meat:**
   - After the curing process, you can store the meat in an airtight container or wrap it in cloth. If you want to extend its shelf life even further, combine salting with sun drying or smoking.

Pro Tip: For additional flavor, mix your salt with herbs or spices like thyme, rosemary, or pepper before coating the meat.

By mastering these natural preservation techniques, you ensure that your harvest supply remains stable and secure, no matter the season or circumstances. Whether you're sun drying, smoking, or salting, these methods give you the ability to extend the shelf life of your meat and fish, allowing you to enjoy the fruits of your labor for months on end. Practice these techniques regularly, and soon you'll find that preserving your harvest becomes second nature.

23. Herbal Remedies for Off-Grid Living

The Role of Herbal Remedies in Off-Grid Living

In an off-grid lifestyle, self-reliance extends beyond just providing your own food, water, and shelter—it includes your ability to care for your health using natural resources. Without easy access to conventional medicine, you need a deep understanding of the natural remedies available to you. Herbal medicine, a time-honored tradition, is an invaluable tool for anyone living off the grid, offering a sustainable, effective alternative to modern pharmaceuticals.

Using medicinal plants for health not only aligns with the principles of sustainability but also connects you to the natural world in a way that's deeply empowering. By learning how to identify, grow, and prepare medicinal herbs, you can treat common ailments, boost your immune system, and manage stress, all while reducing dependency on modern healthcare systems. This section will introduce you to the basics of herbal remedies, helping you integrate them into your off-grid lifestyle and establish a self-sufficient health system for you and your family.

Identifying and Foraging Essential Medicinal Herbs

One of the greatest advantages of living off-grid is the abundant access to nature's pharmacy. Foraging for medicinal herbs is a valuable skill, allowing you to find the ingredients needed for a wide range of home remedies. However, foraging requires knowledge, attention to detail, and respect for the natural environment.

- **Foraging Basics**: Learn the core principles of foraging, including how to correctly identify, harvest, and collect wild herbs. Developing this skill will enable you to confidently source medicinal plants from your surroundings.
- **Essential Herbs to Identify:**
  - **Plantain (Plantago major)**: A versatile herb used for treating insect bites, minor cuts, and inflammation. Often found in most regions, it's a staple in any herbal toolkit.
  - **Yarrow (Achillea millefolium)**: Known for its ability to heal wounds, reduce bleeding, and lower fever. Yarrow's versatility makes it indispensable for off-grid living.
  - **Echinacea (Echinacea purpurea)**: Renowned for its immune-boosting properties, this herb helps prevent and fight infections, making it crucial during cold and flu seasons.
- **Safety and Identification Guidelines**: How to distinguish between beneficial plants and potentially harmful lookalikes. Understanding these differences is critical for safe foraging, especially in unfamiliar environments.
- **Seasonal and Geographic Considerations**: Learn when and where to find these herbs, ensuring you can harvest them in their optimal conditions throughout the year.

Growing Your Own Medicinal Herbs at Home

Cultivating your own medicinal herb garden ensures you always have access to vital remedies. Whether you're dealing with a seasonal illness or preparing for long-term health needs, a well-planned herbal garden can sustain your wellness efforts in any off-grid scenario.

- **Herb Garden Design**: Discover the principles of designing an efficient herb garden that thrives in an off-grid environment. Learn how to select the best location, manage soil health, and maximize sunlight and water use to grow robust medicinal plants.
- **Key Medicinal Herbs to Grow:**
  - **Chamomile (Matricaria chamomilla)**: A gentle, calming herb known for its ability to soothe nerves and promote restful sleep. Chamomile is easy to grow and offers a reliable source of relaxation and relief from anxiety.
  - **Lavender (Lavandula angustifolia)**: Lavender is celebrated for its soothing properties and effectiveness in treating stress, skin issues, and sleep disturbances. Having this plant in your garden will provide a multipurpose remedy for various ailments.
  - **Calendula (Calendula officinalis)**: This powerful healing herb is essential for treating cuts, burns, and skin irritations. Calendula's easy growth and wide range of uses make it a must-have in any herbal garden.
  - **Aloe Vera**: Renowned for its remarkable healing properties, Aloe Vera is invaluable for soothing burns, cuts, and irritated skin. It requires minimal maintenance and provides continuous benefits throughout the year.
- **Sustainable Growing Practices**: Learn how to propagate herbs using seeds, cuttings, and transplants to ensure long-term sustainability. These techniques will allow you to continually replenish your garden and expand your herbal resources.

Herbal remedies represent a commitment to living in harmony with nature, using what's around you to maintain both physical and mental well-being. Whether you're treating a small wound or managing stress, these herbs will empower you to take control of your health in a sustainable, self-reliant way.

Storing and Preserving Herbs for Long-Term Use

In an off-grid lifestyle, your access to fresh herbs may not always be guaranteed year-round. To maintain a self-sufficient approach to health, it's essential to know how to properly store and preserve your herbs for long-term use without losing their potency. With the right techniques, you can ensure your herbal remedies remain effective when required, offering a dependable source of healing and care in any season or situation.

Here, we'll guide you through proven methods to dry, store, and preserve herbs. These practices will allow you to maintain your herbal supply, whether you're dealing with a humid environment or other off-grid challenges. Proper preservation ensures that your herbs retain their medicinal properties, allowing you to create salves, teas, tinctures, and oils anytime.

Drying Herbs: Techniques to Preserve Potency

Drying herbs is one of the most reliable methods to ensure they last and maintain their effectiveness. Here's how to do it right:

- **Air Drying**: The simplest method, ideal for sturdy herbs like rosemary, thyme, and sage. Tie small bunches of herbs together and hang them in a dry, well-ventilated area. Avoid direct sunlight, as it can diminish the potency of the oils within the plants.
- **Dehydrators**: For quicker and more controlled drying, a dehydrator works well, especially in humid conditions. Set your dehydrator to a low temperature (95-115°F) and allow the herbs to dry over several hours.
- **Oven Drying**: If you're off-grid and using solar ovens or wood-fueled stoves, you can dry herbs by placing them on low heat for a few hours. Ensure the herbs don't cook, which can reduce their effectiveness.

Storing Dried Herbs

Once your herbs are properly dried, storing them is key to preventing moisture and mold from spoiling your hard work. Here's how to ensure their long-term preservation:

- **Airtight Containers**: Store dried herbs in airtight glass jars or metal tins. Glass jars are preferred as they are non-reactive, keeping your herbs pure.
- **Cool, Dark Storage**: Herbs should be kept in a cool, dark place to preserve their potency. Exposure to heat and light will cause the herbs to lose their essential oils over time.
- **Labeling and Dating**: Always label your jars with the name of the herb and the date it was stored. Most dried herbs maintain their potency for 1-2 years.

Creating Herbal Oils and Tinctures for Long-Term Use

Making herbal oils and tinctures is a great way to preserve the benefits of herbs over extended periods. These preparations are easy to store and ready to use whenever needed:

- **Herbal Oils:**
  - Combine your dried herbs with a carrier oil (such as olive or coconut oil) in a glass jar.
  - Seal the jar and place it in a warm spot (but not in direct sunlight) for 2-6 weeks, shaking it daily to release the herbs' essential oils into the carrier oil.
  - After infusing, strain out the herbs and store the oil in a cool, dark place.
- **Tinctures:**
  - Tinctures are made by soaking herbs in alcohol or vinegar to extract the medicinal properties.
  - Fill a glass jar with dried herbs and cover them with alcohol (vodka or brandy) or apple cider vinegar for a non-alcoholic option.
  - Let the mixture sit for 4-6 weeks, shaking it every few days. Afterward, strain and store the tincture in a dark glass bottle for up to several years.

Avoiding Degradation: How to Maintain Herb Effectiveness

Proper storage is vital to preventing your herbs from losing their medicinal properties over time. Here are a few tips to ensure they stay potent:

- **Avoid Moisture**: Dried herbs should remain dry. If they get exposed to moisture, they could mold or degrade. Regularly check your stored herbs, and if any moisture is detected, you may need to re-dry them or discard compromised portions.
- **Rotate Stock**: Use your oldest stored herbs first to ensure nothing is left to degrade over time. Follow a first-in, first-out rotation method.
- **Keep Oils and Tinctures Cool**: Herbal oils and tinctures should be kept in a cool, dark place. Excessive heat can cause them to go rancid or lose potency.

Preparing Salves, Teas, and Tinctures

Creating herbal preparations allows you to make the most of your stored herbs. Whether you need relief from a headache, aid for digestion, or a treatment for burns, herbal salves, teas, and tinctures offer powerful solutions.

Salves: Step-by-Step for Healing Ointments

Salves are healing ointments made by combining herbal oils with beeswax. They are excellent for treating skin irritations, bruises, and muscle pain. Here's how to make a basic salve:

1. **Infuse Oil**: Start by making an herbal oil infusion as described above, using herbs like comfrey for bruises or arnica for muscle soreness.
2. **Melt Beeswax**: In a double boiler, melt beeswax over low heat. As a rule, use 1 oz of beeswax for every 8 oz of herbal oil.
3. **Mix and Cool**: Once the beeswax is melted, slowly stir in your herbal oil. Pour the mixture into jars and let it cool before sealing.

Teas: Simple, Soothing Herbal Remedies

Herbal teas are a comforting and effective method to treat a wide range of ailments. Whether you're dealing with digestive issues or fighting off a cold, teas provide a gentle remedy:

- **Peppermint Tea**: Perfect for soothing nausea and aiding digestion. Steep dried peppermint leaves in hot water for 5-10 minutes and drink as needed.
- **Ginger Tea**: For cold relief and digestive health, steep fresh or dried ginger root in hot water for 10 minutes. Add honey for extra soothing benefits.

Tinctures: Potent and Long-Lasting Herbal Medicine

Tinctures offer a concentrated and long-lasting way to benefit from herbs. Valerian root tincture, for instance, is excellent for reducing stress and promoting sleep. Follow the same tincture-making process outlined above, ensuring you store it properly for long-term use.

Tools and Materials for Herbal Preparations

For off-grid herbal preparations, here's what you'll need:

- **Glass jars** for infusions and storage
- Cheesecloth or strainers for filtering
- **Mortar and pestle** for grinding dried herbs
- **Beeswax** for salves
- **Carrier oils** such as olive or coconut oil
- Alcohol or vinegar for tinctures

Herbal Remedies for Common Ailments

Herbs offer powerful solutions for everyday health issues. Here's a breakdown of effective remedies for common ailments:

- **Cuts and Burns:**
  - **Aloe Vera**: Renowned for its calming and restorative properties, aloe vera is a go-to for burns and minor cuts.
  - **St. John's Wort**: This oil-infused herb accelerates healing for skin injuries and reduces inflammation.

- **Colds and Flu:**
  - **Elderberry**: Packed with antioxidants, elderberry boosts the immune system and helps relieve cold and flu symptoms.
  - **Echinacea**: A powerful herb for strengthening the immune system during cold and flu season.
- **Digestive Issues:**
  - **Fennel**: Helps relieve bloating, gas, and indigestion.

- o **Peppermint**: Calms the stomach and alleviates indigestion.
- **Headaches and Muscle Aches:**
  - o **Lavender**: Known for its calming effect, lavender helps reduce tension and soothe headaches and sore muscles.

Armed with the proper knowledge and strategy, you can be fully prepared to handle common health issues using herbal remedies. Storing, preserving, and preparing herbs is an essential skill for off-grid living, ensuring that you have access to natural and effective solutions whenever needed.

Herbal Remedies for Mental Health

In today's fast-paced world, stress, anxiety, and sleep disorders have become common issues. Off-grid living brings many benefits, such as peace, self-sufficiency, and closeness to nature, but it doesn't make you immune to mental health challenges. Using herbal remedies to support your mental well-being is an excellent way to stay balanced and healthy in your off-grid life.

Stress and Anxiety Relief

Living off the grid requires adaptability and resilience, but it can also come with its own stressors. Herbs can provide natural relief and help manage anxiety without the need for pharmaceutical solutions.

- **Ashwagandha (Withania somnifera)**: This powerful adaptogen is well-known for its ability to reduce stress and anxiety. It's ideal for long-term use as it helps regulate your body's response to stress by balancing cortisol levels. You can take it as a tincture or capsule.
- **Lemon Balm (Melissa officinalis)**: Known for its calming properties, lemon balm is perfect for reducing stress and anxiety. A simple lemon balm tea can help soothe nerves after a long day and create a sense of relaxation. It's also great for lifting mood during stressful times.

Insomnia and Sleep Aids

Good, restorative sleep is crucial for maintaining physical and mental health, especially when you're off the grid and have demanding tasks to manage daily. These herbs can naturally support better sleep quality and help with insomnia.

- **Valerian Root (Valeriana officinalis)**: This herb is a go-to for treating insomnia and improving sleep quality. Valerian works by calming the central nervous system, promoting faster sleep onset and helping you stay asleep longer. It's typically used as a tincture or in capsule form before bed.
- **Chamomile (Matricaria chamomilla)**: A classic herbal remedy for promoting relaxation and sleep, chamomile tea is one of the easiest and most effective ways to unwind before bed. It helps calm both the mind and body, making it easier to drift off into a restful sleep.

Mood Boosting

Maintaining a positive outlook is essential, especially when challenges arise in off-grid living. Herbs that naturally uplift the mood can provide the boost you need to stay positive and focused.

- **St. John's Wort (Hypericum perforatum)**: Known for its ability to support emotional well-being, St. John's Wort is commonly used to alleviate symptoms of mild to moderate depression. It works by increasing levels of serotonin in the brain, helping regulate mood and emotions. Use it as a tincture or capsule for a mood-boosting effect.

Immunity-Boosting Herbs

Maintaining a strong immune system is essential when living off the grid. Access to conventional medicine might be limited, so using herbs to support and strengthen your immune system can be invaluable. These herbs not only help you fight off illness but also act as preventative measures.

Herbs for Strengthening the Immune System

These herbs help boost immunity and protect against infections, especially during cold and flu season or times of heightened exposure to illness.

- **Astragalus (Astragalus membranaceus)**: This herb is an immune-modulating powerhouse, helping to enhance your body's natural defenses. Astragalus supports the immune system by increasing white blood cell production and can be taken regularly as a tincture or tea for long-term immune health.
- **Echinacea (Echinacea purpurea)**: Well-known for its immune-boosting properties, echinacea helps fight off infections, particularly respiratory illnesses. It's most effective when taken at the onset of symptoms or as a daily preventative during flu season.
- **Elderberry (Sambucus nigra)**: Rich in antioxidants and vitamins, elderberry is highly effective for supporting the immune system and treating cold or flu symptoms. You can make elderberry syrup or tea to boost immunity and shorten the duration of illness.

Preventative Use

To maintain overall health, you can integrate these herbs into your daily routine. Teas and tinctures made from astragalus, echinacea, or elderberry are easy to prepare and can be consumed regularly to strengthen your immune system before illness strikes.

Herbal Remedies for Common Ailments

No matter how well-prepared you are, common ailments like colds, digestive issues, or urinary infections can still occur in off-grid living. Here's how to prevent and treat these conditions with herbal remedies.

Colds and Flu

When cold and flu season comes around, these herbs can help prevent illness or reduce the severity and duration of symptoms.

- **Sambucus (Elderberry)**: Helps boost immune function and fight off viral infections, making it an excellent remedy for colds and the flu. Elderberry syrup can be taken daily as a preventative measure or at the first sign of illness.
- **Echinacea**: This herb not only strengthens the immune system but also helps reduce the severity of cold and flu symptoms. Use it as a tincture or tea at the onset of symptoms for best results.
- **Thyme (Thymus vulgaris)**: Thyme is great for easing respiratory congestion and soothing sore throats. It can be used as a steam inhalation or a tea to break up mucus and calm inflamed airways.

Urinary Tract Infections (UTIs)

UTIs can be painful and, if untreated, lead to more serious complications. These herbs are effective in both preventing and treating UTIs.

- **Cranberry**: Long used to prevent UTIs, cranberry helps by preventing bacteria from adhering to the urinary tract walls. Drinking cranberry juice or taking cranberry extract can be beneficial in managing urinary health.
- **Dandelion (Taraxacum officinale)**: As a diuretic and anti-inflammatory herb, dandelion helps flush the urinary system and supports kidney health. You can drink dandelion tea to cleanse your system and promote urinary health.

Digestive Issues

For those occasional bouts of indigestion, bloating, or gas, these herbs can provide fast relief and help keep your digestive system running smoothly.

- **Fennel (Foeniculum vulgare)**: Fennel is excellent for relieving bloating and gas. You can chew fennel seeds after meals or brew fennel tea to ease discomfort.
- **Ginger (Zingiber officinale)**: A well-known digestive aid, ginger helps with nausea, indigestion, and bloating. Drink ginger tea or chew fresh ginger to soothe an upset stomach or prevent nausea.

By incorporating these herbal remedies into your off-grid lifestyle, you'll be able to manage common health challenges with confidence and self-reliance. Whether you're looking to boost your immune system, calm anxiety, or treat digestive discomfort, these herbs offer practical, effective solutions.

Essential Oil Distillation and Preparation

When living off the grid, creating your own essential oils can be a valuable skill. Essential oils not only have therapeutic properties but are also incredibly versatile. They can be used for treating headaches, skin conditions, stress, and even for household cleaning or as insect repellents. The process of extracting these oils from herbs can be done using simple equipment, making it an ideal project for an off-grid lifestyle.

Off-Grid Distillation Techniques

The process of distillation involves extracting the volatile compounds (essential oils) from herbs through steam or water distillation. It requires minimal equipment and is an efficient way to harness the power of plants.

- **Steam Distillation**: This method involves boiling water to create steam, which passes through plant material, carrying essential oils with it. The steam is then condensed into a liquid, where oil and water naturally separate, allowing you to collect the oil. A basic distillation setup includes a heat source, a condenser, and collection jars. Even an off-grid setup with a wood stove can power the process.
- **Water Distillation**: This method works similarly, but instead of using steam, the plant material is submerged in boiling water. The essential oils are extracted as the water evaporates. This method is ideal for herbs with more delicate oils like lavender or chamomile, which can lose potency if exposed to direct steam.

Best Herbs for Essential Oils

Certain herbs are particularly effective for essential oil distillation. These plants are rich in volatile oils and provide numerous benefits:

- **Lavender (Lavandula angustifolia)**: Known for its calming properties, lavender oil is great for reducing stress, relieving headaches, and soothing skin irritations.

- **Peppermint (Mentha piperita)**: This oil is ideal for relieving headaches, improving focus, and soothing digestive discomfort when applied to the skin or inhaled.
- **Eucalyptus (Eucalyptus globulus)**: Eucalyptus oil is excellent for respiratory issues and has antibacterial properties, making it useful in off-grid settings for disinfecting and purifying the air.
- **Rosemary (Rosmarinus officinalis)**: Rosemary oil is energizing and helps improve memory and concentration. It's also useful for promoting hair growth and treating scalp conditions.

Uses of Essential Oils

Once you've distilled your essential oils, there are various practical applications for them, especially when living off-grid:

- **Headache Treatment**: Oils like peppermint and lavender can be diluted in a carrier oil and applied to the temples or inhaled for quick relief.
- **Skin Problems**: Lavender and calendula essential oils are perfect for treating cuts, burns, and other skin irritations, thanks to their soothing and healing properties.
- **Stress Relief**: Diffusing or applying lavender or eucalyptus oils can help reduce stress, making your off-grid life more peaceful and manageable. You can create DIY diffusers using simple materials like clay or wood.

Herbal Skin Care Solutions

Taking care of your skin using medicinal herbs is not only effective but aligns perfectly with the self-sufficient nature of off-grid living. Many herbs are packed with healing properties that can help manage conditions like eczema, acne, and burns without the need for synthetic products.

Herbs for Skin Conditions

- **Calendula (Calendula officinalis)**: Known for its gentle healing properties, calendula is ideal for treating eczema, acne, and other inflammatory skin conditions. You can create calendula-infused oils or balms to soothe irritated skin.
- **Aloe Vera (Aloe barbadensis)**: This plant is famous for its ability to hydrate and soothe the skin. It's particularly useful for burns, cuts, and dry skin. Aloe gel can be harvested directly from the plant and applied as needed.
- **St. John's Wort Oil (Hypericum perforatum)**: St. John's Wort is fantastic for treating burns and scars. An oil infusion of the herb can be applied to the skin to promote healing and reduce the appearance of scars over time.

Remedies for Acne and Psoriasis

For those dealing with more persistent skin issues like acne or psoriasis, herbal remedies can offer significant relief:

- **Calendula and Chamomile Infusions**: A mixture of calendula and chamomile tea can be applied as a toner to reduce acne inflammation and soothe the skin.
- **Tea Tree Oil**: Known for its antibacterial properties, tea tree oil is a powerful remedy for acne. It should be diluted in a carrier oil to prevent irritation before applying to problem areas.
- **Herbal Baths**: Taking herbal baths with lavender, chamomile, or calendula can help reduce psoriasis symptoms and promote overall skin health. Simply steep the herbs in boiling water and add the infusion to your bathwater.

Understanding Herb-Drug Interactions

When using herbs for medicinal purposes, it's crucial to recognize potential interactions between herbs and pharmaceutical drugs. While herbal remedies are natural, they can sometimes interfere with prescribed medications, leading to unwanted side effects or diminished efficacy.

Recognizing Potential Risks

Understanding the possible risks of combining herbs and medications is key to ensuring safe usage:

- **Anticoagulants and Herbs**: Herbs such as garlic, ginkgo biloba, and ginger have blood-thinning properties. When combined with anticoagulant medications like warfarin, they can increase the risk of bleeding.
- **Antidepressants and St. John's Wort**: St. John's Wort is a popular herb for treating mild depression, but when combined with SSRIs or other antidepressants, it can cause serotonin syndrome, a potentially dangerous condition.
- **Blood Pressure Medications**: Some herbs, like licorice root, can elevate blood pressure and interfere with the effectiveness of antihypertensive drugs.

Safe Usage Guidelines

To avoid potential interactions, follow these guidelines when incorporating herbal remedies into your routine:

- **Consult a Healthcare Professional**: Always talk to a healthcare provider before combining herbs with prescription medications, especially if you have a chronic condition.
- **Monitor Dosages Carefully**: Stick to recommended dosages and avoid overuse. Herbs can be potent, and more is not always better.
- **Start with Small Doses**: When trying a new herb, start with small amounts to monitor how your body reacts, especially if you're taking medications.

Final Thoughts on Preparedness and Self-Reliance

Herbal knowledge is an essential part of off-grid preparedness. By knowing how to cultivate, forage, and use herbs, you enhance your ability to live independently and respond to health challenges without relying on pharmaceuticals or outside help. This self-reliance is empowering, giving you confidence that you can manage not just daily health, but also potential emergencies, using the resources around you.

The more you integrate these practices into your routine, the more resilient you become. Your health, your environment, and your preparedness all benefit from this natural synergy, and you are better equipped for long-term sustainability.

In the end, your knowledge of herbal medicine strengthens your off-grid experience, ensuring that you're not just surviving, but living a healthy, empowered, and self-sufficient life. Keep learning, keep practicing, and trust in the power of nature to support you on this journey.

24. Off-Grid First Aid & Medical Preparedness

The Importance of Off-Grid Medical Preparedness

In the world of off-grid living, you can't afford to rely on modern conveniences like hospitals, pharmacies, or even basic sanitation systems. Your health and safety depend on your ability to manage medical emergencies with the resources you have. Just as you learned to harness herbal remedies in the previous book, now it's time to shift your focus to the broader aspects of medical preparedness—one pillar of self-reliance in an off-grid environment.

The key to thriving off the grid is long-term health. A clean environment reduces the risk of infections, while preparedness ensures you can address medical emergencies as they arise. This guide will take you through essential first aid practices, and improvisation techniques you'll need to stay resilient in your self-sufficient lifestyle.

Building a Complete Off-Grid First Aid Kit

Your first line of defense in any medical situation is a well-stocked and well-organized first aid kit. Off-grid living requires more than just a basic kit—yours needs to be comprehensive and tailored to the specific challenges of remote living.

Essentials for Your Kit:

- Standard supplies like bandages, gauze, tweezers, antiseptic wipes, and gloves are a must.
- Include **specialized items** that will allow you to handle more serious situations:
    o Hemostatic agents for controlling severe bleeding.
    o Splints and braces for managing fractures.
    o Sutures or wound closure strips for deeper cuts.
    o Antibiotic ointments to prevent infections in wounds.

Organization Tips: Your first aid kit should be organized so that every item is easy to find in an emergency. Group similar items together, and make sure that frequently needed supplies, like bandages and antiseptic wipes, are easily accessible.

First Aid Techniques for Bleeding, Trauma, and Fractures

Knowing how to handle injuries is critical when you're miles from the nearest hospital. Stopping bleeding quickly and effectively is one of the most important skills you'll need. Here's how you can manage different types of trauma.

- **Stopping Bleeding:** For minor cuts, applying direct pressure with clean gauze will usually suffice. In cases of more severe bleeding, applying a tourniquet or using hemostatic agents may be necessary. Learn to assess the severity of the situation and act accordingly.
- **Handling Fractures:** Broken bones are a common risk in off-grid environments, especially if you're working with tools or hiking rugged terrain. First, assess the injury. Then, improvise a splint using materials you have on hand, such as sturdy branches or boards. Immobilizing the fracture is key to preventing further damage. If available, use cold packs or even natural alternatives like cold water to reduce swelling and alleviate pain.

Heat-Related and Cold-Related Medical Emergencies

When living off-grid, you're exposed to the elements, and extreme temperatures can pose serious threats to your health. Recognizing and treating both heat-related and cold-related emergencies can be lifesaving.

- **Heat-Related Emergencies:** Heat exhaustion and heatstroke are serious risks, especially in warm climates. Key symptoms include dizziness, nausea, heavy sweating, or hot, dry skin. Move the person to a shaded area, cool them down with water and fanning, and provide hydration. In severe cases, call for medical help or transport the person to a cooler environment.

- **Cold-Related Emergencies:** Hypothermia and frostbite can occur if you're exposed to cold weather without proper protection. Hypothermia symptoms include shivering, confusion, and fatigue. In such cases, move the person to a warmer area, remove wet clothing, and gradually warm them with blankets or body heat. Frostbite should be treated by warming the affected area, but avoid rubbing, as it can cause further damage.

Respiratory and Allergy Emergencies

Respiratory problems and allergic reactions are life-threatening if left untreated. Asthma attacks, allergic reactions, and choking incidents can occur anywhere, and having the skills to handle these emergencies is essential.

- **Asthma and Allergies:** If you or someone in your group suffers from severe allergies, carrying an EpiPen is non-negotiable. In the absence of one, there are alternatives like natural antihistamines, though they should never be a substitute in life-threatening cases. Recognize the signs of anaphylaxis early and act fast.
- **Airway Blockages:** Knowing the Heimlich maneuver can save a life if someone chokes, and understanding how to clear a blocked airway is crucial. In more serious situations, you may need to perform CPR or rescue breathing, techniques that every off-gridder should be familiar with.

Burns and Scalds

Burns can be a common injury in off-grid living, especially if you rely on open fires or stoves for cooking and heating.

- **Types of Burns:** Burns are categorized into three degrees. First-degree burns cause redness and minor pain, while second-degree burns blister and are more painful. Third-degree burns are severe, involving deep tissue damage and possibly charring.
- **First Aid for Burns:** Cool the burn area with clean, cool water (but not ice) for a minimum of 10 minutes. Gently cover the burn with a sterile dressing or clean cloth to prevent infection. For severe burns, avoid removing clothing stuck to the burn and seek medical help immediately. Keep the person warm and hydrated until help arrives.

Mental Health Preparedness

While physical health is critical, mental health is equally important in off-grid living. Prolonged isolation, uncertainty, and the challenges of self-reliant living can take a toll on your mental well-being.

- **Recognizing Mental Health Struggles:** Symptoms of mental health issues can include prolonged sadness, anxiety, irritability, or a sense of hopelessness. These can be exacerbated by isolation in remote areas.
- **Self-Care Strategies:** Maintain a routine, engage in physical activity, and make time for relaxing activities like reading or hobbies. Stay connected with loved ones, even if it's through letters or satellite communication. Establish a support system within your group to ensure mental health is addressed proactively.

Improvised Medical Solutions for Off-Grid Living

In remote locations, professional medical tools might not always be available. That's where the ability to improvise comes in. With a combination of natural remedies and makeshift tools, you can manage many medical emergencies.

- **Using Natural Remedies:** As you learned in the herbal remedies guide, plants like yarrow can be used to treat wounds and control bleeding, while willow bark can serve as a natural pain reliever. Knowing which plants can serve as first aid substitutes is essential when pharmaceuticals are out of reach.

- **Makeshift Tools:** You can create effective medical tools with everyday off-grid materials. For instance, a sturdy branch can work as a splint, and clean fabric can be used as a bandage in a pinch. Being resourceful with what you have around you can greatly influence how you manage injuries.

In this guide, we've covered the essential aspects of off-grid first aid and medical preparedness, equipping you with the tools and knowledge to handle emergencies and stay healthy in remote environments. However, medical preparedness is only one part of the bigger picture. In the next book, we'll delve into hygiene management, a topic that's closely linked to maintaining your long-term health off the grid. Proper hygiene practices can drastically reduce the risk of infections and other health complications, making it a critical element of your self-reliant lifestyle. Stay tuned as we explore how to create sustainable hygiene systems that will keep you and your living environment safe and clean.

25. Off-Grid Personal Hygiene and DIY Solutions

Sustainable Hygiene Practices for Off-Grid Living

Without access to modern sanitation, maintaining personal hygiene off the grid requires creative and sustainable methods. Fortunately, many effective solutions require minimal resources and can be created from materials you already have available.

DIY Soap-Making

Soap is a basic necessity for hygiene, but when living off-grid, it may not always be readily available. Luckily, you can make your own effective soap using animal fats and wood ash, both of which are common byproducts of off-grid living. The process is straightforward, though it requires some care.

First, render your animal fat (such as lard or tallow) by heating it slowly and straining out any impurities. Next, create lye water by soaking hardwood ashes in water for about 24 hours, then carefully strain the solution. Combine the lye water with the rendered fat, heating and stirring the mixture until it thickens. Once it's thick enough, pour it into molds and let it set. After it has hardened, cut the soap into bars and allow them to cure for several weeks before using.

This soap is great for cleaning not only your body but also clothes and other household items. It's an essential skill that ensures you can maintain cleanliness no matter your situation.

Grooming

Staying well-groomed is another aspect of hygiene that can be challenging without electricity or running water, but it is essential to prevent infections and maintain health. Regularly trimming your hair and nails is important, especially when working in outdoor conditions where dirt can easily accumulate under your nails.

To maintain your grooming tools, sterilize them by boiling them in water. This helps eliminate bacteria and prevents any infections from spreading when you cut your nails or trim your hair. Additionally, if shaving, use soap as a lubricant to avoid skin irritation, and always clean the razor thoroughly after each use.

Managing Menstrual Hygiene Off-Grid

For those who menstruate, managing menstrual hygiene is a practical consideration, especially in remote areas. Reusable menstrual products such as menstrual cups or cloth pads are the best options for off-grid living. These items reduce waste, last longer, and can be easily cleaned and reused.

Menstrual Cups are a widely preferred option for off-grid living because they are made of durable, medical-grade silicone and can be worn for up to 12 hours. After use, they only need to be rinsed with clean water and soap and can be sterilized by boiling them for a few minutes each month.

Cloth Pads are another option, providing a reusable and eco-friendly solution. These pads can be easily washed with soapy water, dried in the sun for sterilization, and stored in clean, breathable bags for future use. Always wash them immediately after use to prevent staining and maintain hygiene.

Washing Clothes with Minimal Water

Water is a precious resource in off-grid living, and washing clothes with minimal water is crucial to conserving this essential element.

Bucket Washing is a simple method: fill one bucket with soapy water and another with clean water for rinsing. Scrub your clothes using your hands or a simple washboard. Once the clothes are clean, wring out the water and rinse them in the second bucket. This method ensures effective cleaning with minimal water use.

Another approach is the **Plunger Method**. Using a clean plunger as a manual agitator can help mimic the action of a washing machine. Simply place your clothes in a bucket with soapy water, and use the plunger to agitate them for several minutes. This method is particularly useful for heavier fabrics.

For **natural detergents**, you can make a simple mix using ingredients such as washing soda, grated soap, and baking soda. If you have access to soap nuts, they are another excellent natural alternative, as they contain saponins that act as a natural soap when boiled.

Finally, once your clothes are washed, take advantage of **solar drying** by hanging them in the sun. Not only does this conserve energy, but the UV rays also act as a natural sanitizer for your fabrics.

Preventing Infections in Humid or Remote Environments

Living off-grid in humid or remote areas presents unique challenges, especially when it comes to staying healthy. Moist environments can foster fungal infections, increase the risk of insect bites, and generally make it harder to maintain proper hygiene. The key to thriving in such conditions is to be proactive about cleanliness and health management.

Skin Care in Humid Climates

In humid environments, sweat and moisture can lead to fungal infections, particularly in areas like the feet, armpits, and groin. Preventing these infections is crucial, as they can easily escalate if untreated. Here's how you can take care of your skin effectively:

- **Stay Dry**: After washing or sweating, make sure to thoroughly dry yourself using a clean towel, concentrating on spots that are more likely to retain moisture. This step might seem simple, but it's vital for preventing fungal infections.
- **Natural Antifungals**: Dusting cornstarch or baking soda in moisture-prone areas can help absorb excess moisture and act as a natural antifungal agent. These simple powders are invaluable in an off-grid setting, where modern antifungal treatments may not be available.
- **Choose Breathable Fabrics**: Opting for loose, breathable clothing made from natural fibers like cotton or linen helps reduce sweat buildup. Synthetic fabrics tend to trap heat and moisture, so opt for natural materials that allow your skin to breathe.
- **Rotate and Clean Clothing**: In humid environments, changing your clothes regularly is key. Damp, dirty clothes can become a breeding ground for bacteria and fungi. Sun-dry your clothing after washing, as the sun's UV rays help kill bacteria and keep your gear fresh.

Insect Prevention and Bite Care

Insects can be more than just an irritation—they can carry diseases, especially in remote areas. Mosquitoes, ticks, and other pests are common in humid environments, so it's essential to take protective measures.

- **Natural Repellents**: Citronella, eucalyptus, and lavender essential oils are powerful natural insect repellents. Create a DIY repellent by mixing a few drops of these oils with water or a carrier oil like coconut oil. Apply it to your skin before heading outdoors, especially during dawn and dusk when insects are most active.
- **Tick Checks**: After spending time outside, especially in wooded or grassy areas, conduct a thorough tick check. If you spot a tick, use fine-tipped tweezers to carefully remove it by pulling straight out without twisting. Clean the bite area with soap and water, then apply a natural antiseptic like tea tree oil.
- **Insect Bite Treatment**: If you do get bitten, treat the area promptly. Applying a paste of baking soda and water can help relieve itching, while applying lavender oil can reduce swelling and discomfort. Keeping these natural remedies on hand can make a big difference in managing bites.

Wound Care in Remote Locations

Even minor cuts or scrapes can lead to serious infections if not treated promptly in off-grid environments. Here's how to handle wounds effectively:

- **Immediate Cleaning**: The moment you get a cut or scrape, clean it with soap and the cleanest water you have available. This removes dirt and bacteria that could cause infection. If possible, use boiled or filtered water to ensure cleanliness.
- **Natural Antiseptics**: Honey and tea tree oil are excellent natural antiseptics. Apply a small amount to cleaned wounds to prevent infection. Honey, in particular, has been used for centuries for its antimicrobial properties and can help speed up healing.
- **Cover the Wound**: After cleaning and treating the wound, keep it covered with a clean bandage to prevent further contamination. Change the bandage regularly, ensuring the wound remains dry and clean.

Resourcefulness and Creativity

Creative Solutions: Use whatever is at your disposal to maintain hygiene. If soap runs out, make your own. If running water is limited, find ways to stretch your supply. The ability to adapt and be resourceful is essential to staying healthy while living off-grid.

By embracing these resourceful approaches to hygiene, you enhance your self-sufficiency and resilience, ensuring you can thrive even in the most remote environments. These skills are not just about survival—they're about living well and sustainably off the grid.

26. Sanitizing, Cleaning, and Emergency Hygiene Solutions

While personal cleanliness is essential, the cleanliness of your surroundings, tools, and water supply is equally important for long-term health and well-being.

In Sanitizing, Cleaning, and Emergency Hygiene Solutions, you'll dive into the practical and sustainable methods for sterilizing surfaces, utensils, and bedding using natural cleaning agents. This guide explores the power of simple ingredients like vinegar, baking soda, and essential oils for keeping your home free of harmful bacteria. You'll also learn how to distill your own essential oils for cleaning and health, as well as how to maintain personal hygiene in crisis situations when water and supplies are limited. Whether you're dealing with a minor scrape, washing clothes with minimal water, or purifying your tools, this booklet provides essential skills to ensure you thrive, not just survive, in your off-grid lifestyle.

Sterilizing Surfaces, Utensils, and Bedding

Maintaining cleanliness in your living space is just as important as personal hygiene. Off-grid life means you'll need to rely on natural cleaning agents to keep your environment sanitary and free from harmful bacteria.

Natural Cleaning Agents

In place of store-bought disinfectants, nature provides plenty of effective alternatives:

- **Vinegar and Baking Soda**: This duo is highly versatile. Vinegar acts as a natural disinfectant, killing most bacteria, while baking soda works as a gentle scrub for surfaces. Use this combination to clean countertops, utensils, and even tough stains.
- **Tea Tree Oil and Lemon Juice**: These are powerful natural cleaners with strong antibacterial properties. Combine a few drops of tea tree oil or lemon juice with water to create a multipurpose cleaning spray. Tea tree oil is particularly effective for disinfecting areas that might harbor germs.

Sterilizing with Boiling Water

For utensils and tools, boiling is one of the most reliable methods to ensure they are free of germs:

- **Boil for 10 Minutes**: Submerge utensils, knives, and any tools you regularly use in boiling water for at least 10 minutes. This method effectively kills bacteria and viruses that may be lingering on their surfaces.
- **Sunlight Sterilization**: After boiling, let your utensils air dry in the sun. Sunlight's UV rays are a natural disinfectant, helping to ensure your items are thoroughly sterilized.

Sunlight as a Disinfectant

If you're short on cleaning supplies, sunlight is an incredibly effective tool:

- **Sanitizing Linens and Bedding**: Hang your bedding and clothes outside in direct sunlight for several hours. The UV rays kill bacteria, dust mites, and other harmful microorganisms. It's a simple yet effective way to maintain a clean living environment in an off-grid setting.

Using Essential Oils for Cleaning and Health

Essential oils are more than just pleasant-smelling—they pack a powerful punch when it comes to cleaning and maintaining hygiene. If you've ever wondered how to use essential oils off-grid, here are some practical applications.

Distilling Your Own Essential Oils

If you have access to fresh herbs like lavender, rosemary, or eucalyptus, you can distill your own essential oils using a basic steam distillation setup. While this might sound complicated, it's quite simple:

Steam Distillation: Add your plant material to a pot of boiling water. As the steam rises, it carries the essential oils from the plant into a condenser, where the steam cools and separates into water and oil. This process allows you to create your own supply of essential oils for cleaning, health, and insect repellents.

Practical Applications of Essential Oils

- **Lavender**: Excellent for calming, treating minor burns or skin irritations, and even helping with sleep. You can also add a few drops to your laundry to give it a fresh, clean scent.
- **Tea Tree Oil**: Renowned for its powerful antibacterial and antifungal qualities, tea tree oil is a go-to for cleaning surfaces, treating wounds, and combating skin infections.
- **Eucalyptus and Rosemary**: Both of these oils are fantastic for respiratory issues, making them ideal for steam inhalation when you're battling congestion. They also repel insects, which is an added bonus in the wilderness.

Personal Hygiene in Crisis Situations

In a crisis, personal hygiene becomes more difficult but no less crucial. With limited access to water and supplies, maintaining cleanliness can prevent illness and keep you in good shape.

Hand Hygiene

- **Alcohol-Based Sanitizers**: If water is scarce, an alcohol-based hand sanitizer is your best bet. If you don't have any available, you can make your own using isopropyl alcohol and aloe vera gel.
- **Minimal Water Handwashing**: If you have just a small amount of water, use it wisely. Pour a little water over your hands, scrub with soap, and rinse with the same water. This method conserves water while still allowing you to clean your hands properly.

Improvised Showers

Bucket Showers: With just a bucket of clean water and a scoop, you can take an effective shower. Use the scoop to pour water over yourself, lather with soap, and rinse off. It's simple but effective, allowing you to stay clean without wasting water.

Sterilizing Water

If you're uncertain about the quality of your water, ensure it's safe for cleaning by boiling it:

Boiling or Solar Sterilization: Boil water for at least 10 minutes to kill bacteria and viruses. Alternatively, you can use solar sterilization by placing water in clear plastic bottles and leaving them in direct sunlight for several hours.

Staying Healthy Off-Grid

Your overall well-being off-grid hinges on how consistently you can stick to hygiene routines. In a self-sufficient lifestyle, your health is your greatest asset, and prevention is always better than cure.

Routine Hygiene Practices

- **Consistency**: Regular handwashing, especially after using the bathroom, handling food, or dealing with wounds, is non-negotiable. A consistent routine is your best defense against illness.
- **Wound Care**: Any minor injury should be treated with immediate care to avoid infection. Keep wounds clean, dressed, and monitored for signs of infection.

In this compact guide you've gained practical, sustainable methods to keep your off-grid environment clean, safe, and healthy. From natural disinfectants to DIY essential oils and emergency hygiene practices, these tools ensure you can maintain cleanliness and prevent illness, no matter the circumstances. By mastering these techniques, you're not only safeguarding your health but also reinforcing your independence. As you continue your off-grid journey, these skills will be key to creating a resilient, thriving lifestyle that prioritizes both personal and environmental well-being.

27. DIY Off-Grid Home Security Systems

Securing your property when living off-grid isn't just about protecting your possessions—it's about ensuring your safety and peace of mind in an environment where help may be hours or even days away. Whether you're dealing with wildlife, trespassers, or opportunistic theft, a well-designed, DIY security system is a critical part of off-grid living. It gives you control over your surroundings and ensures that you're prepared for whatever challenges come your way.

Basic Perimeter Security Systems

Your first line of defense in off-grid security is establishing a strong perimeter. This doesn't have to be complex or costly. In fact, with a few simple tools and natural resources, you can set up an effective security boundary around your property.

- **Natural Barriers**: Start by using nature to your advantage. Plant dense hedges or strategically place thorny bushes along property lines to create natural barriers. Fences made from locally sourced materials like wood or stone can further fortify your perimeter. These barriers not only block access but also signal that your land is occupied and protected.
- **Perimeter Alarms**: Simple, homemade alarms can be highly effective. You can create noise-making alarms with cans, strings, and bells that will alert you to any movement around key entry points. These alarms may not look high-tech, but they can make a big difference in warning you of approaching threats.
- **Tripwire Alarms**: Setting up basic tripwire alarms around gates, pathways, or other access points adds an extra layer of detection. These alarms can be rigged to create a sound or even trigger lights when activated, making it harder for intruders to go unnoticed.

By creating a strong perimeter, you set up the first defense layer that requires minimal investment but provides excellent protection.

DIY Laser and Motion-Activated Alarms

If you're looking for a more advanced level of security, adding laser and motion-activated alarm systems can give you that extra peace of mind, especially in vulnerable areas like entrances or storage sheds.

- **Laser Tripwire Alarms**: A laser tripwire system is a great addition to your security plan. You can build one using affordable, easy-to-find components. Set up a laser beam across critical entry points, connected to a sensor that triggers an audio or visual alert if interrupted. It's a nearly invisible line of defense, ideal for nighttime protection.
- **Motion-Activated Alarms**: Using PIR (Passive Infrared) sensors, you can set up motion detectors around high-traffic areas like driveways, doorways, or garages. These sensors detect body heat and movement, triggering alarms, lights, or even recorded messages. They're perfect for alerting you of any unexpected movement around your property.
- **Solar and Battery Power**: Both laser and motion alarms can be powered using solar panels or rechargeable batteries, making them ideal for off-grid setups. With no need to rely on the grid, these systems will keep running as long as they have sunlight or a charged battery source.

These high-tech systems offer additional security that is sustainable and reliable, allowing you to be aware of activity around your property at all times, without the need for constant oversight.

Setting Up Visual Deterrents for Off-Grid Security

Creating visible deterrents is one of the simplest and most effective ways to prevent potential threats before they even reach your property. The goal is to make intruders think twice by giving the impression that your property is well-protected and constantly monitored, even when it's not. These strategies help avoid direct confrontation, which is crucial when living in a remote, off-grid location where help might not be readily available.

Decoy Cameras and Warning Signs

The power of deterrence starts with psychological tactics. One of the most effective ways to make intruders hesitate is by installing decoy cameras around your property. These fake cameras are inexpensive but can look realistic enough to make someone think twice before entering your space.

- **Decoy Cameras**: You can buy inexpensive, battery-powered decoy cameras that have blinking red lights to simulate recording. Place these in visible areas like near your entry points or any other high-traffic areas to create the impression of constant surveillance. It's an easy and affordable way to deter potential intruders.
- **Warning Signs**: Simple signs indicating that your property is monitored or protected can also be a strong deterrent. Messages like "Warning: 24/7 Surveillance" or "Beware of Dog" suggest to trespassers that they will be detected if they attempt to break in. Even if these threats aren't real, the possibility alone can be enough to make someone reconsider.

Light-Based Deterrents

Illumination is a powerful tool for off-grid security. Motion-activated lights not only make it harder for intruders to move undetected, but they also make your property feel more secure.

- **Solar-Powered Motion Lights**: These are particularly effective and sustainable for off-grid living. Install solar-powered motion lights around key entry points like doors, gates, and windows. When triggered, the sudden flood of light will not only alert you to movement but also startle potential intruders, making them feel exposed.
- **Pathway Lighting**: Setting up low-energy pathway lights around your property can further increase visibility at night and make it difficult for intruders to approach unnoticed. These lights can also be connected to a small solar panel system, making them completely off-grid and self-sustaining.
- **Scarecrows or Reflective Objects**: In more rural or wooded areas, wildlife might pose a threat to your garden or livestock. Setting up scarecrows or reflective objects (like old CDs or foil) can deter animals from coming too close. These reflections are particularly effective at night when they catch the light, creating an illusion of movement or unnatural presence.

By employing these light-based deterrents, you're creating a highly visible barrier that increases both security and peace of mind, making sure you can detect and respond to threats before they reach your home.

DIY Surveillance Systems

Installing a DIY surveillance system is a smart move when living off-grid. While traditional surveillance systems often rely on the grid, you can create a fully functional, off-grid solution using simple components and solar energy. These systems enable you to monitor your property in real-time or review recorded footage when needed, adding another layer of protection to your home security plan.

Building a DIY Camera System

With the technology available today, setting up a basic surveillance system doesn't require high costs or professional installation. Using old smartphones or affordable wireless cameras, you can set up a DIY system that monitors key areas of your property.

- **Repurposed Smartphones:** If you have old smartphones lying around, they can be turned into makeshift security cameras. By downloading free or low-cost surveillance apps, you can set up the phones in strategic locations to record footage. Many of these apps offer live streaming or cloud storage options, allowing you to check your property remotely if you have a mobile data connection.

- **Wireless Cameras:** Affordable wireless security cameras are also an option. Many models are battery-operated or solar-powered, making them perfect for off-grid environments. Place them in high-visibility areas to monitor potential access points, like gates, driveways, or front porches.

Powering Your Surveillance System

Since you're living off-grid, ensuring that your surveillance system has a reliable power source is crucial. Luckily, there are simple and effective ways to power these devices.

- **Solar Power**: Connect your surveillance cameras to solar panels for a steady, renewable power source. Small, portable solar panels can keep your cameras running without needing to connect to the grid. This method works well, especially in areas with consistent sunlight.

- **Low-Energy Solutions**: Consider energy-efficient cameras or devices that have motion-triggered recording to save battery life. These systems only record when movement is detected, helping conserve power while still maintaining security.

By installing a DIY surveillance system, you create an additional safeguard to your home, allowing you to keep an eye on your property whether you're there or not. This also gives you the ability to document any unusual activity for later review, which is valuable if any intrusions occur.

Fortifying Your Home and Shelter

Beyond securing your perimeter, it's essential to ensure that your home or shelter is well-protected against both intruders and natural threats.

- **Reinforcing Doors and Windows:** Reinforce doors with heavy-duty locks, or install metal bars or wood barricades for added protection. You can use scrap materials to create sturdy shutters or barriers for windows, securing them against both intruders and severe weather.
- **Creating a Safe Room:** Designating a safe room within your home is another critical step. This room should be heavily reinforced, with secure locking mechanisms, and stocked with emergency supplies. It's a place you can retreat to if your security is compromised, giving you time and space to call for help or prepare for defense.

Using a Dog for Home Security

When it comes to off-grid security, a well-trained dog can be one of the most effective and natural additions to your overall plan. Dogs have been trusted for centuries to protect homes, livestock, and their owners, and they offer a unique advantage in any off-grid setting. With their incredible senses of hearing and smell, they serve as early warning systems and powerful deterrents. In an environment where advanced technology or quick human response may not be readily available, a dog's natural instincts can play a critical role in keeping your property safe.

The Benefits of a Dog for Off-Grid Security

A well-trained dog can provide several key benefits, particularly in a remote, off-grid setting:

- **Early Warning System**: A dog's acute senses allow them to detect potential threats long before you or any electronic system would. Whether it's an intruder, an approaching animal, or an unfamiliar sound, they will alert you early, giving you valuable time to react.
- **Deterrence**: A barking dog can stop intruders before they even attempt to cross your property line. The presence of a dog, especially one that appears alert and ready to defend its territory, can be an effective psychological barrier. Many intruders will opt to move on rather than risk dealing with an aggressive guard dog.
- **Around-the-Clock Protection**: Unlike alarms or surveillance systems that might have limitations, a dog provides continuous protection, day or night. They're not dependent on power, making them an ideal companion in off-grid environments where energy conservation is key.

Training Your Dog for Security

To maximize the security benefits a dog can offer, proper training is essential. With the right techniques, you can transform your dog into a reliable partner in your off-grid defense plan.

- **Basic Commands**: Start with foundational obedience training. Commands such as "sit," "stay," "come," and "quiet" are crucial. These will ensure your dog is disciplined and able to follow your instructions in high-stress situations.
- **Patrolling the Perimeter**: You can train your dog to patrol specific areas of your property, reinforcing boundaries and ensuring they remain alert. This can be done by taking them on regular walks along the perimeter, rewarding them for staying within the designated area.
- **Alert Training**: Encourage your dog to alert you through barking or another behavior when they sense something unusual. Positive reinforcement is key here. When they successfully alert you to an approaching person or animal, reward them immediately to reinforce this behavior.

Integrating Your Dog into a Security System

To get the most out of your dog's security instincts, you should integrate them into the broader context of your off-grid security plan. This means combining their abilities with other tools and strategies.

- **Perimeter Security**: Place your dog in areas where they can freely monitor the perimeter of your property. If you have a fenced-in area or gates, ensure your dog is aware of their boundaries and has full access to patrol key areas.
- **Supporting Other Security Measures**: Your dog can act as the first layer of defense, complementing other systems like motion sensors, alarms, and surveillance cameras. For instance, when paired with motion-activated lights, a barking dog can further deter potential intruders.
- **Controlled Visitor Handling**: While your dog may be trained for security, it's important to balance this with socialization. You don't want them to bark or react aggressively to familiar guests or neighbors. Teach your dog to recognize friendly faces and how to behave appropriately around visitors.

Caring for Your Security Dog Off-Grid

Your dog's health and well-being are essential to maintaining their effectiveness as part of your security strategy. Ensuring they are well-fed, healthy, and comfortable is crucial in any off-grid scenario.

- **Adequate Nutrition and Water**: Keep your dog's food and water supplies well-stocked. In an off-grid setting, it's smart to have a backup supply of dog food or the ability to create homemade meals using ingredients you have on hand. Fresh water is also critical, especially if they're patrolling outside during hot weather.
- **Comfortable Shelter**: Just as you ensure your off-grid home is secure and comfortable, your dog will need appropriate shelter. A well-built doghouse or a designated indoor space will protect them from extreme weather conditions and keep them safe and ready to guard your property.
- **Routine Health Checks**: Your dog's health is a priority. If regular vet visits aren't possible, ensure you have a basic pet first-aid kit and know how to handle common issues like cuts, ticks, or minor infections. Regular grooming and tick checks are essential, especially in rural environments where pests are more common.

Choosing the Right Dog for Security

Not all dog breeds are equally suited to off-grid security. The best guard dogs are not only protective but also adaptable to the unique challenges of off-grid living.

- **Size and Strength**: Larger breeds like German Shepherds, Rottweilers, or Mastiffs are known for their protective instincts and physical presence. They make great deterrents and are naturally alert to their surroundings.
- **Temperament**: While you want a dog that will protect your home, it's crucial to select one that won't be overly aggressive. Look for breeds that balance protection with calmness, so they can differentiate between a real threat and normal activity.
- **Adaptability**: Off-grid living can present extreme weather conditions and rugged terrain. Select a breed that can thrive in these environments without becoming fatigued or overwhelmed.

A well-trained dog is far more than just a pet—it becomes a loyal partner and a crucial part of your off-grid security system. With its incredible senses and natural instinct to protect, it offers unwavering vigilance, acting as your first line of defense against intruders, wildlife, and unforeseen dangers.

By properly training, nurturing, and integrating your dog into your security strategy, you not only enhance the safety of your home but also build a deep, trusting bond with a creature that will stand by your side through thick and thin. Your dog won't just alert you to threats—they'll patrol your perimeter and offer a level of loyalty and protection that no piece of technology can match. With the right care and training, your security dog becomes not only an irreplaceable asset for your off-grid life but also a cherished companion who enriches your journey in ways beyond protection.

Ensuring Your Off-Grid Property Remains Secure

Securing your off-grid property is an ongoing responsibility that requires thoughtful planning, consistent vigilance, and adaptability. By implementing the strategies outlined in this guide—from setting up basic perimeter defenses to integrating modern DIY surveillance and employing trained dogs for protection—you can create a strong, reliable security system that will stand up to the unique challenges of off-grid living. The key is not only in the tools and technologies you use but in your mindset: staying prepared, aware, and proactive in addressing potential threats.

By combining practical solutions, like tripwire alarms and reinforced shelters, with smart deterrents like decoy cameras, you ensure that your property remains a difficult target for both wildlife and human intruders. Your dog, as a loyal companion and first responder, adds an irreplaceable layer of protection, making your system complete.

As you grow more familiar with your off-grid environment, remain flexible and willing to refine and adapt your strategies. Continuous improvement and attention to detail will keep you, your property, and your loved ones safe.

No system is perfect, and no one becomes an expert overnight. Seek further learning opportunities through books, online courses, and community forums to expand your knowledge. Sharing experiences with others who have embarked on similar off-grid journeys can provide invaluable insights and tips.

Your off-grid security is your responsibility, but it's also a project you can take pride in. Stay safe, stay vigilant, and continue to build a secure future.

28. Surviving Extreme Weather Off-Grid

When you're living off the grid, your security encompasses much more than safeguarding your home from intruders or setting up advanced alarm systems. As critical as these elements are, extreme weather poses an equally significant threat to your off-grid lifestyle. From freezing winters to scorching heatwaves, or powerful storms, your ability to adapt and prepare is essential to ensure long-term safety and resilience. To thrive in such environments, you need to prepare your shelter and survival strategies meticulously for a wide range of environmental challenges.

Essential Preparations for Extreme Weather

The first and most important step in protecting your off-grid shelter from harsh weather conditions is assessing the specific climate risks in your location. Understanding what types of extreme weather are most likely to impact you will help guide your preparation efforts and ensure your shelter is equipped to handle those challenges. Whether you're facing hurricanes, wildfires, snowstorms, or prolonged droughts, each presents unique risks that demand tailored solutions.

Identifying Climate Risks

Begin by thoroughly researching the historical weather patterns in your area. Are you in a region prone to hurricanes, floods, wildfires, or heavy snowfall? Understanding these risks allows you to implement targeted protection measures for your off-grid home.

- **Wildfire Zones**: If your home is located in a region prone to wildfires, your priority will be fireproofing. This includes creating defensible space around your home by clearing away flammable vegetation, installing fire-resistant materials, and ensuring access to water for fire suppression.
- **Hurricane and High Wind Zones**: For those living in hurricane-prone areas, it's essential to reinforce your home against high winds and potential debris. Focus on securing your roof, reinforcing windows with storm shutters, and ensuring the overall structure can withstand gale-force winds.
- **Flood-Prone Areas**: If flooding is a concern, elevate your living space and critical infrastructure to minimize water damage. Build your home on higher ground if possible, and ensure that your foundation is sturdy and well-protected against water ingress.

Reinforcing Your Shelter

Once you've identified the specific threats your region faces, it's time to fortify your off-grid home. This is especially important for off-grid dwellers, as your home must stand strong without immediate access to external help. Focus on reinforcing doors, windows, and walls with materials that can withstand your region's particular weather challenges.

- **Storm Shutters**: Install storm shutters to shield your windows from debris in strong winds or hurricanes. These can be made of metal or heavy-duty wood, depending on the severity of storms in your area.
- **Waterproofing**: If your area is prone to heavy rainfall or flooding, ensure your home is equipped with water-resistant barriers, and seal any cracks in the walls or foundation.
- **Roof Reinforcement**: High winds can easily damage roofs, so ensure yours is securely fastened. Consider using hurricane straps or other durable fasteners to anchor your roof to the walls of your home.
- **Insulation**: For areas with extreme temperatures, both hot and cold, proper insulation is crucial. Not only does insulation help maintain a consistent internal temperature, but it also reduces energy consumption by keeping your shelter naturally cooler or warmer.

Cold Weather Survival

Living in an off-grid environment during freezing winters presents unique challenges that can be life-threatening if you're not adequately prepared. Winterizing your shelter and ensuring access to reliable heat and water sources are key to surviving cold weather.

Winterizing Your Shelter

Insulation is one of the most important steps in preparing for cold weather. Without proper insulation, your home will lose heat quickly, making it difficult to stay warm.

- **Seal Cracks**: Seal any cracks or gaps in windows, doors, and walls to prevent drafts. Drafts can lead to significant heat loss, making it harder to maintain a warm living space.
- **Add Insulation**: If your home lacks adequate insulation, consider adding more to your walls, floors, and roof. This will help retain heat and lower your fuel usage.
- **Window Treatments**: Install heavy curtains or thermal blinds to keep cold air out and retain warmth inside.

Off-Grid Heating Options

Heating your home off-grid can be challenging, but with proper systems in place, you can remain warm even in extreme cold. Wood stoves are a popular choice because they are efficient, reliable, and use a renewable resource. Ensure you have enough firewood stockpiled to last through the coldest months.

- **Wood Stoves**: A well-maintained wood stove can heat your entire living space, and the fuel is often readily available. Make sure you have proper ventilation and a reliable chimney to avoid carbon monoxide build-up.
- **Propane Heaters**: Propane heaters are another off-grid option. They are simple to use and need very little effort to maintain. However, be sure to store propane safely and use heaters that are rated for indoor use.
- **Rocket Mass Heaters**: If you're looking for an energy-efficient option, consider installing a rocket mass heater. These heaters use minimal fuel and are designed to retain heat for long periods, making them ideal for cold climates.

Water Management in Freezing Conditions

In freezing temperatures, maintaining access to clean water is crucial. Frozen pipes and water storage systems can cut off your water supply, so it's essential to take preventive measures.

- **Insulate Water Pipes**: Insulate your water pipes to prevent freezing. You can also install heat tape to keep pipes warm and ensure water flow during extremely cold weather.
- **Solar Water Heaters**: Solar water heaters can be an excellent solution for maintaining access to warm water during winter months. These systems use sunlight to heat your water supply and reduce your reliance on firewood or propane.
- **Emergency Water Storage**: Always have emergency water stored in case your main supply freezes. Collect rainwater in insulated tanks or barrels and store it in a location where it's unlikely to freeze, such as a basement or insulated shed.

Essential Winter Gear

Surviving in cold weather isn't just about preparing your shelter—it's about protecting yourself. Having the right winter gear is crucial for staying warm and safe.

- **Thermal Clothing**: Invest in high-quality thermal clothing, including base layers, mid-layers, and insulated outer layers. Layering is key to retaining heat and wicking away moisture to avoid hypothermia.
- **Insulated Boots**: Cold feet can quickly lead to frostbite. Insulated, waterproof boots are essential for maintaining warmth and protection in freezing conditions.
- **Cold-Weather Survival Tools**: Keep emergency blankets, fire-starting materials, and additional heating sources accessible. In case of power loss or heating system failure, these tools could be life-saving.

By taking these measures to prepare for extreme weather, you can safeguard your off-grid lifestyle from the harshest conditions. Proper planning, insulation, and heating systems are the foundation of cold-weather survival, ensuring you remain resilient and self-sufficient even in the most extreme environments.

Heatwave and Hot Weather Survival

When living off the grid, one of the most challenging environments to endure is extreme heat. Without access to traditional air conditioning or modern cooling systems, managing heat and maintaining adequate hydration becomes a critical focus. Surviving a heatwave requires thoughtful planning around your home, water management, and daily routines to ensure your health and well-being. Let's dive into the strategies that will help you stay cool, safe, and prepared during hot weather.

Cooling Your Home

One of the first steps to surviving a heatwave is creating a livable, cool environment within your home. Traditional air conditioning may not be an option off-grid, so implementing passive cooling techniques is essential. These methods utilize natural ventilation, shading, and insulation to control temperatures without relying on external power sources.

- **Ventilation**: Proper ventilation is key to keeping air circulating in your home. Install vents at both the top and bottom of your home to allow hot air to escape while cooler air flows in. Cross-ventilation, where air can flow freely from one side of the house to the other, is particularly effective.
- **Shading**: Shading your home is another highly effective way to reduce indoor temperatures. Planting trees or installing overhangs can block direct sunlight from hitting your home during the hottest part of the day. Additionally, exterior shutters or blinds can block heat before it enters through windows.
- **Reflective Barriers**: Installing reflective materials on your roof or walls can significantly reduce the heat absorbed by your home. Reflective barriers work by bouncing sunlight away from your home, preventing the structure from heating up as quickly. Aluminum foil or specialized reflective coatings are common choices for this technique.
- **Insulation**: Proper insulation isn't just for cold weather; it's crucial for hot climates, too. Insulating your walls, floors, and roof can help keep the cool air inside and prevent the heat from seeping in. Materials like foam boards, reflective bubble wrap, and even thick curtains can act as barriers to heat, maintaining a more stable indoor temperature.

Managing Water in Hot Weather

Water is an invaluable resource when living off the grid, and its importance increases significantly during a heatwave. Staying hydrated and managing your water supply effectively can be the difference between comfort and danger in extreme heat. Here's how to ensure you have sufficient water for drinking, cooking, and other essential uses.

- **Rainwater Harvesting**: Setting up a rainwater harvesting system is one of the best ways to secure a consistent water supply in hot weather. Collect water from rooftops or other surfaces and store it in large, covered tanks. During dry periods, having a well-planned storage system can help you maintain access to water when rainfall is scarce.

- **Water Storage**: In addition to rainwater harvesting, use storage tanks and barrels to hold excess water. Store water in cool, shaded areas to prevent evaporation and contamination. If possible, insulate your storage tanks to keep the water cooler for longer.
- **Water Conservation**: During a heatwave, it's essential to conserve water. Implement greywater systems that allow you to reuse water from sinks, showers, and washing for purposes like irrigation. In hot climates, reducing water waste is critical to maintaining a reliable supply for longer durations.
- **Hydration Strategy**: Always have plenty of potable water available. Drink frequently, even if you don't feel thirsty, to prevent dehydration. Store bottled water in a shaded, cool area and keep emergency supplies on hand. Recognize the early signs of dehydration—such as headaches, dry mouth, and fatigue—and address them immediately by increasing your water intake.

Heat-Safe Cooking Methods

Cooking indoors during a heatwave can raise your home's temperature, making an already hot situation worse. Instead of using indoor stoves or ovens, it's smart to adapt your cooking methods to avoid adding heat to your living environment.

- **Solar Ovens**: Solar ovens are an excellent off-grid solution for cooking in hot weather. These ovens use the sun's energy to cook food without requiring any fuel, and they don't produce additional heat in your living space. Solar ovens are also an eco-friendly and sustainable cooking option.
- **Rocket Stoves**: Rocket stoves are another energy-efficient method for cooking outdoors. They require very little wood to produce high heat, making them ideal for conserving resources while keeping your home cool. Cooking outside prevents the heat from building up indoors, allowing your home to stay more comfortable.
- **Fireless Cooking**: Utilize methods such as dehydrating or cold-prep meals that require minimal or no cooking. Prepping salads, sandwiches, or other no-cook meals can keep you well-fed without generating excess heat inside your home.

Hot Weather Essentials

Surviving a heatwave also requires having the right tools and resources to keep yourself cool. Along with home management and water conservation, personal cooling strategies are essential for staying safe.

- **Emergency Cooling Tools**: Battery-operated fans, cooling towels, and ice packs are indispensable during extreme heat. Cooling towels, in particular, can be dipped in cold water and placed on your neck or head to lower your body temperature quickly.
- **Shaded Rest Areas**: In the hottest part of the day, it's important to seek shade and rest. If possible, create an outdoor shaded area where you can relax without direct exposure to the sun. Whether you use tarps, natural trees, or a canopy, having a shaded space can provide relief during peak temperatures.
- **Hydration and Electrolytes**: In addition to water, it's important to replenish electrolytes lost through sweating. Keep electrolyte tablets or sports drinks on hand to prevent heat exhaustion and dehydration. These supplements help maintain the balance of salts in your body, which is crucial for avoiding heat-related illnesses.
- **Recognizing Heat Stroke and Dehydration**: Understanding the warning signs of heat stroke and dehydration is critical. Early symptoms of dehydration include dizziness, dry mouth, and dark-colored urine. Heat stroke, on the other hand, is far more dangerous and is characterized by confusion, nausea, and the cessation of sweating. If you or anyone else shows signs of heat stroke, it's vital to cool down immediately and seek medical attention if symptoms worsen.

Surviving High Winds and Storms

Just as important as dealing with heat is being prepared for the possibility of high winds and severe storms. These weather events can be devastating if you're not adequately prepared, especially for off-grid homes that may be more exposed to the elements.

Wind proofing Your Home

In areas prone to high winds, reinforcing your home is a top priority. Storm-proofing measures include securing your roof, walls, and windows to withstand the pressure from high winds and flying debris.

- **Securing the Roof**: Your roof is often the most vulnerable part of your home during high winds. Use hurricane straps or other heavy-duty fasteners to anchor it securely to the frame of your house. Reinforce the edges and seams to prevent wind from lifting shingles or panels.
- **Strengthening Walls and Windows**: Storm shutters or boards can provide extra protection for windows. If strong winds are forecasted, ensure that all doors and windows are securely latched and reinforced with strong materials.

Securing Outdoor Equipment

Loose outdoor items can become dangerous projectiles in high winds. Before storms hit, secure outdoor furniture, tools, and equipment. Store smaller items in enclosed spaces like sheds or garages, and use heavy-duty straps or anchors for larger objects.

Building a Storm Shelter

In extreme cases, having a designated storm shelter is a lifesaving measure. Whether it's a basement, a reinforced room within your home, or a standalone structure, your storm shelter should be able to withstand powerful winds and keep you safe from flying debris.

Evacuation Planning for Severe Storms

Sometimes, the best way to stay safe during a severe storm is to evacuate. Make sure you have a clear evacuation plan in place, know the location of the nearest shelters, and have your go-bags ready with essential items such as food, water, first aid kits, and important documents.

By focusing on these essential survival strategies, you'll be well-prepared to handle extreme heat and high winds, ensuring the safety of both your home and yourself.

Flood Preparedness

Flooding is one of the most significant risks for off-grid living, particularly in low-lying or flood-prone areas. Floods can occur suddenly, caused by heavy rainfall, snowmelt, or nearby water bodies overflowing their banks. For those living off-grid, preparedness is key to safeguarding both property and lives. Ensuring that your home is well-equipped to handle flood risks will significantly improve your chances of avoiding devastating damage. Here's how to effectively prepare for floods and protect your off-grid home.

Floodproofing Your Home

The first and most critical step in flood preparedness is floodproofing your home. One of the best strategies is to elevate critical areas of your living space to avoid potential water damage. For example:

- **Elevating Living Areas**: If possible, elevate your home by building it on stilts or platforms, particularly in flood-prone zones. This extra height can keep rising floodwaters from entering your main living areas and damaging valuable possessions. It's a major investment, but it can save your home from catastrophic damage in the long run.
- **Elevating Utilities**: Keep essential utilities such as electrical systems, heating units, and water heaters above potential flood levels. If you have an off-grid power system, ensure your solar panels, batteries, and generators are either raised or installed on higher ground.
- **Furniture and Appliances**: Elevate furniture and appliances when a flood warning is issued. Move them to higher levels or secure them in waterproof storage. Consider storing items in floating waterproof containers, which can prevent damage even in cases of extreme flooding.
- **Location Matters**: If you're still in the planning stage of your off-grid life, consider placing your home on a hill or higher ground. While it may take more effort to haul materials, the protection it offers from flooding is invaluable. Homes built on a slope have a natural drainage system that keeps water from pooling around the structure.

Waterproofing Supplies

Being prepared for a flood also means protecting your essential supplies and possessions. Storing your most critical items in waterproof containers and ensuring that your emergency equipment is flood-resistant are essential steps in flood preparedness. Here's what you can do:

- **Waterproof Storage**: Keep important documents, such as property deeds, insurance papers, and emergency contacts, in waterproof containers. This also applies to essential electronics, tools, and other equipment necessary for your survival. Ensure you have an inventory of your most critical supplies in a floodproof location.
- **Stock Up on Tarps and Covers**: Have waterproof tarps and rain covers available to protect outdoor equipment and critical structures. If heavy rain is forecasted, you can quickly cover any vulnerable areas of your property, helping to minimize water damage.
- **Essential Flood Gear**: Invest in flood-specific gear like waterproof boots, waders, and rain gear. These items will keep you dry if you need to move around your property during heavy rain or rising water. Portable waterproof bags are also useful for securing valuables during an emergency.

Building Water Diversion Systems

An essential part of flood preparedness is controlling and diverting the flow of water away from your home. By creating barriers and trenches around your property, you can prevent water from pooling near your home and potentially entering it. Here are some practical water diversion strategies:

- **Trenches and Channels**: Dig trenches or drainage channels around your property to direct water away from your home. Ensure the trenches are deep enough and slope away from the house, allowing water to flow naturally to lower ground.
- **Berms and Barriers**: Build earth berms or raised barriers around the perimeter of your property to keep water at bay. Berms can be particularly effective in areas with flat terrain, creating a flood barrier that prevents water from reaching your home.
- **Sump Pumps**: Consider installing a sump pump system to divert water from lower levels of your home, such as basements or cellars. A sump pump will automatically remove water from your property, helping prevent flooding in critical areas.

Evacuation Strategies in Flood Situations

Even with the best preparations, some floods can become overwhelming. That's why it's crucial to have a clear evacuation strategy, including a well-stocked emergency kit. Here's how to prepare:

- **Evacuation Routes**: Identify safe evacuation routes that won't be compromised by flooding. This includes planning alternate routes in case your primary path is blocked by rising waters or fallen trees. Keep local emergency services informed about your location and plans, so they can assist if needed.
- **Emergency Kits**: Prepare an evacuation kit with waterproof boots, rain gear, non-perishable food, water purification systems, first-aid supplies, and essential tools. Include portable, waterproof containers for important documents, cash, and communication devices such as a satellite phone or two-way radios. Your evacuation kit should be easy to grab and transport in case you need to leave quickly.
- **Keep Vehicles Ready**: If flooding is imminent, move your vehicles to higher ground. Ensure they are fueled and ready for evacuation. Floodwaters can rise rapidly, and having your vehicle prepared can make the difference between a timely escape and becoming stranded.

In the off-grid lifestyle, nature's unpredictability requires preparedness and adaptability. From surviving the biting cold of winter to staying safe during scorching heatwaves, high winds, and floods, proactive planning and the right strategies are essential. By understanding your specific climate risks and fortifying your home against these environmental threats, you can protect your off-grid sanctuary. Ensuring access to vital resources like water, shelter, and heat, while maintaining the flexibility to respond to extreme weather events, will ensure you not only survive but thrive in even the harshest conditions.

29. Sustainable Off-Grid Income: Growing and Raising for Profit

Living off-grid doesn't mean you have to disconnect from financial sustainability. Generating income while living off the land is a key element of maintaining your off-grid lifestyle. This book focuses on two crucial income streams: selling surplus produce and raising livestock for profit. These methods not only support self-reliance but also integrate seamlessly into the off-grid ethos by emphasizing sustainability, resourcefulness, and local community engagement.

Selling Surplus Produce: Direct to Consumer

One of the most straightforward ways to generate income off-grid is by selling excess produce from your self-sustaining garden. Even if you're just starting out with a small plot, the surplus you grow can quickly turn into a reliable income stream. Here's how to get started:

Growing and Selling Fresh Produce

Start Small but Strategically:

Begin by cultivating a variety of fruits, vegetables, or herbs that your local market demands. Identify crops that grow well in your region and are in high demand. As you harvest your garden, set aside the surplus that exceeds your own consumption needs. This excess produce is where your income opportunity lies.

- **Local Markets and Farmers' Markets:**

The most common avenue for selling surplus produce is at local farmers' markets. Many off-grid growers find that local communities are eager to purchase fresh, organic, and chemical-free produce. This direct-to-consumer model not only provides income but also builds relationships with your neighbors, fostering community support for your off-grid efforts.

- **Bartering Opportunities:**

In addition to selling, bartering is a valuable way to exchange your surplus produce for goods or services you need. Barter with other local farmers, ranchers, or artisans for essentials like livestock feed, seeds, or even farm equipment. Bartering can be a practical income alternative, allowing you to sustain your off-grid lifestyle without relying on cash transactions.

Maximizing the Appeal of Your Produce

To make your produce stand out in a competitive market, focus on highlighting the quality and sustainability of your growing methods. Consumers increasingly value organic, chemical-free, and locally grown food, and your off-grid produce can meet this demand.

- **Emphasize Organic Growing Methods:**

Make sure your customers know that your crops are grown without synthetic pesticides or fertilizers. Consumers who care about their health and the environment are often willing to pay a premium for produce grown using sustainable and eco-friendly practices.

- **Offer Seasonal Produce:**

By offering a rotating selection of seasonal fruits, vegetables, or herbs, you can keep customers coming back throughout the year. This not only ensures steady income but also helps you manage the natural rhythms of your off-grid garden.

Tip: Use your market stall as an educational platform. Explain the benefits of organic gardening, and offer tips on how customers can grow their own small gardens. By positioning yourself as an expert, you can build trust and increase sales.

Livestock and Animal Products

If your off-grid homestead includes livestock, there's great potential to generate income from animal products like eggs, dairy, meat, and wool. Here's how to turn your animals into a reliable source of revenue:

Raising Livestock for Profit

Eggs, Meat, and Dairy Products:

Chickens, goats, and cows are among the most common livestock on off-grid homesteads, and they provide a wealth of products that can be sold directly to consumers.

- **Eggs**:
  Free-range, organic eggs are always in demand. If you're raising chickens, selling eggs can be a steady source of income, especially if you promote the natural, humane conditions in which your hens are raised.
- Milk and Dairy:

If you're raising goats or cows, selling raw milk or homemade dairy products like cheese and yogurt can be very lucrative. Many people seek out raw, organic dairy products because of their nutritional value and the fact that they aren't mass-produced.

- **Meat**:
  Selling ethically raised, hormone-free meat can also generate significant income. Whether it's chicken, goat, or pork, there is a market for meat from animals that have been raised naturally in a free-range, humane environment.

Local Community Networks

Building a loyal customer base within your local community is key to success in selling animal products. Word of mouth is often the best form of marketing in smaller communities, and once people know they can trust your products, they'll keep coming back.

- **Build Trust with Transparency:**

One way to foster a loyal customer base is by inviting them to visit your homestead. Offering tours or open houses allows potential customers to see firsthand how your animals are raised. When customers understand the care and attention you put into raising your livestock, they're more likely to support your farm and pay premium prices for your products.

- **Emphasize Ethical and Sustainable Practices:**

Today's consumers are more aware of where their food comes from and how it's produced. Emphasize the ethical treatment of your animals, and highlight the fact that your products are free from antibiotics and growth hormones. This appeals to health-conscious customers who are willing to pay more for quality.

Bartering Livestock and Animal Products

Similar to produce, livestock and animal products can also be used in bartering. Trading eggs, milk, or even livestock itself can help you obtain goods or services that you need to maintain your off-grid lifestyle.

- **Barter for Tools, Feed, or Labor:**

Livestock can be traded for practical goods like farming tools, feed for your animals, or even labor to help with larger projects on your homestead. In an off-grid community, this exchange system allows you to thrive without relying heavily on cash transactions.

Tip: Consider offering a farm membership or subscription model where locals can receive a regular supply of eggs, milk, or other products in exchange for upfront payment. This provides you with steady income while ensuring your customers always have fresh products on hand.

Beekeeping and Honey Products

Another excellent way to generate income off-grid is through beekeeping. Bees are beneficial not only for their honey but also for pollination services, which can increase crop yields in your area. Beekeeping aligns perfectly with sustainable living, as it encourages biodiversity and contributes to the health of your environment.

Profiting from Apiculture

Honey Sales:

Raw honey is a highly sought-after product, particularly among customers who prioritize natural, unprocessed foods. Beekeeping requires minimal land and resources, making it an ideal off-grid income source. Honey can be sold locally at markets, to health food stores, or directly to consumers.

- **Beeswax Products:**

In addition to honey, beeswax can be used to create a variety of profitable products such as candles, lip balms, and skin lotions. These items are always in demand and can be sold year-round. Making beeswax products adds value to your beekeeping operation and provides additional income streams.

Tip: Highlight the environmental benefits of beekeeping to your customers. By educating them on how bees contribute to healthy ecosystems and crop production, you can foster a sense of responsibility that encourages them to support your bee products.

Pollination Services

Bees are excellent pollinators, and by offering pollination services to local farmers or gardeners, you can further increase your income. Pollination services involve moving your hives to different locations to help with crop pollination, in exchange for goods, services, or payment.

- **Bartering Pollination Services:**

Offering pollination services can be an excellent way to barter for goods such as crops, seeds, or even livestock. By establishing relationships with local farmers, you create a mutually beneficial arrangement where both parties gain value without the need for money.

Generating sustainable income while living off-grid is not only achievable but can also enhance your self-reliance and support your local community. By selling surplus produce, raising livestock, and engaging in beekeeping, you can create multiple income streams that align with your off-grid lifestyle. Emphasizing organic, ethical, and sustainable practices will help you build trust and loyalty among customers, while bartering offers a valuable alternative to traditional transactions. These methods allow you to maintain financial stability without compromising your principles, ensuring that your off-grid journey thrives both practically and sustainably

30. Crafting and Services: Off-Grid Income from Handwork and Expertise

Following the insights from Sustainable Off-Grid Income: Growing and Raising for Profit, where we explored how surplus produce and livestock can fuel your off-grid income, we now dive into another rewarding avenue for generating income—handcrafting and offering essential off-grid services. In Crafting and Services: Off-Grid Income from Handwork and Expertise, we'll shift the focus to leveraging the natural resources around you and honing practical skills to create high-demand, handmade goods. From woodworking and textiles to renewable energy installations and water systems, this book highlights how craftsmanship and expertise can create sustainable financial independence while living off-grid.

By tapping into the demand for authentic, eco-friendly products and vital services, you can build an income stream that not only supports your off-grid lifestyle but also contributes to a thriving local community.

Handmade Goods from Natural Resources

One of the most rewarding and sustainable ways to generate income while living off-grid is by crafting and selling handmade goods using the natural resources around you. These products are not only eco-friendly but also align perfectly with the off-grid ethos of self-reliance and sustainability. By utilizing wood, stone, clay, wool, cotton, or leather, you can create high-quality artisanal items that appeal to customers seeking unique, handmade alternatives to mass-produced goods.

Craftsmanship and Artisanal Products

Natural Crafting: Maximizing Local Resources

You can start by using the materials that are readily available in your environment, such as wood, stone, or clay. Whether it's furniture, pottery, baskets, or utensils, handmade goods from natural resources have significant market appeal due to their authenticity, durability, and sustainability.

- **Woodcraft**:
  If you have access to a sustainable wood supply, consider crafting furniture, utensils, or decorative items. Wood is highly adaptable and can be utilized to produce a variety of products, from simple kitchen tools to intricately carved furniture pieces. Highlighting the fact that your items are handcrafted from natural, locally sourced materials adds value and differentiates your products from those made using industrial processes.
- **Pottery and Clay Items:**

Using locally sourced clay, you can create pottery that serves both functional and decorative purposes. Whether it's bowls, mugs, or more artistic pieces, pottery appeals to those looking for unique, handmade items for their homes. Firing clay in an off-grid environment can be done using a wood-fueled kiln, making this a sustainable option for income generation.

- **Stone Crafting:**

If your area has a good supply of natural stone, consider crafting stone products such as mortar and pestle sets, garden statues, or even small building materials like stepping stones. Stonecraft is labor-intensive but can yield products that last for generations, offering a timeless appeal to buyers.

- **Baskets and Woven Goods:**

Basket weaving is an ancient skill that is still highly valued today. You can use materials like willow, reeds, or even vines to create durable and functional baskets for storage, gardening, or decorative purposes. Baskets are popular at markets and fairs, where people appreciate their practicality and beauty.

Clothing and Textiles: Handmade and Sustainable

If you have access to wool, cotton, or leather, you can expand your offerings by creating handmade clothing or accessories. These natural materials allow you to craft high-quality, durable goods that customers can't easily find elsewhere.

- **Wool Products:**

Wool is a fantastic material for making clothing, blankets, and accessories. If you're raising sheep or alpacas, spinning your own wool into yarn adds another layer of value to your products. From there, you can knit or weave warm clothing or soft blankets, which are always in demand during the colder months.

- **Leather Goods:**

If you raise cattle or goats, using the hides to create leather products is another way to maximize the resources on your homestead. Leather is a durable, versatile material that can be used to make everything from belts and wallets to shoes and bags. Handmade leather goods have a premium market appeal due to their longevity and craftsmanship.

- **Handmade Clothing:**

Creating clothing from natural materials like cotton or wool appeals to those who value sustainable, eco-friendly products. Whether you focus on simple, functional designs or more elaborate garments, handmade clothing is always in demand at local markets or among eco-conscious consumers.

Tip: When selling textiles or clothing, emphasize the ethical production methods you use. Highlight that your products are made from natural, renewable resources, and appeal to buyers who prioritize sustainable fashion.

Hosting Craft Workshops or Classes

Sharing your skills with others is another way to generate income. Hosting workshops or classes in your community not only provides you with another revenue stream but also teaches valuable, self-reliant skills to others.

- **Basket Weaving Workshops:**

Teach others the art of basket weaving using locally sourced materials. This skill is easy to learn and can be a rewarding activity for people interested in sustainable living. By charging a fee for the workshop and providing materials, you can turn a single skill into a profitable event.

- **Leatherworking Classes:**

Leatherworking can be an attractive skill to teach, especially in off-grid or homesteading communities. Offering hands-on classes where participants create their own belts, wallets, or simple accessories can attract those looking to learn practical crafting skills.

- **Crafting Events:**

Organizing events around crafting, where participants can learn multiple skills such as woodworking, pottery, and leatherworking, is another way to bring in income. These events can attract families, local businesses, or groups interested in sustainable craftsmanship.

Preserved and Fermented Goods: Turning Surplus Into Income

In off-grid living, food preservation is a necessity. Preserving surplus produce not only extends the shelf life of food but also provides an additional income stream. With the growing interest in natural, homemade, and long-shelf-life products, preserved and fermented foods are highly marketable.

Canning and Preserving Surplus Produce

If you're producing more fruits, vegetables, or herbs than your household needs, preserving them can help you generate income while reducing food waste.

- **Preserves, Pickles, and Sauces:**

Canning excess produce into jams, pickles, sauces, or chutneys allows you to sell products with a long shelf life. These homemade goods are highly valued, especially if they're made with organic, chemical-free ingredients. Setting up a stall at local markets or selling directly to customers can help you turn your garden's surplus into consistent income.

- **Dried Herbs and Spices:**

Drying herbs and spices is another way to preserve your garden's bounty. Dried herbs are durable and can be sold in small, affordable packages at local markets. You can also create herb blends or spice mixes to add variety to your product offerings.

Tip: Make sure to market your preserved products as organic and sustainable, emphasizing the handmade, small-batch nature of your goods. This will appeal to customers looking for wholesome, locally produced foods.

Fermented Foods: High-Value, Health-Conscious Products

Fermented foods, such as sauerkraut, kombucha, and kefir, are gaining popularity due to their health benefits and unique flavors. Fermentation not only preserves food but also adds value by creating probiotic-rich products that appeal to health-conscious consumers.

- **Sauerkraut, Kimchi, and Pickled Vegetables:**

Fermenting vegetables is a simple and effective way to preserve them while adding nutritional value. Sauerkraut, kimchi, and other fermented veggies are highly marketable products. You can sell them at farmers' markets, local health food stores, or directly to customers seeking gut-friendly, fermented foods.

- **Kombucha and Kefir:**

These probiotic-rich drinks are increasingly popular, and making them off-grid is a viable business option. By producing small batches of kombucha or kefir, you can cater to the growing demand for natural, fermented beverages. With the right marketing, your off-grid fermented drinks can become a staple at local markets or within health-conscious communities.

Tip: Hosting fermentation workshops can further increase your income while sharing essential off-grid food preservation techniques with others. This not only generates revenue but also fosters a stronger sense of community and self-reliance among your customers.

Providing Off-Grid Services to the Community

Living off-grid presents numerous opportunities to offer valuable services to those in your community. Whether it's helping others transition to off-grid living or providing essential systems for those already off-grid, your skills and knowledge can become a significant source of income. Here's how you can leverage your expertise to benefit both your community and yourself.

Renewable Energy Installation: Solar and Wind Power Systems

Mastering the installation and maintenance of renewable energy systems is a highly sought-after skill, especially in off-grid living. As more people seek to minimize their dependence on conventional energy sources, there's a growing demand for professionals who can install and maintain systems like solar panels and wind turbines.

- **Solar Panel Installation:**

If you're proficient in setting up photovoltaic solar power systems, you can offer your services to help others transition to solar energy. Many off-grid homes rely on solar power, and as an expert, you can assist with the full setup, from selecting the right panels to installing the inverter and battery storage systems.

- **Wind Turbine Installation:**

In regions where wind is steady, small-scale wind turbines can be a reliable source of energy. Offering wind turbine installation services, especially in combination with solar, provides a comprehensive solution for off-grid energy needs. Ensuring turbines are correctly installed, maintained, and optimized for performance can be a valuable service for your local community.

Tip: Consider offering consultation services as well. Many people interested in going off-grid may not know where to begin. You can provide them with assessments and recommendations, helping them design energy systems tailored to their specific location and energy needs.

Carpentry and Construction: Building Off-Grid Structures

With your experience in building off-grid homes, cabins, yurts, and other sustainable structures, you can offer your carpentry and construction skills to those looking to develop their own off-grid properties.

- **Eco-Friendly, Sustainable Building:**

Many people are searching for eco-friendly alternatives to traditional construction methods. Focus on using sustainable materials, like reclaimed wood or locally sourced natural resources, to construct energy-efficient homes. Whether it's building full homes or smaller structures like storage sheds, greenhouses, or workshops, your construction expertise can be a huge asset.

- **Yurts and Tiny Homes:**

Smaller, mobile, and sustainable homes are becoming more popular. Yurts, in particular, are a staple in off-grid living due to their durability and low environmental impact. Offering yurt-building services or pre-made kits can cater to a niche market of people looking to live off-grid or transition to smaller, more sustainable living spaces.

Tip: Create packages for clients that include both consultation and construction services, guiding them through the process from start to finish. You can also offer training workshops for those who want to build their homes themselves, providing them with the hands-on skills they need to be successful.

Water Collection Systems: Building Rainwater Harvesting and Purification Systems

Water is one of the most critical resources in off-grid living. You can leverage your knowledge to design, build, and maintain rainwater collection and filtration systems for others in your community. These systems are essential for sustainable living, especially in areas where water access may be limited.

- **Rainwater Harvesting:**

Setting up rainwater harvesting systems allows homeowners to collect and store water for everyday use. Whether it's for drinking, irrigation, or general use, these systems can help off-grid residents become more self-sufficient. Offering custom rainwater harvesting systems that cater to the unique needs of each household is an excellent way to serve your community.

- **Water Filtration Systems:**

Purification is critical to ensure that water is safe for consumption. If you're skilled in building or installing filtration systems—whether they're gravity-fed filters, solar distillation setups, or simple DIY systems—you can offer this service to off-grid families. Ensuring safe and clean water for the long term is a necessity for off-grid sustainability, and your expertise can help others achieve this.

Tip: Bundle water collection and filtration services with energy system installations. Providing a comprehensive solution for both energy and water needs will add value to your offerings and attract clients looking for a one-stop solution.

Handcrafted Soaps, Herbal Remedies, and Natural Products

Living off the grid opens up a wide range of opportunities to create valuable products directly from nature. Handcrafted soaps, herbal remedies, and natural skincare products are in high demand, particularly among people who prioritize natural, chemical-free options. In this section, we'll explore how to leverage these natural resources to create valuable products that not only serve your needs but can also be sold for profit in local markets or through barter systems.

Soap and Skincare Products: A Natural Approach to Self-Sufficiency

Creating your own soap and skincare products from natural ingredients like herbs, beeswax, and essential oils is not only a fulfilling process but also a practical one. With these products, you can ensure your family's health and hygiene while tapping into a growing market for natural, eco-friendly skincare.

- **Soap Making**

Making natural soap is a straightforward process that involves combining fats (such as vegetable oils or animal fats) with a lye solution, which triggers a chemical reaction called saponification. You can customize your soap with various additives, including dried herbs, essential oils, or clays, to provide specific benefits like exfoliation or aromatherapy. For example, lavender-infused soap can promote relaxation, while peppermint adds a refreshing cooling effect.

Start small by making soap for personal use, and once you've mastered the process, consider selling your handcrafted soaps at local markets. Highlight that your soaps are made using sustainable, off-grid practices, which can attract eco-conscious customers.

Tip: Packaging plays a big role in marketing your products. Use eco-friendly, recyclable materials and emphasize the handmade, chemical-free aspects of your soap to appeal to health-conscious consumers.

Crafting and offering services off the grid presents limitless opportunities for sustainable income. By mastering skills like woodworking, soap making, and renewable energy installations, you're not only creating valuable products but also providing solutions that align with the ethos of self-reliance and sustainability. Whether you're selling handcrafted goods, hosting workshops, or helping others transition to off-grid living, your expertise becomes a powerful tool for both financial and personal growth.

Ultimately, success in this field relies on creativity, resourcefulness, and community engagement. By continuing to refine your craft, expand your services, and build strong connections with your local network, you'll ensure that your off-grid lifestyle remains both fulfilling and financially stable.

Thank You

Thank you for choosing the No Grid Survival Projects Bible and for joining us on this journey toward true self-reliance. It has been a privilege to share these projects and solutions with you, and we hope you've found them both practical and inspiring as you work to build your off-grid life.

Creating this series of books has been a labor of love, driven by our passion for sustainable living and helping others achieve self-sufficiency. We understand how challenging—but also incredibly rewarding—this path can be, and our goal was to ensure you feel equipped with the knowledge and confidence to take on each project, step by step.

If this guide has been helpful to you, we would love to hear about your experiences. Whether it's a quick review, a few sentences, or sharing what you've built so far, your feedback not only helps us improve but also inspires others who are beginning their own off-grid journey.

Thanks again for letting us be a part of your off-grid adventure. Stay resilient, keep pushing forward, and enjoy the freedom and satisfaction that come from living a truly independent life!

Scan the QR code below to leave your review:

Your feedback not only helps us refine and enhance future content but also guides others in finding the right resources to effectively prepare themselves. By sharing your thoughts, you contribute to a community of like-minded individuals working toward self-reliance and off-grid success.

Unlock Your Exclusive Bonus Content

Thank you for picking up the No Grid Survival Projects Bible! Along with your purchase, you now have access to a set of exclusive bonuses—created to give you critical tools and insights for mastering every facet of off-grid life. These bonuses build on the book's foundation, giving you an extra edge for mastering off-grid living in any scenario.

Here's What You'll Receive:

1. **Survival Mindset**: Develop the mental resilience needed to tackle off-grid challenges with composure and determination. This guide will empower you with the mindset crucial for thriving in independent living.

2. **Physical Preparedness**: Master strength and endurance techniques that are vital for self-reliant living. Designed to build real-world fitness, this bonus ensures you're ready for anything life off the grid throws your way.

3. **Delicious Off-Grid Recipes**: Discover how to create hearty, nourishing meals from limited resources. These recipes bring together simplicity, nutrition, and taste, so you stay fueled, strong, and satisfied in any condition.

4. **Off-Grid Canning Recipes**: Learn the essential skill of preserving your food independently. These canning recipes allow you to maximize your food supply without relying on refrigeration or modern conveniences.

SPECIAL VIDEO TUTORIALS

Dive deeper with our collection of step-by-step selected videos led by experienced survival experts. These visual guides simplify complex off-grid projects—from building solar panels to mastering core survival techniques—so you're truly prepared to tackle every challenge of self-sufficient living.

Ready to Access Your Bonuses?

Scan the QR code to unlock your exclusive resources!

Or navigate to → rebrand.ly/ng-go

These powerful tools are here to support you at every step of your journey toward a resilient, resourceful, and self-sufficient lifestyle. Don't miss out—get started now!

Made in the USA
Coppell, TX
09 December 2024

42045246R10118